Further praise for *Jarhead*

'By turns profane and lyrical, swaggering and ruminative, *Jarhead* is not only the most powerful memoir to emerge thus far from the last gulf war, but is also a searing contribution to the literature of combat, a book that combines the black humour of *Catch-22* with the savagery of *Full Metal Jacket* and the visceral detail of *The Things They Carried*' Michiko Kakutani, *The New York Times*

'If you want a clear-eyed sense of what might be going on today in the staging areas surrounding Iraq, a view stripped of cant, hypocrisy, and the bloated lies of officialdom, read *Jarhead*' Malcom Jones, *Newsweek*

'An incomparable document of military record . . . I believe it will be read by millions' Jonathan Kaplan, author of *The Dressing Station*

'*Bravo Two Zero* rewritten by Schopenhauer' *Time Out*

'Powerful, compelling, deeply disturbing' *Mail on Sunday*

'Swofford delivers, in the furious impassioned prose of a lost soul who sought poor odds and a likely death but was cheated of them both. Eloquent, searing, thoroughly ambivalent' Boyd Tonkin, *Independent*

'Rare is the marine who is willing to share the raw experience, and rarer still is one like Swofford – the marine who can really write. *Jarhead* is some kind of classic, a bracing memoir of the 1991 Persian Gulf War that will go down with the best books ever written about military life. It is certainly the most honest memoir I have read from a participant in any recent war. His voice isn't pretty – it's just terribly and despicably beautiful' Mark Bowden, *New York Times Book Review*

'Not just the finest memoir to emerge from Operation Desert Storm, but one of the most honest and compelling accounts of men-at-arms in a generation. With a keen eye and biting wit, Swofford has rendered the true face of the battlefield – what it looks and sounds and tastes like – as only one who has been there can. In an age when politicians are again talking about good and just wars, *Jarhead* should be required reading for all those who would believe them' Scott Anderson, author of *Triage*

'This is a book that smokes and screams in your hands. With a sniper's cold and unforgiving eye, Swofford has found the nexus between nihilism and language, a language ripped, home-grown, American-made, trashy and lyrical and bold . . . Brash, honest and most unnerving, *Jarhead* delivers coruscating and unpleasant truths about war and warriors' Joy Williams

'Extraordinary: full of insight into the minds and rucksacks of our latter-day warriors' *Kirkus Reviews* (starred)

'A sometimes funny but mostly provocative, intensely honest look at life and death in Desert Storm' *USA Today*

JARHEAD

A SOLDIER'S STORY OF MODERN WAR

ANTHONY SWOFFORD

Scribner

First published in Great Britain by Scribner, 2003
This paperback edition published by Scribner, 2004
An imprint of Simon & Schuster UK Ltd

A CBS COMPANY

Scribner and design are trademarks of Macmillan Library Reference
USA, Inc., used under licence by Simon & Schuster,
the publisher of this work.

Designed by Erich Hobbing

Text set in Granjon

9 10

Simon & Schuster UK Ltd
1st Floor
222 Gray's Inn Road
London WC1X 8HB

www.simonsays.co.uk

Simon & Schuster Australia
Sydney

A CIP catalogue record for this book is
available from the British Library

ISBN: 978-0-74323-919-6

Printed and bound in Great Britain by
CPI Cox & Wyman, Reading, RG1 8EX

This book is for
the U.S. Marines of Surveillance and Target Acquisition
Platoon, Second Battalion, Seventh Marines,
August 1990–April 1991

and

in memory of my brother.

But if you want to go on fighting
go take some young chap, flaccid & a half-wit
to give him a bit of courage and some brains
                    —Ezra Pound, *Canto LXXII*

I go to the basement and open my ruck. The basement is in Iowa, after a long, harsh winter, and deep in the ruck where I reach for my cammies, I still feel the cold of February. We were supposed to turn in our desert cammies, but I kept mine. They're ratty and bleached by sand and sun and blemished with the petroleum rain that fell from the oil-well fires in Kuwait. The cammies don't fit. While in the Marines, I exercised thirty hours a week. Since I've been out, I've exercised about thirty hours a year. The waist stops at my thighs. The blouse buttons, but barely. I pull out maps of Kuwait and Saudi Arabia. Patrol books. Pictures. Letters. My journal with its sparse entries. Coalition propaganda pamphlets. Brass bore punch for the M40A1 sniper rifle. A handful of .50-caliber projectiles. I think of what I must look like to the late-night walker peering through the basement windows: the movie cliché, the mad old warrior going through his memorabilia, juicing up before he runs off and kills a few with precision fire. But, no, I am not mad. I am not well, but I am not mad. I'm after something. Memory, yes. A reel. More than just time. Years pass. But more than just time. I've been working toward this—I've opened the ruck and now I must open myself.

It would've been easy to sell my gear to a surplus store. After the war, when I spent most of my monthly pay in the bars in Palm Springs and Newport Beach, Las Vegas and Santa Monica, I'd steal a case or two of MREs (meals ready to eat) from Supply each week, and on my way out of town for the weekend I'd sell the meals for $80 per case in an army/navy store in San Bernardino. And occasionally I'd steal more than meals. Or I wouldn't necessarily steal. Sometimes I'd happen along a Sergeant Smith's ruck, and he'd be nowhere near, and I'd remember the saying *Gear left adrift, must be a gift,* and I knew that the ex-marine who ran the army/navy store would give me $300 for the sergeant's misfortune.

So my ruck didn't have to be here, in my basement, six or seven moves and eight and a half years after my discharge. I could've sold it for one outrageous bar tab or given it to Goodwill or thrown it away—or set it afire, as some jarheads did.

I open a map of southern Kuwait. Sand falls from between the folds.

As a lance corporal in a U.S. Marine Corps scout/sniper platoon, I saw more of the Gulf War than the average grunt. Still, my vision was blurred—by wind and sand and distance, by false signals, poor communication, and bad coordinates, by stupidity and fear and ignorance, by valor and false pride. By the mirage.

Thus what follows is neither true nor false but *what I know.* I have forgotten most of the statistics and must look them up. I remember the weapons, though not their capabilities, so I must look those up as well. For the place names I refer to maps. For unit deployments and order of battle, I must consult published charts. I search through congressional reports and presidential statements at the Federal Depository Library. I remember most of the names and faces of my platoon mates. I remember the names and faces of some of their girlfriends and wives. I think I know who cheated and who stayed faithful. I remember who wrote letters and who drove their men mad with silence. I remember some of the lies and most of the questions. I remember the dreams and the naive wishes, the pathetic pleas and the trouser-pissing horror.

I remember some of the sand, but there was so much of it, I should be forgiven.

I remember about myself a loneliness and poverty of spirit; mental collapse; brief jovial moments after weeks of exhaustion; discomfiting bodily pain; constant ringing in my ears; sleeplessness and drunkenness and desperation; fits of rage and despondency; mutiny of the self; lovers to whom I lied; lovers who lied to me. I remember going in one end and coming out the other. I remember being told I must remember and then for many years forgetting.

On August 2, 1990, Iraqi troops drive east to Kuwait City and start killing soldiers and civilians and capturing gold-heavy palaces and expensive German sedans—though it is likely that the Iraqi atrocities are being exaggerated by Kuwaitis and Saudis and certain elements of the U.S. government, so as to gather more coalition support from the UN, the American people, and the international community generally.

Also on August 2, my platoon—STA (pronounced *stay*), the Surveillance and Target Acquisition Platoon, scout/snipers, of the Second Battalion, Seventh Marines—is put on standby. We're currently stationed at Twentynine Palms Marine Corps Base, in California's Mojave Desert.

After hearing the news of imminent war in the Middle East, we march in a platoon formation to the base barber and get fresh high-and-tight haircuts. And no wonder we call ourselves jarheads—our heads look just like jars.

Then we send a few guys downtown to rent all of the war movies they can get their hands on. They also buy a hell of a lot of beer. For three days we sit in our rec room and drink all of the beer and watch all of those damn movies, and we yell *Semper fi* and we head-butt and beat the crap out of each other and we get off on the various visions of carnage and violence and deceit, the raping and killing and pillaging. We concentrate on the Vietnam films because it's the most recent war, and the successes and failures of that war helped write our training manuals. We rewind and review famous scenes, such as Robert Duvall and his helicopter gunships during *Apocalypse Now,* and in the same film Martin Sheen floating up the fake Vietnamese Congo; we watch Willem Dafoe get shot by a friendly and left on the battlefield in *Platoon;* and we listen closely as Matthew Modine talks trash to a streetwalker in *Full Metal Jacket.* We watch again the ragged, tired, burnt-out fighters walking through the villes and the pretty native women smiling because if they don't smile, the fighters might kill their pigs or burn their cache of rice. We rewind the rape scenes when American soldiers return from the bush after killing many VC to sip cool beers in a thatch bar while whores sit on their laps for a song or two (a song from the fifties when America was still sweet) before they retire to rooms and fuck the whores sweetly. The American boys, brutal, young farm boys or tough city boys, sweetly fuck the whores. Yes, somehow the films convince us that these boys are sweet, even though we know we are much like these boys and that we are no longer sweet.

There is talk that many Vietnam films are antiwar, that the message is war is inhumane and look what happens when you train young American men to fight and kill, they turn their fighting and killing everywhere, they ignore their targets and desecrate the entire country, shooting fully automatic, forgetting they were trained to aim. But actually, Vietnam war films are all pro-war, no matter what the supposed message, what Kubrick or Coppola or Stone intended. Mr. and Mrs. Johnson in Omaha or San Francisco or Manhattan will watch the films and weep and decide once and for all that war is inhumane and terrible, and they will tell their friends at church and their family this, but Corporal Johnson at Camp Pendleton and Sergeant Johnson at Travis Air Force Base and Seaman Johnson at Coronado Naval Station and Spec 4 Johnson at Fort Bragg and Lance Corporal Swofford at Twentynine Palms Marine Corps Base watch the same films and are excited by them, because the magic brutality of the films celebrates the terrible and despicable beauty of their fighting skills. Fight, rape, war, pillage, burn. Filmic images of death and carnage are pornography for the military man; with film you are stroking his cock, tickling his balls with the pink feather of history, getting him ready for his real First Fuck. It doesn't matter how many Mr. and Mrs. Johnsons are antiwar—the actual killers who know how to use the weapons are not.

We watch our films and drink our beer and occasionally someone begins weeping and exits the room to stand on the catwalk and stare at the Bullion Mountains, the treacherous, craggy range that borders our barracks. Once, this person is me. It's nearly midnight, the temperature still in the upper nineties, and the sky is wracked with stars. Moonlight spreads across the desert like a white fire. The door behind me remains open, and on the TV screen an ambush erupts on one of the famous murderous hills of Vietnam.

I reenter the room and look at the faces of my fellows. We are all afraid, but show this in various ways—violent indifference, fake ease, standard-issue bravura. We are afraid, but that doesn't mean we don't want to fight. It occurs to me that we will never be young again. I take my seat and return to the raging battle. The supposedly anti-war films have failed. Now is my time to step into the newest combat zone. And as a young man raised on the films of the Vietnam War, I want ammunition and alcohol and dope, I want to screw some whores and kill some Iraqi motherfuckers.

When the Iraqi army of Saddam Hussein invades Kuwait City, Kuwait's Emir Sheikh Jabir al-Ahmad as-Sabah flees to Saudi Arabia and establishes his government either in a Saudi palace or the Ad Dammam Hilton, depending on what paper you read. At a press conference on August 3, President George Bush calls Saudi Arabia, Kuwait's southern neighbor, a "vital U.S. interest." Defense Secretary Dick Cheney visits Saudi Arabia on August 5 and brokers a historic deal allowing U.S. troops on Saudi soil for the first time ever. On August 6 the UN Security Council passes Resolution 661, imposing an economic embargo on Iraq and occupied Kuwait. On August 7 the deployment of American fighting troops begins.

I'm in the base gym at noon on August 7, lifting a few hundred pounds over my chest, working off the days-long damage from our Vietnam War Film Fest, when I hear an announcement over the public address system: *All personnel from STA 2/7 are ordered to report immediately to battalion headquarters. Get some, jarheads!* Now we're locked down on base. Our deployment is inevitable.

On August 8, Iraq formally annexes Kuwait, and two days later twelve of the twenty-four Arab League countries vote to send troops to help defend Saudi Arabia. Iraqi and Kuwaiti assets are frozen by the United States, Great Britain, France, and West Germany. On

ANTHONY SWOFFORD

August 14, two days after my twentieth birthday, the Seventh
Marines arrive in Riyadh, Saudi Arabia.

As I debark the plane, the oven heat of the Arabian Desert grips my
throat. In the distance the wind blows sand from the tops of dunes,
cresting beige waves that billow like silk through the mirage. The
tarmac is full of American civilian jumbo jets—American, Delta,
United; we flew United. The scene on the airfield is like that at any
busy international airport, only we passengers are wearing fatigues
and carrying loaded rifles, our gas masks strapped to our hips. Just
beyond the tarmac, artillery batteries point their guns east and
north. Fighter jets patrol the sky. During the twenty-hour flight our
mode of debarkation was debated—tactical or general—and I'd
hoped for the tactical approach—live rounds and a defensive perimeter could be the only authentic introduction to a theater of war. This
won't be like jumping off a Huey at Green Beach in the Philippines,
trading an MRE for a plate of hot noodles and blood pork. We
received our rounds, but we exit the plane in an orderly single-file
line, and I realize that we'd surely look ridiculous surrounding a
civilian jetliner with our weapons drawn, the cabin crew performing inventory in the galley while we scream for war.

We're marched toward a series of large, bright green Bedouin
tents. Inside the tents marines drink bottled water and attempt to
stay cool by draping wet skivvy shirts over their heads. Jarheads
from other units who've been in-country a few hours affect the air
of grungy desert veterans, pointing to the pallets of European spring
water and saying, "You better drink a lot of that. It's hot here," as if
offering us religious insight.

After we sit for an hour in the hydration tents, the colonel calls a
battalion formation and proudly announces that we are taking part
in Operation Desert Shield. He explains that the Kuwaiti-Iraqi
conflict is not yet our concern, but that currently our mission is to
protect, to shield, Saudi Arabia and her flowing oil fields. We'll be
shielding enough oil to drive hundreds of millions of cars for hundreds of millions of miles, at a relatively minor cost to the American

10

consumer. We joke about having transferred from the Marine Corps to the Oil Corps, or the Petrol Battalion, and while we laugh at our jokes and we all think we're damn funny jarheads, we know we might soon die, and this is not funny, the possibility of death, but like many combatants before us, we laugh to obscure the tragedy of our cheap, squandered lives with the comedy of combat and being deployed to protect oil reserves and the rights and profits of certain American companies, many of which have direct ties to the White House and oblique financial entanglements with the secretary of defense, Dick Cheney, and the commander in chief, George Bush, and the commander's progeny. We know this because Kuehn, one of our representatives from Texas, says, "All those old white fuckers from Texas have their fat hands in Arab oil. The motherfuckers drink it like it's beer."

And at this point we also know that the outcome of the conflict is less important for us—the men who will fight and die—than for the old white fuckers and others who have billions of dollars to gain or lose in the oil fields, the deep, rich, flowing oil fields of the Kingdom of Saud.

By late September the American troop count in Saudi reaches 150,000 and the price of crude oil has nearly doubled since the invasion. Millions of Kuwaiti guest workers from the Philippines, Vietnam, Sri Lanka, and India have humped across the dry desert to the relatively safe haven of Jordan.

Our days consist of sand and water and sweat and piss. We walk and drive over the sand and we drink water, gallons of water. And as we drink, we sweat, and as we sweat, we drink. Six times a day we gather for formation and swallow two canteens per man, and between formations we ingest more water, and we piss and sweat and walk the desert and drink and piss and sweat. We look north toward what we're told is a menacing military, four hundred thousand or more war-torn and war-savvy men. Some of the Iraqi soldiers who fought during the eight-year Iran-Iraq war (September 1980 to August 1988) began tasting combat when we were ten years old. The Iraqi dead totalled more than 120,000, with 300,000 or more wounded and 60,000 prisoners of war. An army capable of sustaining such damage and invading another neighbor two years later sounds like a truly menacing force. And the civilian population that supports this army and its missions, that accepts such a staggering mutilation and loss of fathers and sons, must be extremely devoted to the country and the protection of its leader. While fighting Iran, the Iraqis became experts at fortifying their border using mines and obstacles, such as the thirty-kilometer-long and eighteen-hundred-meter-wide artificial lake used to defend the city of Basra. We're forced to wonder what the Iraqis are preparing for us at the Saudi-Kuwaiti border. And in 1981 and 1984 the Iraqis used mustard and nerve gas against the Iranians, including civilians, and since then they've dropped nerve gas on the Iraqi Kurds. We believe they'll do the same to us. Gas! Gas! Gas! We wait for the Iraqi army. This is our labor. We wait.

We've been in Saudi Arabia for six weeks, and we're currently operating in the training/security area called the Triangle: on my map, its coordinates form a rough triangle, the tip of which points toward Kuwait; twenty miles rear of our position the pogues (regiment and division-level headquarters and support personnel) eat three hot meals a day in a chow hall and sleep in an air-conditioned oil-company barracks while we're boonies-stuck and out of luck, no showers, no hot chow, no rack, no wadi in sight, no oasis. We can't see the superhighway and the Saudis and Kuwaitis driving toward Egypt and safety, though we know the road runs just to our south and we hear their Mercedes diesel engines racing through the night, their sound like some kind of muffled cosmic laughter.

We're excited this morning because the reporters are finally coming. It's late September and we've each received newspaper clippings from parents or grandparents or siblings, neat cutouts of stories in our hometown papers about other hometown boys deployed to the Arabian Gulf, the margins penciled in by a parent or grandparent or sibling: *Didn't you know Private Douglas from school? Is William Wesley the kid you beat up in fourth grade? I thought Hall was in jail?* Now the clippings will end. The reporters will write about us, and when you're written about, you don't need the clipping. You stand tall and have your picture taken and you say wise, brave things that your family and friends read and they become even more proud of you, and girls not your girlfriend read about you, the ones you almost had, and they become sorry for having said no, because now you are brave and wise and your words and photo are in the newspaper. And people will take time out of their busy days to read the article and send it to someone else serving in the U.S. Marines, in Operation Desert Shield, and they'll write in the margin—*Wasn't Swofford an altar boy with you? Is Swofford the kid who stole your third-grade science project? Is he of the Swoffords recently divorced in Carmichael, the father arrested for chasing the mother's boyfriend out of the house and down the street with a pistol?* You never know what other people know about you, what they remember, what they write in the margins.

Knowing the reporters will arrive soon, we shave for the first time in a week, pull new cammies from the bottoms of our rucks, and helmet-wash our pits and crotches and cocks. Vann's wife recently sent him a bottle of cologne, and we each dab a bit on our neck and our chest.

Sergeant Dunn gathers the platoon in a school circle under the plastic infrared (IR) cover. It's before zero nine and already one hundred degrees. Our platoon commands three Humvees, and the vehicles are under IR cover. Ideally, weapons, vehicles, and personnel shielded under the netting will avoid detection by enemy infrared devices. We're not convinced. Why believe in the effectiveness of IR netting when the drink tube on your gas mask breaks every time you don-and-clear during a training nerve-gas raid? When the best method of maintenance for the PRC-77 radio, the Prick, is the Five-Foot Drop?

We've known about the press visit for a few days, and Sergeant Dunn has already recited a list of unacceptable topics. We're prohibited from divulging data concerning the capabilities of our sniper rifles or optics and the length and intensity of our training. He's ordered us to act like top marines, patriots, shit-hot hard dicks, the best of the battalion. As the scout/snipers, we've been hand-picked by the executive officer and the S-2 officer to serve as the eyes and ears of the battalion commander.

"Listen up," Dunn says. "I've gone over this already. But the captain wants you to hear it again. Basically, don't get specific. Say you can shoot from far away. Say you are highly trained, that there are no better shooters in the world than marine snipers. Say you're excited to be here and you believe in the mission and that we'll annihilate the Iraqis. Take off your shirts and show your muscles. We're gonna run through some calisthenics for them. Doc John, give us a SEAL workout. Keep it simple, snipers."

Kuehn says, "It ain't simple. This is censorship. You're telling me what I can and can't say to the press. This is un-American."

As we begin arguing about the gag order, Staff Sergeant Siek arrives. He says, "You do as you're told. You signed the contract. You have no rights, you can't speak out against your country. We call that treason. You can be shot for it. Goddamnit, we're not playing around. Training is over. I'm sick of hearing your complaints. Tell your complaints to Saddam Hussein. See if he cares."

I want to come to the defense of free speech, but I know it will be useless. We possess no such thing. The language we own is not ours, it is not a private language, but derived from Marine Corps history and lore and tactics. *Marine Corps birthday? 10 November 1775, the Marine Corps is older than the United States of America. Birthplace? Tun Tavern, Philadelphia, a gang of drunks with long rifles and big balls. Tarawa? Bloodiest battle of World War II. Dan Daly? He killed thirty-seven Chinese by hand during the Boxer Rebellion. Deadliest weapon on earth? The marine and his rifle. You want to win your war? Tell it to the marines!* When you are part of that thing, you speak like it. Reporters are arriving to ask me what I think about sitting in a desert, waiting for war. I'll answer that I like it; I'm prepared for any-thing that might come my way; I have supreme confidence in all of my leaders, from my team leader to the president.

The reporters are due at our position at 0900.

Staff Sergeant Siek says, "You are marines. There is no such thing as speech that is free. You must pay for everything you say. Especially the unauthorized crap."

I leave the free speech argument and walk to our straddle trench. I enjoy shitting in the desert. There's no seat in a straddle trench, but I've been punished many times, for hours on end, in the squat position, so I could sleep while straddling the trench. Also, it reminds me of Korea, where we spent a month of our last deployment. Most public rest rooms in Korea had straddle holes, and I enjoyed shitting there as well, often drunk, often having just walked away from a bar booth where I'd been buying a prostitute five-dollar Lady Drinks.

I look at the sky, blue like no blue I've known before, and at the desert that will not stop. This is the pain of the landscape, worse than the heat, worse than the flies—there is no getting out of the land. No stopping. After only six weeks of deployment, the desert is in us, one particle at a time—our boots and belts and trousers and gas masks and weapons are covered and filled with sand. Sand has invaded my body: ears and eyes and nose and mouth, ass crack and piss hole. The desert is everywhere. The mirage is everywhere. Awake, asleep, high heat of the afternoon or the few soft, sunless hours of early morning, I am still in the desert.

The Desert will become the popular moniker of Operation Desert Shield and the forthcoming Desert Storm, the Gulf War, the Operation to Free Kuwait—whatever else the war, the mass staging and movement of personnel and weapons of destruction might be called, it is the Desert. Were you in the Desert? Who were you with in the Desert? They kicked ass in the Desert. Those jarheads didn't do shit in the Desert but sit on their asses and chow down on pogey bait.

I wipe myself and turn to kick sand over the waste. A Land Rover crests the rise, an enlisted man in the driver's seat, a marine colonel next to him, and two reporters in the back.

The press-pool colonel and his driver wait in the Land Rover, the air-conditioning blowing the colonel's hair into fine white wisps of artillery smoke.

We gather under the IR netting and the reporters introduce themselves. The man is from the *New York Times* and the woman from the *Boston Globe*. They shake our hands and urge us to speak freely, but they know we've been scripted; they know our answers to their questions have already been written on our faces, though maybe not in our hearts. The *Boston Globe* woman looks bored, or at least not very interested in what we might tell her. She just heard the same stories a few miles away.

"Yes, ma'am, I believe in our mission. I believe we will quickly win this war and send the enemy crawling home."

"Yes, ma'am, I'm proud to be here serving my country. I'm proud of our president standing up to the evil. Them ragheads is gonna go down."

"I'm from Texas, ma'am. I joined when I was eighteen rather than go to jail for a few years. Petty stuff. I finds out later my dad talked to the judge the night before and set the whole thing up. How 'bout that shit? But I'm proud of what the Corps has made me."

"This is about freedom, not about oil. This is about standing up to aggression, like the president says. Nobody wants to go to war. We just got to be ready. We can shoot out someone's eyeball from a klick away. Ain't no better shot in the world."

"I'm proud to serve my country. This is what I signed for. I'm gonna make my pop and mom and my girl proud. I come from a little town in Missouri. They're gonna make a parade for me, they got the ribbons up already. My mama says the whole town is behind us."

"My uncle, he was in the Vietnam and he don't feel good about me being over here, but still he writes me letters about watching my ass and don't try being a hero and watch out for your buddies."

"I think the mission is valid and we have all the right in the world to be here and the president has all the right to deploy us and we are well trained and prepared to fight any menace in the world. They can bomb us and gas us and shoot and we'll keep at them. Many of us have been preparing for this since birth."

The *Times* reporter has brought a football. Kuehn and I toss the ball back and forth and speak with the reporter. He stands between us and his eyes follow the ball. He looks like an anthropologist, an expert in primate behavior. He's a kind man, soft-spoken, eager to hear from us what we really think about the operation, to see how we live through a single day. He wants a look at the psyche of the frontline infantryman, and I can only offer him processed responses. I've been ordered to give him SPAM. I wish to speak with him honestly and say: I am a grunt, dressed up in fancy scout/sniper clothes; I am a grunt with limited vision. I don't care about a New World Order. I don't care about human rights violations in Kuwait City. Amnesty International, my ass. Rape them all, kill them all, sell their oil, pillage their gold, sell their children into prostitution. I don't care about the Flag and God and Country and Corps. I don't give a fuck about oil and revenue and million barrels per day and U.S. jobs. I have a job. I'll walk the rest of my life. I'm a grunt. I'm supposed to walk and love it. I'm twenty years old and I was dumb enough to sign a contract and here I sit, miserable, oh misery oh stinking hell of all miseries, here I sit in the hairy armpit, swinging in the ball sack, slopping through the straddle trench of the world, and I can hear their bombs already, Mr. *Times,* I can hear their bombs and I am afraid.

I go out for a long pass, over the straddle trench, and I catch the ball with one hand, a diving catch with one hand, and I slam my left shoulder and my face against the desert. I am proud of my difficult catch. Kuehn yells, "Touchdown!" Sand is in my mouth, it feels gritty against my teeth and gums, and I run my tongue over my teeth, clearing the sand, and as if the particles of sand were particles of luck, I swallow them. As I jog the ball in, I hear bitching and moaning.

Vann yells, "Swoff, quick, throw the ball in the shitter!"

The colonel, on seeing the football, has exited his vehicle and instructed Staff Sergeant Siek that better than a workout of calisthenics, we should play football for the reporters, wearing full MOPP (Mission Oriented Protective Posture) gear and gas masks.

We were issued the MOPP suits at 29 Palms and have been humping them in our rucks ever since. They weigh ten pounds and were once hermetically sealed, but after six weeks of being beaten around in our rucks, most of the suits aren't even in their original packaging but bound together with duct tape and nylon rip cord. The MOPP is supposed to protect us from skin contamination during a chemical attack. We're happy to use the suits for this foolish game, because now they'll really be useless; we'll burn them in the straddle trench and it will take Supply months to issue replacements.

Grunt mathematics: ruck minus ten pounds equals happy grunt. What else can I burn?

Doc John Duncan, our navy corpsman, reports that the temperature has reached 112 degrees.

In combat, we'd wear our cammies under the suit, but we'll cut down the heat by wearing only skivvies, and those of us, like me, who wear none will go naked beneath. Siek assures us that the colonel has guaranteed him that the next day the shower trucks will visit our position. The next day.

With just the bottoms on, I begin to roast; I feel as though I've stepped into an oven. Dunn orders us into formation, and before we don our masks, we each drink a canteen of water. We put our masks on and tie the hoods.

We're all in great shape. Stateside, we'd run two or three 10Ks a week, swim three thousand yards four days a week, and spend at least a few hours a day in the weight room. In the desert, we've been performing Doc John's SEAL workouts every morning and running three or four miles a night, not to mention the battalion humps of seven or fifteen or twenty miles.

The MOPP suits are in jungle camouflage, so we look like a movable forest, something from a Monty Python skit. We break up, scout teams one and three versus teams two and four. We use five-gallon water jugs to mark the goals. This football game will kick our asses, but it might be better than standard-issue boredom.

I drop a touchdown pass. Dickerson and Fowler argue back and forth across the line of scrimmage and throw sand at one another and insult each other's mother. *Hut, hut, hike.* My team makes ten yards, good enough for a first down. Combs and Johnny Rotten get into a pushing match, and a few of us pull them apart. The drama of the scene is catching, our audience is entranced. The reporters are taking notes and Siek looks happy with our performance. We've been forced into this inhumane game and we're going to play. We have no lines. MOPP improv. The heat is intense: 125, 130, 140 degrees inside our suits.

Combs intercepts a pass and runs it in for a touchdown. We're all bent over at the knees, trying to catch our breath, and Siek shouts at us to continue the game. The Pentagon insists that warriors can fight at 100 percent in full MOPP and gas mask for eight hours. Siek wants us to play ball for an hour.

After a few more changes of possession and no change in score, Siek calls halftime. To demonstrate to the reporters the usefulness and practicality of the drinking tube, he orders that with our gas masks on we drink from our canteens, as if to say, *Aren't we smart, we've thought of everything.*

The gas mask and hood cause your hearing to lengthen and stretch, so that words enter your brain in slow motion, and it takes a moment to formulate just what it is you're hearing. I hear Siek telling the reporters that our gas masks are high-tech pieces of equipment, that combined with the MOPP suits we are virtually an unstoppable fighting force, that the only chance the Iraqis have is to drop an A-bomb on us. We retrieve our canteens from inside the IR net, and a few of us break the seals on our masks to catch fresh air. The air tastes sweet. It swirls around my face and cools my lungs and I think of fighting with this gear on and I hope, more than anything, that if we are going to war, and they are going to kick our asses, that they'll do it with an A-bomb, scatter us dead with the flames and fierce winds of a Little Boy or a Fat Man. And soon.

We stand in line and Siek issues instruction on using the drink tubes. Of course, we know the directions, but this is part of his show. The problem is, even if your drink tube is intact, the device on your canteen cap designed to interact with the drink tube will probably be broken. The atmosphere is one of glee.

When talking with a gas mask on, it sounds like you have a styrofoam cup over your mouth.

Kuehn yells, "I'm fucking dead already. The cap is broken on my canteen. If I drink this, I'm gonna drink some fuckin' mustard gas. I been saying for three months I needed a new canteen cap."

Vegh says, "My drinking tube is broken. I'm not going to break the seal on my mask, because that would kill me. I'll die of dehydration. Sir, thank you, sir."

"Staff Sergeant," I say. "I requested a new gas mask four months ago. My drinking tube fell off in the gas chamber at the Palms and Kuehn stepped on it. And we have unserviceable filters in our masks. We're all dead. We are the ghosts of STA 2/7."

Fowler has been wrestling with his drink tube and canteen, and finally he rips his mask off his face and punts it down the field. We're breaking up with laughter, but Siek is not happy. He tells us to take our masks off and drink from our canteens, and that he'll talk to Supply about replacement parts. He whistles like a referee and we resume the game.

Vann returns the kickoff. Kuehn decides to switch from touch to tackle, and he takes Vann down hard. Vann punches Kuehn in the side of the head, Combs kicks Kuehn in the ass, and we all jump on the pile, punching each other, and it doesn't matter whom you punch, because you're not punching hard, you're not punching to hurt, but only to punch. The half-speed fight degenerates into a laughter-filled dog-pile, with guys fighting their way from the bottom to climb back to the top, king of the pile, king of the Desert. We're sweating and shouting and shrieking through our masks. This is fun, plain mindless fun, the kind grunts are best at. Siek doesn't like our grab-ass, and he yells at us to resume the game, but we do not listen. He must know what terrible treat will soon be played out for the colonel and the reporters.

Field-fuck: an act wherein marines violate one member of the unit, typically someone who has recently been a jerk or abused rank or acted antisocial, ignoring the unspoken contracts of brotherhood and camaraderie and esprit de corps and the combat family. The victim is held fast in the doggie position and his fellow marines take turns from behind.

Combs pulls Kuehn from the bottom of the pile and yells, "Field-fuck!" Fowler starts the fun, thrusting his hips against Kuehn's ass, slapping the back of his head; when you aren't field-fucking, you're shouting support and encouragement or helping secure Kuehn.

Dickerson yells, "Get that virgin Texas ass! It's free!"

"I want some of that. I ain't seen boy ass this pretty since Korea."

"*Semper fi!* Scout-sniper!"

"Somebody get a picture for his wife. Poor woman."

Kuehn yells, "I'm the prettiest girl any of you has ever had! I've seen the whores you've bought, you sick bastards!"

"Scout-sniper! STA 2/7!"

We continue to scream, in joy, in revelry, still wearing full MOPP and gas mask, and we look like wild, hungry, bug-eyed animals swarming around disabled prey, and we sound thousands of miles away from ourselves.

The reporters have stopped taking notes. Siek runs toward us, yelling, "Stop! Stop, you assholes!"

I stand back from a turn with Kuehn. I feel frightened and exhilarated by the scene. The exhilaration isn't sexual, it's communal—a pure surge of passion and violence and shared anger, a pure distillation of our confusion and hope and shared fear. We aren't field-fucking Kuehn: we're fucking the press-pool colonel, and the sorry, worthless MOPP suits, and the goddamn gas masks and canteens with defective parts, and President Bush and Dick Cheney and the generals, and Saddam Hussein, and the PRC-77 radio and the goddamn heavy E-tools that can't help us dig deep enough holes; we're fucking the world's televisions, and CNN; we're fucking the sand and the loneliness and the boredom and the potentially unfaithful wives and girlfriends and the parents and siblings who don't write and the bad food and the fuckhead peaceniks back home, the skate punks and labor unionists and teachers and grand-mothers and socialists and Stalinists and Communists and the hung-over hippies grasping their fraudulent sixties idealism; we're fucking our confusion and fear and boredom; we're fucking our-selves for signing the contract, for listening to the soothing lies of the recruiters, for letting them call us buddy and pal and dude, luring us into this life of loneliness and boredom and fear; we're fucking all of the hometown girls we've wanted but never had; we're angry and afraid and acting the way we've been trained to kill, violently and with no remorse. We take turns, and we go through the line a few times and Kuehn takes it all, like the thick, rough Texan he is, our emissary to the gallows, to the chambers, to death do us part.

We stop the field-fuck and rip our gas masks from our faces and throw them in the air, as football players might do with their helmets after an especially grueling victory. We're bent over at the waist, hands on knees, breathing hard, breathing free. We pile our charcoal-lined MOPP suits in the straddle trench. We're standing around the trench either naked or in skivvy bottoms. We look like burn victims. The fires, the smoke and mirrors of history have been transposed to our skin.

The colonel and his driver jog at double time toward the Land Rover, the woman from the *Boston Globe* in tow. The *Times* reporter will stay on a few days.

Kuehn douses the suits with fuel and strikes a match. He says, "May God please save us, because these MOPP suits won't," and he drops the match, sending the pile into raging flames that burn black and sooty, choking the blue sky gray.

A few guys stand in line in front of a Humvee while Vegh pours water over them in a useless attempt at replicating a shower. Noth-ing other than an honest, power-driven shower will clean this muck from our bodies. I rub water over my face, and as the water runs down my forearms and mixes with the charcoal MOPP protectant, I recognize an odd formation on my skin, like a tattoo of fish scales. My thoughts return to my childhood in Japan. The world expands and contracts. My temples begin to throb and my ears ring a piercing rhythm through my brain. It's the heat, or breathing through the gas mask for an hour, or desert exhaustion, but I must sit down, and as I do, I stare at my forearms as though they are a map.

One day, as a child in Tachikawa, Japan, I sneaked off the air force base where my family lived and entered the city, hoping to find a nearby candy store. I was nervous. When shopping with my mother, Japanese women constantly stopped us on the street to look into my blue eyes, and the attention confused and aroused me and I often pissed my pants while a Japanese lady giggled and tickled my stomach or stroked my hair. But my younger sister's birthday was soon, and I wanted to surprise her with a long necklace of whistle gum, her favorite novelty from our preferred candy store. I'd never been off base alone, and I quickly lost my way. I knew the store was in an alley, and so I wandered from alley to alley, as they all looked alike with noodle houses and teahouses and sake bars and fish shops and electronics stores and candy stores that weren't the one I wanted. I ended up in a tattoo shop.

Two artists were busy on skin, one needling a man, his partner needling a woman. The artists were smoking and talking and hard at work, so they didn't notice me enter their shop. The clients looked at me and the woman smiled. They were naked above the waist, and their bodies were covered with ink, dragons and fish and ancient, wicked shogunal faces. Their tattoos were identical. I didn't even notice the woman's breasts. At the navel they each had a tattoo of a mushroom cloud. As the artists worked, in the middle of the man's chest an image of the woman's face began to appear, and in the middle of the woman's chest an image of the man's face began to appear. The man was ugly, with the face of a kicked dog, but the woman was beautiful and I thought him lucky to have her face painted on his chest, though I didn't understand the permanence of the shared act.

The artists still hadn't noticed me, and I continued to stare. I stood watching for an hour at least, as the faces were finished and the artists moved to their clients' forearms. They painted fish scales, and the electric needles continued to hum in the air like mad flies. The couple stared at one another and the woman occasionally smiled at me. The artists worked and smoked and talked back and forth in quiet, harsh whispers, aware only of the skin canvases in front of them. The woman's work was completed first, and when her tattooist noticed me, he hissed and threw his cigarette at me. The burning cigarette missed and I picked it up and threw it back at him, then I ran from the shop. The woman screamed. I didn't stop running until I made it home.

I awake hours later on a cot under the infrared net, with an IV in my arm. I passed out, as did a few of my platoon mates. We'll be sick for five days with dysentery. Yesterday, Fowler had gone to the rear on a fuel run and stole a vat of food from the chow hall, hoping it was hot food—lasagna or beans and rice or beef stew or any of the slop they make in those hideous chrome kitchens, but it was a plain green-leaf salad with no dressing. Only those of us desperate enough to eat the salad are down with the sickness. The lettuce came from Jordanian fields where they use human feces as fertilizer. So here we are, defending a country none of us gives a shit about, eating its neighbors' shit, and burying ours in the sand.

Prior to leaving the platoon, the *Times* reporter asks us what we want from the States, and we give him a list: European or Asian porn mags of any size, shape, content, and function; Oreo cookies; canned tuna; saltine crackers; Gatorade; Truth; a rotate-to-the-states date; ham; turkey; salami; a month of the *New York Times;* condoms just in case; canned soups; letter-writing gear; batteries; powdered chocolate; actual coffee, not crystals; candy bars; pop; beef jerky; whiskey; mouthwash; rubber bands; duct tape; corned beef hash; Sterno; Jolly Ranchers; the names and addresses of women incarcerated at federal correctional facilities; mail-order Filipino-bride catalog; cigars; baby-name book; marijuana; methamphetamines; cocaine; LSD; penis enlarger; pocket-pussy; blowup doll; butt beads; Vaseline;

baby powder; shaving cream; boot laces; toothpaste; shower soap; needles and thread.

We don't believe he'll come through, but a month after his visit, a cardboard box the size of two footlockers arrives, full of some of the items on our list and others we didn't request. We're surprised, and a few of us walk around the box and choose not to remove anything, having forgotten what we'd requested and feeling that if we reach into the box, we'll spoil the magic.

Kuehn thumbs through a smut mag and says, "He's an all right motherfucker. I didn't believe him for a second. He's all right for a reporter."

On the second day of boot camp I was selected for the platoon scribe position. My job would be to assist the drill instructors in administrative duties such as completing sick-call chits, training schedules, and travel manifests. My first task required me to draw on the barracks chalkboard the proper layout of our footlockers. Drill Instructor Burke handed me a photocopy of the footlocker display and ordered me to create a masterpiece.

Burke, like most DIs, didn't speak as much as growl. His chest was as thick as a butcher block. His eyes looked dead, as though he'd lost them for a few years and found them washed up on the beach. When he yelled, every vein in his body jumped. He wore, I would learn, the Charlie Uniform: olive-drab wool trousers and short-sleeve beige shirt with ribbons and badges. Expert badges for rifle and pistol were pinned to his left pocket flap. Above the badges he wore ribbons from Beirut. Later that night he'd tell us "Beirut bedtime stories" about digging dead buddies from the rubble.

I suppose there was confusion over what capabilities a scribe should possess, and drawing had never been my strong suit. I struggled through a poor representation of the schematic I held in my hand. I attempted to concentrate on the task while Burke ran up and down the squad bay, agitating and insulting my fellow recruits, making accusations about bestiality and other dark secrets the recruits were hiding. I took some pleasure in that scribe duty might keep me out of the line of verbal fire.

He yelled to a recruit, "I can't believe my fucking eyes! Did you piss your trousers, boy? Did you piss your trousers like a little girl?"

"Sir, no, sir!"

"You had an orgasm, is that it? You think I'm so sexy you jizzed in your trousers? Where are you from, boy?"

"Sir, Olympia, Washington, sir."

"Fuck me standing! My mother lives in Olympia. She don't piss her pants. Where'd you learn to piss your pants, boy? From your mama?"

"Sir, the recruit's mother is dead, sir."

"One less bitch I got to worry about her calling her senator because her cunt son can't handle my Marine Corps!"

"Sir, my mother was not a bitch, sir. Sir, I am not a cunt and I can handle your Marine Corps, sir."

Burke punched the recruit square on the forehead. He swayed but his knees did not give. The recruit had made the mistake of using personal pronouns, which the recruit is not allowed to use when referring to the drill instructor or himself. The recruit is *the recruit*. The drill instructor is *the drill instructor* or *sir*.

Burke surveyed the platoon, hands clasped behind his back.

He yelled, addressing us all, "I am your mommy and your daddy! I am your nightmare and your wet dream! I am your morning and your night! I will tell you when to piss and when to shit and how much food to eat and when! I will teach you how to kill and how to stay alive! I will forge you into part of the iron fist with which our great United States fights oppression and injustice! Do you understand me, recruits?"

"Sir, yes, sir!"

"If your daddy is a doctor or if you come from the projects in East St. Louis or a reservation in Arizona, it no longer matters. Black. White. Mexican. Vietnamese. Navajo. The Marine Corps does not care! Your drill instructors do not care! You are now green! You are light green or dark green. You are not black or white or brown or yellow or red. Do you understand me, recruits?"

"Sir, yes, sir!"

Burke approached me and the chalkboard. "What in the fuck is that, scribe?"

"Sir, it's the recruit's drawing of the footlocker, sir," I said.

"Jesus, Joseph, and doggy-style Mary, that looks like a pile of dogshit! My three-month-old daughter can draw better than that."

"Sir, the recruit has never been good at drawing, sir."

"Why the fuck are you my scribe? Isn't my scribe supposed to know how to draw?"

"Sir, the recruit doesn't know. The recruit thought the scribe was supposed to *write,* sir."

"Of course the recruit doesn't know! The recruit doesn't know because I haven't told him! And don't fucking tell me what my shithead scribe is supposed to do. You are my shithead scribe because someone fucked up! You should be in the retard platoon, learning how to draw with crayons and throwing your shit on the bulkheads!"

While he spoke, he spit in my face, and he bashed the brim of his Smokey Bear cover into my nose and pressed his index finger into my chest. He asked me to read what I'd written and point out exactly where the skivvies and running shoes were supposed to go. I couldn't decipher my chalk drawing. He slapped me on the back of the head a few times, as though slowly contemplating some further violence, winding me up, and then he shoved my head into the chalkboard. The board was affixed to the cinder-block barracks wall, so that after my head broke through the chalkboard, it stopped at the cinder block. I did not really feel the assault. It's possible it was minor enough, and that's why I didn't feel it, or I was in shock. The large bump on my head would fade away by the end of the week.

Burke leaned in close to my face and I could feel his moist, cruel breath in my ear, and he said, "Boy, you just entered my killing zone."

He continued berating me, and he complained that I'd ruined his goddamn perfectly good chalkboard, which was, according to Marine Corps Logic 101, absolutely true. He ordered me to prepare my own footlocker as a model for the rest of the platoon. While I labored over this task, he allowed my platoon mates to write letters home.

Eventually I finished, and did not a bad job, for the first time in my life attempting to fold skivvies into four-by-six-inch squares, for the first time in my life actually referring to underwear as *skivvies,* pants as *trousers,* a hat as a *cover.* Now, hands were *dickskinners,* the mouth was a *cum receptacle,* running shoes were *go-fasters,* a flashlight was a *moonbeam,* a pen was an *ink stick,* a bed was a *rack,* a wall was a *bulkhead,* a bathroom was a *head,* a shirt was a *blouse,* a tie was still a *tie,* and a belt a *belt,* but many other things would never be the same.

Burke didn't touch me again, but he beat on other recruits. I'm sure he had only the best intentions, and now when I consider him and his acts of violence, they seem petty, not severe enough. I wish that that night at the chalkboard, after he'd shoved my head into the wall, he'd have put me to the floor with a swift knee to the stomach, followed by a boot to the face, and another boot, and that he'd have continued beating me, while the other recruits watched, horrified, observing their future. Perhaps this is only the luxury of distance and time and the reemergence of the blind stupidity and dumb loyalty that first led me into the Corps and helped carry me out alive. But a further beating wouldn't have damaged me, a further beating wouldn't have caused me to run.

One morning during a heavy rain, we shoved our racks to the bulkheads and turned our barracks into a mini-drill-field and practiced close order drill. We'd been issued our weapons the day before, and even for a farm boy raised with a rifle in his lap, the particulars of COD are difficult. You don't throw the weapon over your shoulder and a piece of straw into your mouth, like you used to do before diddying down to the local hot spot for squirrels.

We dropped our rifles, confused *port arms* with *shoulder arms,* and along the way Burke became angrier and angrier, until he grabbed a recruit's rifle and rifle-butted him in the chest. The recruit fell backward a few ranks, and Burke threw the recruit's weapon at him and stormed out of the barracks. Unfortunately for Burke, the company commander stood at the back stairwell and had watched him train us and eventually lose his temper.

A few hours later, a command lieutenant spoke to our platoon and ordered anyone who'd been physically assaulted by Burke to come forward. Along with others, I chose to speak, and I wrote a report of what had occurred the first night of training when Burke had introduced me to the chalkboard. Partly I did this because I believed that no one had a right to put his hands on me. I briefly fantasized that the Marine Corps would apologize to me and buy me a ticket home, no questions asked. But mostly I hoped that reporting Burke's brutality might somehow put me in danger, increase the odds against my survival, that his fellow DIs would fuck me further and longer than anyone else, and I welcomed this imagined challenge. I'd increased the likelihood of my failure.

Burke was transferred to another platoon in our training company, and we rarely saw him. The matter didn't surface again, and I left boot camp and never spoke about the event. Sometimes I'd think that my reporting Burke would surface and reflect poorly on me. I had daydreams of running into Burke in a bar on Okinawa, where I'd apologize to him for being so weak, ask his forgiveness, and let him beat on me more, as I assumed he'd have liked to that second night at boot camp.

Like most good and great marines, I hated the Corps. I hated being a marine because more than all of the things in the world I wanted to be—smart, famous, sexy, oversexed, drunk, fucked, high, alone, famous, smart, known, understood, loved, forgiven, oversexed, drunk, high, smart, sexy—more than all of those things, I was a marine. A jarhead. A grunt.

I hated the Marines and I hated being a marine. I wore earrings while on leave and liberty, grew sideburns, hung out with gay navy guys who knew the best straight clubs anywhere—San Diego, L.A., Olongapo, Angeles City, Barrio, Kinville, Naha, Pusan, Seoul—jarhead-free clubs where I'd lie to pretty local girls and say I was a college student visiting my parents.

When I partied in enlisted clubs, things went poorly. I remember one night in particular—an enormous fight between jarheads and airmen at Kadena Air Base on Okinawa; we tore the place apart, tables and chairs and people airborne, broken bodies, broken bottles, broken skulls; one jarhead was punched for good reason and we all poured ourselves into the dumb, brutal stew. I made it out the back and missed the MPs.

I ducked into a sex show downtown, where a beautiful, young Filipino girl assaulted bananas and stacks of yen with her crotch.

Bored and saddened by the show, I ventured into the warm night, steering clear of the Japanese police, the JPs, masters of the baton.

I found a jarhead-free restaurant and bar I'd eaten at before, and I drank Asahi and sake and ate broiled mackerel with the owner's daughter, whose name was Yumiko. Her hair was dyed wine-red. When she laughed, three small wrinkles appeared on the bridge of her nose. She wore deep red lipstick and her lips were like waves and I imagined them crashing against my thin lips, crushing me. Her chin was rather sharp, and I would come to enjoy lightly kissing it while she slept.

I'd retained spotty Japanese from living in Tachikawa from age four to seven, and Yumiko had rough English from the Tokyo business school she'd dropped out of. I told her I went to college in America but I was taking a semester off, visiting my parents up north. We carried a big bottle of *nigori* sake upstairs to her convenience apartment, and we drank the sweet, cloudy liquor and listened to Japanese pop for hours before helping each other out of our clothes.

In the morning, in the kitchen downstairs, she made omelette-rice and miso and more mackerel. We sat on the spotless floor and ate from dark lacquerware. She called me Prince An-tony, the name of a popular Japanese cartoon character. Later, we drank beers on Red Beach between snorkeling missions, the ocean blue like a welder's flame, the tide soft against the white sand. We'd driven to the beach in her father's three-cylinder Suzuki van, and we had sex in the van, to the smell of burnt engine oil and seaweed, and to the slow slap of the ocean on dark volcanic rocks. We snorkeled again. I forget the names of the fish we saw, though I remember the fresh urchin bleeding through Yumiko's fingers as she opened them for me on the beach, and I remember the taste of the urchin and her skin.

I asked her, "Have you ever climbed Fuji-san?"

She laughed. "No Fuji on Okinawa, dumb-dumb. Fuji-san means, what you say, vacation? No vacation for my family. Work and work and don't stop to work more. Vacation is time to work. If restaurant is slow, I go work in uncle's butcher. If butcher is slow, I go work in uncle's laundry. If laundry is slow, I go back to restaurant, fold napkins, fold *gyoza,* sweep."

I could tell she didn't want to talk about Fuji. The Japanese I'd known either loved to talk about Fuji or refused, and either way, they were talking about Fuji. The mountain is blight or jewel. The topic of Mount Fuji is like the topic of war.

But I told Yumiko the story of my family climbing Mount Fuji on July 4, 1976, and the confusion this caused for me, as the two hundredth anniversary of my nation, a nation I wasn't currently living in, had been celebrated by my family with a rigorous two-day hike up the side of a treacherous (to my five-year-old eyes) foreign mountain. My father explained to me the history of the American Revolution, and that because of wars that had been fought, and mostly won, America was everywhere, that the base we lived on, in Japan, was a piece of America, and that similar little Americas thrived all over the world.

I stayed with Yumiko on weekends, taking a $30 cab from the north to Naha on Friday evening and returning to base late Sunday night. She told me about her boyfriend, who was still enrolled at business school in Tokyo. We stayed out of the fashionable bars because he was known around Naha. Mostly we drank sake in her apartment and beers on the beaches. When not drinking, we were snorkeling or making love. I'd wake early in the morning, at four-thirty or five, and go on a city run. The streets of Naha were wet at this hour, the sweepers having just rumbled through; shopkeepers, grocers, and fish merchants were opening their chained storefronts. I never saw another white person this early, and I would catch the shopkeepers' eyes as I pounded through the streets and alleys.

After a few months, Yumiko's boyfriend returned from Tokyo. We bought each other drinks. His name was Saturo, and we became friends. I never asked Yumiko what, if anything, she'd told him about me. It wasn't important. I told them I was not a dependent but an active-duty marine. Yumiko said, "No shit, Tony-san. I knew that from the get and go. Let's still be friends, no?"

I continued to leave base on the weekends. The three of us would go to clubs and drink immense amounts of alcohol. It would have been easy for me to leave a club with a woman, but I always kept the integrity of our triumvirate intact. We'd return to Yumiko's parents' restaurant early in the morning and eat breakfast together, and often I'd stay awake all day, playing poker with the cook while Yumiko and Saturo slept through the afternoon. The cook taught me how to cheat at cards, and also how to drink sake without your boss knowing you're drunk. His family had relocated to Okinawa after the bombs, and he showed me pictures of the devastation in his old neighborhood in Hiroshima. He would say, "Fucking Americans. You okay, Tony-san. Fucking Americans." And he'd tend to his curry or *yakisoba* or other coarse country meals.

That May I rotated back to the States. The night before my battalion left, Yumiko took a cab to Camp Hansen and slept in the barracks with me. She brought a pear that I sliced and fed her, and we made love all night in silence. When not caressing or kissing, we stared at our bodies, entwined like the histories of our nations. Her hands, as she loved me, felt like rose petals against my skin. On my tiny government-issue rack, in a concrete barracks built just after World War II, I experienced more passion than I had ever before in my life. We raced against the sunrise, the sure death of our affair, and every second that I was inside her, we both burned. I sucked her breath from her mouth and she bit my tongue until it bled. As the sun broke into the barracks, we wept, and she kissed my chest softly.

I walked her to the taxi stand, and Saturo was there, waiting in Yumiko's father's van, along with the cook. The cook exited the van and walked toward me, and he handed me a bag of dried shiitake mushrooms and a bottle of *nigori* sake and we bowed toward one another. Yumiko jumped into the van, Saturo cursed at her and shook his head, and they drove away.

I felt bad that Saturo had discovered us, but I also assumed that he'd known, and that when he'd gone to Yumiko's apartment the prior night and she wasn't there, the cook had told him what he hadn't wanted to hear.

*   *   *

I wrote Yumiko a few letters from Saudi Arabia; she was in Japan and Japan was everything Saudi Arabia could never be. I was in the Desert, sending out messages worldwide, clamoring for love with my pen. And with each letter I wrote and sealed, parts of me escaped the Kingdom of Saud. At times I thought I might write myself away, fit my entire body and mind into a few thick envelopes, and that way, as a stowaway, escape the ghastly end that awaited me.

My father served in the jungles of Vietnam from February of 1969 to February of 1970. He was twenty-eight and had been in the air force since the age of seventeen, so to him Vietnam mostly meant packing another seabag, Indochina being another duty station, like Travis or Seville or Moses Lake. But this time, a chance to break away from the wife and kids.

My father's age and the family back home and his proclivities toward Scotch and beer placed him in the population rarely depicted in the literature and films of the Vietnam War. He was not a crazed, fucked-in-the-head grunt, stoned on uppers or nodding on H, not a stealthy Special Forces guru, nineteen or twenty, the perfect age to die; he was a father and a lifer, and while he wasn't necessarily a patriot, he wouldn't be fragging anyone over orders he didn't *groove on* or *dig*—he'd build the fucking landing strip in the middle of the gookthick jungle and at the end of the day hope for Chivas and Budweiser, write a few letters home, maybe screw a whore in the ville. (What happens overseas stays overseas, until someone writes about it. I don't know what my father did in the villes of that bombed-out, fucked-out country, but I'll assume.)

One night between the thirteenth and twentieth of November 1969, I was conceived at the Honolulu Hilton. My father had received a surprise week of R&R. He called my mother from Saigon and told her to be in Honolulu in ten hours, and she called my aunt and asked her to watch my brother and sister. Not expecting my father home until February, she'd been off the pill. I am that old practical joke, the mistake. No one saw me coming.

The hotel room: orange shag carpet, one king bed, ocean view. Wet bar (my father empties the Scotch each night). The painting above the bed is of sailboats or sea horses. Snorkel equipment still wet, hanging from the balcony rail. Two 35mm cameras, four spent rolls of film, seventeen shots left on one camera, five on the other. On the dresser, a framed picture my mother brought from California— my soon-to-be father, mother, brother, and sister on the street in Seville, Spain, a donkey and a pretty Spanish girl behind them. In my mother's basket: grapes, red peppers, meat, wine. My brother and sister are dressed like a flamenco couple. My father is wearing jeans and a black, button-up shirt and black, dusty brogans; my mother wears a pretty yellow sundress.

In the bed, in Hawaii, my parents are fornicating. I cannot watch, and neither can you.

My father could've flown to Vietnam the next day and been shot dead, on the street or in the jungle. But he wasn't shot: the bullets and shrapnel missed him, and he arrived home three months later, a few more ribbons and medals on his chest, a pregnant wife sitting on the porch, nervously smoking.

My father returned from Vietnam only partially disturbed. For many years he suffered migraines, and at social events he wandered away from the crowds to pace. In Japan, in 1975, I played Pee-Wee football on base. My father filmed our games with Super 8. But at some point in the action he'd stop the camera, break down his tripod, pack his gear, and pace behind the bleachers during the remaining quarters, smoking, my handsome father. Years later my mother insisted that the possibility of me breaking a bone was too much for him, weak-stomached man, afraid of his own blood, vomiting over nosebleeds. I'm sure my mother was wrong, that her hypothesis was a product of the divorcée's caustic revisionist history. I think my father couldn't stand still in one place for too long because if you do, a bomb lands there. And then you are dead.

In 1981, when his migraines tapered off, his hands locked in fists. At this time, I delivered a paper route. I'd wake at five-thirty, before anyone else in the house. I'd have about half of my papers folded, and my father would emerge from my parents' bedroom. He'd find me in the garage and sit next to me on the cold concrete floor, fisted hands on his knees.

He'd say, "Sorry, Tone, wish I could help."

Some mornings he'd be fine, and he'd help me fold and load my papers onto my bike, and I'd return from delivering my ninety papers and he'd be dressed in uniform, but usually when I returned, he was still sitting on the floor of the garage, reading, turning the pages of the paper with his fists. I suppose my mother helped him dress on these mornings.

After breakfast, I'd walk with him to his Jaguar and jump in the passenger seat, and I'd work his right fist over the clutch ball and his left fist over the steering wheel, and I'd start the car and in winter turn the headlights on.

His doctors weren't able to explain these ailments, or at least that's the story I received. Agent Orange, maybe? Plain and simple madness? My father once told me that after Vietnam he'd been ordered numerous times to visit the base psychiatrist, something he never did. I suppose he had enough rank to cover his insubordination. Of course he needed help. Not only because of Vietnam, but because his mother had died when he was three months old and his closest half brother died while a marine on embassy duty in 1967. My father was thirty-nine years old and the world seemed a dead, cold place, void of promise. The problems of his psyche had become manifest in his hands. With his fists he beat at the thick chest of the world, but the world ignored him. Of course the world ignored him.

Not long after being birthed through the bloody canal of boot camp, my mind still cluttered with the junk of my military incarnation— Ribbons and Medals, Rifle Badges, Nomenclature, Marine Corps History, Policies and Procedures, Laws of War—this knowledge and these dangling accessories wrapped around my neck like a yolk stalk, I realized that joining the marines had been a poor decision. I had, not unlike Céline's Bardamu, stood from my seat at the café— where with a friend I'd been busy smoking, drinking, and looking at the ladies—and joined the colonel's march, his insane parade through the brick streets. I waved and said good-bye to my friend, but for the sounds of bugles and tank tracks, he did not hear my farewell.

While at Barracks Duty School I further decided my enlistment was a poor decision. I performed morning calisthenics, cleaned my weapons, shot my rifle, shotgun, and pistol expertly, and then, during the sixth week of barracks-duty training, the captain called me to his office.

There'd been a budget cut, and the school had to rid itself of three trainees and send them to the infantry, the Fleet Marine Force, the ready combat force of the Marine Corps. Now, rather than standing guard duty in my handsome uniform, in front of a navy nuclear or missile facility, I'd be doing what I was supposedly made for—humping up steep mountains or through thick jungles with a hundred pounds on my back, sweating and cussing in my wrinkled fatigues, with a large target on my chest: USMC GRUNT.

I was number three. Number one had been Private So-and-So, who for weeks tried for a psych discharge and had in his latest act of defiance masturbated on the captain's desk; number two was a young man, Private So-and-So, who tried for an admin homosexual discharge, making passes at the base MPs, wearing a pink bolo while on guard duty, but during the captain's weeklong review of the paperwork, he discovered that the young marine had been screwing the captain's daughter. So it goes when you screw the captain's daughter. When you're in, you're in.

And when you're out, you're out. The captain had found my drug waiver.

At boot camp, during in-processing, I'd confessed to using drugs, something I hadn't disclosed prior to signing my enlistment contract. Part of the reason I'd spoken up was that, on the third day of boot camp, I wanted, more than anything, not to be in boot camp. I'd slept six hours in two days; they'd shaved my head and insulted me with hundreds of spectacularly profane phrases and shoved my shaved head into the chalkboard. I wanted to go home and screw my girlfriend and paint houses for my father and drink beer with my buddies, who were screwing their girlfriends (and maybe mine) and painting houses for my father and drinking beer. I remember the room: gray industrial carpet, blue plastic seats, scarlet and gold paint, Marine Corps and U.S. flags. Ten or fifteen of us were in this last phase of being administratively harassed, the Final Flushing Out. All day recruits had been standing up and admitting things they hadn't told their recruiters: gay, asthmatic, sleepwalker, illegal alien, felon, fraudulent high school diploma, bed wetter.

Drill Instructor Burke exercised us to keep us alert. He barked the orders and paced in front of us.

"I know you cum receptacles have something to tell me. I know you've lied to my Marine Corps. If it's drugs, we'll find it. If you're a puffer, we'll catch you ass-dorking in the shower or we'll find the cock magazine under your rack. Ya'll ain't faggots, are you? Your faggot bus to Hollywood left ten minutes ago. Let me guess. You keep exercising, ladies, and I'll figure you out. Don't do me any favors. Don't help me out here.

"You, California boy. Swofford. You sure are pretty. Them's pretty blue eyes you got. You sure you ain't a homo? I know you lied about something. Every one of you lied. It's my job to find it out of you. Push-ups!

"Honestly, fellows, what I'm doing here is a favor to you. I'm giving you an option. You tell me now, we write it down in our book, and if it's nothing major, we forget about it. Once you're in the Fleet Marine Force and they find out you lied on your contract, they'll put you in the brig. Do you want to go to the brig someday, Swofford?"

"Sir, the recruit will admit something, sir."

"Don't lie to me, you worthless cum receptacle."

I admitted to formerly using cocaine (four times), methamphetamines (twice), LSD (twice), and marijuana (once).

I closed my eyes and pissed my pants as Drill Instructor Burke screamed in my ear the words *faggot, addict, cumsucker, bitchmaster, dickskinner, dickfuck, fuckforbrains, nopecker,* and *lilywhitebitch.*

I spoke to the colonel about my drug revelation. I hoped he'd send me home. But he ordered me to perform one hundred push-ups and said it was embarrassing for everyone that I'd pissed my pants and to save pissing my pants for combat. He said he thought I'd be a good marine someday, and he'd try to keep my barracks-duty contract for me.

But after fourteen weeks of boot camp and six weeks of barracks-duty training, the captain sent me to the infantry. This was unfortunate for many reasons. From the roll call of local Vallejo women, I'd recently found a girlfriend, a Vietnamese woman new to the country by a few years. She worked at the club on base, and after serving me drinks for a few weeks, she asked me out on a date. I told her I had a girlfriend, but she said that didn't matter, and I couldn't argue with her. She was poor and honest about her desire to acquire a husband from the Marines who'd take care of her while serving his country honorably and with valor and concurrently fathering numerous children. In the military, the more children, the bigger the check. At the same time that she cultivated dreams of pulling herself from the muck of immigrant poverty with the good love of a good man, my girlfriend understood I had no intention of fathering her plan. She only asked that I not marry my other girlfriend, down the road, Kristina in Sacramento.

I enjoyed the sex we shared, and I looked forward to sleeping, on weekends, on the living room floor of her family's house, a filthy ramshackle tumble of wood and stucco, home to three generations of Vietnamese. I loved her, more than I ever did Kristina, and for many months after my training and duty at Mare Island ended, I sent her money orders of $50 and sometimes $100 to help with groceries or rent. So my forced departure from the posh, velvet-lined concertina wire of Barracks Duty School was not well received.

I considered masturbating on the captain's desk, but instead I called him a faggot addict cumsucker bitchmaster dickskinner dickfuck fuckforbrains nopecker lilywhitebitch. He laughed as he signed my orders to the Seventh Marines.

During the long bus ride to Camp Pendleton, I confirmed for myself that joining the Marines had been a mistake. At a breakfast stop in Bakersfield, I considered fleeing, but decided this was my lot, to serve, and I would handle it like a man—I would do my duty wherever they might send me, accomplish all missions, honor my contractual obligation. And besides, Bakersfield looked like a place where people were dying slowly without knowing it—to the east, oil derricks and miles of flat, dead desert, and to the west, strip malls and designer suburban neighborhoods.

I spent my first few days at Camp Pendleton in the base hospital, faking a stomach flu. I chewed Ex-Lax gum and this kept me shitting and dehydrated. A few times a day, I sneaked away to the hospital café and ate their good hamburgers and meat loaf; though I knew the food was not long for my body, I relished the almost civilian flavors.

I pursued a sweet, young candy striper during my stay at the hospital, daughter of an artillery major. She was more than giving with the pinochle and poker cards and small boxes of hard candy, but she did not concede her body, not even a kiss. I felt like an old pervert, though I was merely eighteen and she sixteen, the age of consent in most sane countries. When I'd try to kiss the major's daughter, she'd laugh at me and say, "You funny marine," or, "Wait until I tell the major," or, "My boyfriend is a linebacker for the Camp Pendleton High School Mustangs." I missed her when I left and I knew she missed me. She knew I was not like her father.

After my stool solidified, I spent three days on a work crew. My single duty was changing the marquee at the base theater. I don't recall the titles of the movies I advertised, though I'm sure they were either hyperpyrotechnic combat stories or sorry love stories. Morale builders. On the third and final day of my duty I spelled FUCK IT, SHOWING ALL DAY. An officer's wife noticed the marquee as she left the base beauty parlor or a wives' meeting, and she called the theater manager, a grungy first sergeant, and complained.

I corrected the marquee and performed calisthenics the rest of the day, long into the evening, in the back parking lot, the first sergeant sauntering out every fifteen minutes to alter my punishment from push-ups to sit-ups to cherry pickers and back. When the projectionist took her smoke breaks, she'd laugh at me, calling me a greenie and a newbie and a bitch; she was a hagish marine wife, and while the popular literary compulsion is to tell seedy rumors about female projectionists or to recollect filthy encounters involving such a poor hag, I cannot, for to do so would be pure fiction.

I arrived at Seventh Marine headquarters early on a Monday morning. The Seventh Marines were headquartered at San Onofre, the farthest-north subcamp on Camp Pendleton. This was the real Marine Corps, and to be sure, I had not yet experienced the real Marine Corps. Marines ran all around the place, saluting and shouting and spitting and cussing. I was assigned to the Second Battalion. The battalion had just returned from predeployment leave, and they'd be departing in three weeks on a West-Pac, a six-month training tour of Okinawa, the Philippines, and Korea. The duty staff sergeant who checked me in was a short, harsh man. Most of his ribbons were for individual valor in Vietnam. As he looked over the battalion roster, deciding which grunt platoon to send me to, he spoke through his cigar.

"Swofford. What kind of fucking name is that?"

"It's English, Staff Sergeant."

"You sound like a goddamn choirboy. Do you play any instruments?"

"I played the trumpet in third grade, Staff Sergeant."

"The trumpet? Can you still play?"

"Maybe, Staff Sergeant."

"Maybe my ass. I need a bugler to blow taps and reveille and the battle march. It'll get you out of the grunts. Headquarters and Support Company. You won't have to carry a rifle. We'll give you a sidearm and a bugle. Your pack will be light. If you're interested, I'll try you out."

"Yes, Staff Sergeant, I'd like to try."

I thought the chance of being a bugler was rather a stroke of luck and to not at least try for the position would be ignorant, even indicative of a certain stupidity, a love for the grunts that many boots professed because they thought the grunt held Spiritual High Ground in the Corps. I didn't need Spiritual High Ground. I needed a bugle and a sidearm and a featherlight pack. The staff sergeant told me to stow my gear in the rec room and meet him at the flagpole at 0900 for battalion formation and my bugle tryout.

The rec room was full of grunts playing cards and billiards. They all looked at me but no one spoke. They didn't need to speak, I was the new guy, I was fucked, and they were going to do the fucking. "Bend over, sweet cheeks," I heard someone whisper as I left the room. I met the staff sergeant at the flagpole. He seemed giddy, oddly excited for a man who'd fought in one of the more senseless wars of the century.

"Swofford, do you wonder why I look old enough to be your grandpop but I'm still a goddamn staff sergeant?"

"No, Staff Sergeant."

"Because in Vietnam I beat a lieutenant over the head with my E-tool. He wanted to send my platoon into a gook valley, and I told him to fuck himself, to which he told me he'd send me to the brig, to which I pulled out my E-tool and split open his fucking head before calling in a medevac for his dumb ass. I didn't go to the brig but I lost my stripes. An hour later another platoon went up that valley and got carved to fuck. Poof, the sorry fuckers were dead and gone. My platoon mates still send me birthday cards, did you know that?"

"I didn't know that, Staff Sergeant."

"Well, now you do. And stop calling me staff sergeant. Was your old man in the war?"

"He was in the air force. He built hot runways."

"The fucking air farce. He ever tell you about it? Did he live?"

"Yes, he lived. He spoke once about Vietnam."

"If he only spoke once, he wasn't lying."

The battalion poured onto the parade deck in a U formation. After the company commanders reported to the major, "All present and accounted for," the staff sergeant left me at the flagpole and joined the colonel and the major and the other staff officers.

The sergeant major used a bullhorn to address the men, welcoming them home from leave, reminding them he had granted an extra seventy-two hours of liberty, a bonus three days of freedom, and he expected recompense for his charity, in the form of gallant behavior overseas.

He said, "No rapes of village girls, marines. No beating up old Okinawan women for a free plate of *yakisoba* or a bowl of jungle juice. If you're gonna screw working girls, make sure they're clean. And if you're married, don't let me hear about it, don't let the docs tell me you're on treatment, because I'll give you office hours, minimum of one stripe and two months' pay. Goddamnit, check their Clean-Crotch cards. Last West-Pac we had over two hundred cases of the clap, seven herpes, one syphilis, and possibly one AIDS. Don't bring dirty members home to America. Right now on Kadena Air Base there's a flyboy who's got some disease they've never seen before. His little pecker is falling off in pieces. He's quarantined. The horny bastard's going to die."

The sergeant major ordered the battalion to return to the barracks and commence with field day.

The staff sergeant joined me at the flagpole and said, "You still want that bugle job? There isn't a bugle job, you fucking monkey! I could've humiliated you in front of the battalion, called you out there to make bugle noises with your mouth. But I didn't because for some reason I like you. Swofford, you are a goddamn Marine Corps grunt. You are the most savage, the meanest, the crudest, the most unforgiving creature in God's cruel kingdom. You are a killer, not a goddamn bugle player. That bugle shit is from the movies. You ain't Frank Fucking Sinatra."

"Aye, aye, Staff Sergeant."

"You're in Third Platoon, G Company. Third is full of drunks and half-wits. Maybe you can bring some respectability to the sons of bitches."

"Thanks, Staff Sergeant."

"Don't thank me. Just don't fucking die."

I was being forced into the Spiritual High Ground of the Marine Corps grunt. I appreciated the staff sergeant's generosity in not ordering me in front of the battalion for the mouth bugle tryout. I thought that perhaps I reminded him of a son he'd lost contact with or never had.

I retrieved my gear and the G Company duty sergeant told me I was assigned to room 325, with Private Bottoms and Private Frontier. I entered the room and saw a large crowd gathered around an unmade rack, my rack. One marine was biting his fist as another used a propane torch to heat wire hangers bent to form the letters USMC. I dropped my gear and watched.

Someone said, "Fucko is here."

When the hangers pulsed red-hot, the branding marine shoved the four-letter contraption against the other marine's outer calf. The marine bit his fist until he broke skin and began to bleed. Tears streamed from his eyes and the room filled with the dank stink of his flesh. I vomited into the shitcan and the room erupted in cheers. Before I could speak, the men piled on top of me and bound my hands behind my back with an electrical extension cord and gagged me with dirty skivvies.

The marine at the torch reheated the hangers, and as he did, flesh and hair from the prior man smoked on the metal. At first I struggled and then I did not. The burning-hot metal was extremely painful, but the psychological tumult of the morning took over, from battalion bugler to Fucko, and the pain slowly receded and a deep euphoria took over. The smell of my own burnt leg-flesh did not make me ill, in the same way a man can smell his own shit and not mind the stench, while the smell of another man's waste is vomitous. I was in the stink and the shit, the gutter of the Marine Corps, the gutter of the world, and I knew I had made a mistake, but perhaps I'd discover ME in the gutter, perhaps I'd discover ME in the same way centuries of men had discovered themselves, while at war, while in the center of the phalanx, drowning in the stink and the shit and the rubble and the piss and the flesh.

The men left the room and I fell asleep and didn't wake until it was dark and the man named Frontier untied and ungagged me and offered me a plate of food and a bottle of whiskey to drink from. I reached down to feel my branding wound but my skin was smooth. My branding had been a fake; they'd placed a cold piece of metal against my skin!

Frontier said, "That's a little fuck-fuck trick we play on the new guys. Someday you'll rate a branding. You gotta be a crazy motherfucker first. That sergeant we branded, he's one crazy bitch. He spent six months in Honduras on patrol and all he ate was cocoa and rehydrated pears. He screwed about ten jungle whores a day. Didn't even catch the clap. In the PI he paid a jeepney driver a hundred bucks to drive through the gate at Subic Bay while he fucked a bar girl doggy-style on the hood, and he and the whore both were wearing gas masks. You gotta pull some shit like that before we brand you."

Bottoms and Frontier were drunks and not the simple drunks

who are concerned only with their own drunkenness, their own sad stupor, but social drunks, the poor bastards who feel it is their duty to fill every mouth in the house with drink. So nightly they filled me up, with decent whiskey mostly, but as their funds ran low, they switched to generic gin and powdered Gatorade. The two were pleased with hydrating themselves and catching a drunk at the same time.

I was happy to drink with Frontier and Bottoms; they were decent young men, ruined early by the Marine Corps and dedicated to debasing the standards and policies of the institution that had struck them nearly dead in the moist tracks of youth. I enjoyed hearing their manifestos against the Corps—the Suck, as they called it, "because it sucks dicks to be in it and it sucks the life out of you."

After spending time around Frontier and Bottoms, I realized the grunt holds Spiritual High Ground because he creates it; through constant bitching and inebriation he creates his own Grunt Island, and the poor, sad, angry grunt on the outside is actually a happy and contented grunt on the inside, because he has been heard, someone understands his misery: through profanity and disgrace he has communicated the truth of his being—an awful life punctuated by short bursts of mostly meaningless action, involving situations where he might die horribly or watch his friends die horribly. The very real possibility of dying at any moment—that is the grunt's magic, his Spiritual High Ground.

The constant clatter of the discarded liquor bottles and the cackles and howls from my roommates helped me forget that I'd made a mistake by joining the Corps.

A few weeks after my fake branding we deployed on our West-Pac.

I spent a lot of my time on Okinawa working out. I went to the gym with Graycochea, a huge Hawaiian guy who hated running and swimming and shooting rifles and every other marine duty except lifting weights. The few gyms on Camp Hansen were primitive and small, one end of a barracks stuffed as full with free weights as possible. Graycochea was much stronger than me, but we were good partners. I could max bench-press 350 pounds, and I started my sets with 225; he could max 450 and he started with 300. We pushed each other, and we screamed at and insulted each other, and after our workouts we walked slowly back to our barracks, tired and cussing the world and our loneliness.

I learned from Graycochea that just because you're a marine, it doesn't mean you must like other marines or even care about them. I was in awe of the Fleet Marine Force—the fighting Corps, hard Corps—definitely a boot. I wanted to talk to everyone and find out where they were from, ask questions about their hometown, buy them a beer, just hang out; I thought I'd been invited to one big party, and we should all be friends. One day after we left the gym (I'd been talking with some tankers between sets), Graycochea told me flatly, "Swoff, stop that socializing. You think these guys give a fuck about you? They flap their lips' cause you ask questions. You're too nice. Stop smiling. Stop acting like a girl on her first date. This is the Fleet, motherfucker, this ain't high school. These guys will backstab you in a second. Third Platoon, that's all you can trust, no one else. No one else in the whole Suck."

Graycochea told me about his village and his girl waiting back home. We shared a barracks cubicle, and her pictures hung from our walls, and I knew that nothing mattered in the world to him but loving his girl. I wanted to love like that. After our West-Pac, Graycochea still had eighteen months on his contract. He took his leave to Hawaii and stayed. I hope they never caught him, that he's still free, in his village, loving his girl.

About a month into the deployment a Corporal Wagner from the battalion Surveillance and Target Acquisition Platoon, STA, visited me in the barracks. He said he'd heard I was a hard bastard, that on humps my platoon handed the heaviest gear to me and I carried it without complaint; he'd heard that I'd fallen from a cliff in the Northern Training Area, with full ruck on my back, fifty feet to the ground, and walked away; he'd heard that I spent time in the library when I wasn't in the gym. He looked over my stack of books, *The Myth of Sisyphus, The Anabasis, The Portable Nietzsche, Hamlet,* and said, "I don't know what the fuck any of these books are, and I don't care, but if you're tough and don't complain and you're at least a little smart, I want you to take the STA indoc. I think you could be a scout/sniper. The major doesn't want us recruiting, so let's just say a bird told you to start running more and lifting less and studying patrol orders and weapons nomenclature and the history of sniping."

I asked Graycochea about Wagner, and he told me I could trust him. He told me he wouldn't let me lift with him anymore, he wanted me to improve my cardio. But I told Graycochea I wasn't interested in STA, that I liked being Third Platoon's mule, and I liked everyone in the platoon. He told me I was stupid, that I should try for STA because after the deployment most of Third was discharging anyway, and in a grunt platoon you never knew what kind of new assholes would be in charge of you, but with STA you were at least assured that the assholes could kill the enemy with one bullet from a thousand yards. I didn't know anything about STA—they'd been the guys who wore different physical-training gear and flew in Hueys while the rest of the battalion humped, while the line platoons walked up and down hills, and up and down hills. I talked to the battalion weapons officer and acquired training materials and articles on STA and scout/snipers.

Now I would learn what a sniper really was. The term was first applied to a rifleman during the eighteenth century by British army personnel serving in India. The snipe was a bird so difficult to shoot that only the most disciplined, well-trained, and artful hunters could take it down.

The reticle telescope, invented in 1640, had already initiated the birth of sharpshooting. During the Revolutionary War, the navy employed marines as "fighting tops"—the men who fought from the mast rigging aboard ships and used their overhead vantage to harass and kill the enemy with precise fire. Americans tried to develop a sniper rifle, but the weight of the gun and its recoil proved problematic. The scopes were as long as the rifles and would often break free from the weapons.

During the Civil War, both sides used sharpshooters on the battlefield. The Union's best shots were recruited for Berdan's Sharpshooters, a distinction that required the member to shoot ten rounds in a five-inch group. Most of the men owned their own weapons, heavy rifles that weighed as much as thirty pounds. General Lee used sharpshooters as well, most notably at the battle for Fredericksburg.

Prior to World War I, most military professionals thought the Gatling gun had nullified and made useless the precision fire of the sniper. The stream of bullets that the Gatling gun created was assumed to be far more effective than the sniper's single, concentrated shot. But the M1903 Springfield, first manufactured at the turn of the century, and capable of repeated accurate fire, boosted the competition between and within the services for marksmanship expertise.

During World War I, trench warfare was ideal for the sniper—grouped enemy soldiers, often bored and in low morale, unwilling to stay put in defensive positions, proved ripe targets. The Germans, using scopes made by their superior optical factories, deployed their snipers with verve and bravado, eschewing cover and camouflage for open firing positions and body armor! There also exists the apocryphal story of the German sniper who disemboweled a felled horse and fired from within the remains of the carcass, the muzzle protruding through the mouth of the corpse, the sniper acquiring his targets through the dead animal's eyeholes.

The British established a sniper, observer, scout school in France during the war, in hopes of countering the great German sniper advantage. The instructor, Major Hesketh-Prichard, combined the hunting and tracking skills of the Scottish gamekeeper, the ghillie, with the marksmanship skills of the British competitive shooters. The ghillies captured wild game and introduced the animals to preserves. The ghillie suit, the modern sniper's principal camouflage uniform, derives its name from these Scottish game hunters. The training developed at this British school also included the craft of hide building, and much that the British learned in World War I concerning hide construction and sniper employment is still, in modern times, essential to the proper utilization of snipers.

The marines fighting at Belleau Wood in 1918—where the Germans bestowed upon the Corps the infamous moniker *Teufel-Hunden* (devil dogs)—used sharpshooters to eradicate the deeply and lethally entrenched German machine gunners.

During World War II, marine snipers used a 1903A4 Springfield with a German scope, the 12x Unertl, for the first time. The Marines also introduced night-vision devices into the sniper's trade, and during one battle on Okinawa 30 percent of the casualties were due to this capability.

The Marines used many different weapons for sniping during Vietnam, and more than a few of the guns hit out to one thousand yards. Despite the distance efficiency, the first-shot kill—the sniper's goal—was not a constant in the jungle until the introduction of the M40 weapons system, a commercial Remington M700 with a heavy barrel equipped with a Redfield 3x9 scope. Marine snipers started working in highly successful and cost-effective two-man teams. It is said that for every fifteen thousand rounds fired by an infantryman, the United States scored one fatality; for every 1.2 rounds fired by a sniper team, the United States scored one fatality. Still, marine snipers emerged from the jungle as beaten as the rest of the U.S. military, and the command knew that many of their snipers were cowboys who simply loved to shoot, which didn't necessarily mean they were skilled technicians.

The most often repeated sniper stories came from Vietnam. A couple of my favorites, which may or may not be true, though whatever the facts, they are true in nature and design: The sniper who was in a duel with a VC sniper that ended when the marine sniper caught the reflection of the enemy sniper's scope and delivered a round that penetrated the enemy's scope and then his eyeball and skull, thus killing him. The sniper who saved a young Vietnamese boy's life by shooting out the front tire of the boy's bike seconds before a five-ton truck would have rumbled over him.

After Vietnam, the Marine Corps realized they needed a new weapon for sniping, and comprehensive training for the contemporary scout/sniper. The new weapon, the M40A1, was concocted in the bowels of the Marine Corps Marksmanship Training Unit at Quantico, Virginia. Now the best shooters in the world fired the best rifle in the world, one-shot/one-kill out to one thousand meters. Point of aim, point of impact.

Too much time and energy are expended during boot camp and subsequent rifle-training sessions convincing the marine that he must covet his weapons system just as he does his girl back home, his girl back home a beautiful and noble creature, and so too his weapons system a beautiful and noble creature, capable of both saving the marine's life and jeopardizing the marine's life, causing him either joy or grief. The paradoxes of love are the paradoxes of war, the lesson goes, the thing you love most deeply might someday fail you. But when men are at war, the weapons system is simply a *system,* and those who understand and maintain the system understand and maintain order, and they are more likely to survive, and those who fail to understand the system, they might die faster. This has nothing to do with naming your weapon after your girl or your wife, or likening the deadly system to the tight insides of the girl or the wife. Most weapons systems are made of steel and hard plastic, material nothing like the soft great insides of the woman the marine loves. Systems management. We might just as well call marksmanship training by this name. Anyone can be taught a system. And anyone can wreck a system.

The M40A1 (steel and hard plastic) was the result of all of the work done in the fields of sniping and rifle manufacturing since the invention of the reticle scope. When the sniper looks through his ten-power Unertl, he's looking through the history of the sniper, the history of the art. The reticle is his window onto sniper history, and if he's lucky, the picture of his future, and in that picture will emerge the figure of the enemy—the quartered head, the medulla shot, the pink mist, the confirmation that the sniper's training and history and tactics are not all for naught.

In all of the literature I read, certain words reappeared: *uncompromising, highly trained, elite, cruel, shrewd, calculating, hard-nosed, sacrificial, light.* But there was constant debate within the Marine Corps regarding the effectiveness of the STA Platoon and scout/snipers. Leaders who adhered to the idea that mechanization was the future of the Corps discounted the scouts and snipers, while others cried that the art of scouting and sniping helped sustain the Corps and its mythos. The STA Platoons were filled with men who worked in highly disciplined pairs, who gladly took on poor odds and likely death to fulfill thankless missions. I wanted a thankless mission; I wanted poor odds and likely death; I wanted to give myself over to beliefs that were more complex than the base beliefs of the infantry grunt. The grunt dies for nothing, for fifteen thousand poorly placed rounds; the sniper dies for that one perfect shot.

Flyers announcing the indoc appeared around the battalion in early December:

STA INDOC
ONE SHOT ONE KILL
LEAVE YOUR MOTHER IN KINVILLE
19–23 DEC, 1989
MUSTER AT O-COURSE, 0300 ON 19 DEC
GEAR LIST FROM S-2

No one else from my platoon showed any interest in taking the indoc. Graycochea tried to put me in contact with guys he knew who'd tried out in the past, but anyone who'd failed a STA indoc didn't want to talk about it. The common response to my inquiry was "Fuck STA Platoon, they're hard-assed pricks. And fuck you for wanting to be part of them." I signed up at S-2 (the intelligence shop, the entity that commanded STA) and requested leave from my platoon sergeant.

The indoc was run by enlisted STA marines. They were all talented men who assumed we had nothing to offer their platoon, and their first priority was ensuring the continued honor and high standards of STA. Their preference was that none of us pass: our failure would confirm the elite status of the unit.

Twenty-three grunts showed up for the indoc. It was the rainy season in Okinawa. I slept one hour each night on the floor of the wet jungle. I ate crackers and nothing else. The lesson was, if you're going to be in STA, you must want it, you must travel light and sleep little and eat only what you can carry in your cargo pockets. We spent most of five days on a forced march through hundreds of miles of trails in the Northern Training Area, where some of the most vicious battles of World War II had occurred. They teargassed us and stripped us and starved us. During moments of high delirium, I thought I heard screaming from the jungle, the voices of Japanese and American dead.

When the march ended, we were given classes on stalking and camouflage and observation, the scout/sniper's trade secrets. The fundamental work of a sniper is rather simple: Go to this spot, shoot these personnel, extract yourself. We weren't allowed to touch the sniper rifles, but we had our own M16s with us, and we stalked with those far less tactical weapons. In the ideal situation, the sniper will be inserted one thousand meters away from the shooting position. The low crawl is the sniper's chief mode of movement, elbows and knees and belly.

We low-crawled across a thousand-meter-long wet field, trying to move undetected while STA personnel attempted to locate us using binoculars and scopes. The rain came on hard, and then harder, which was good for tactical movement, but I was miserable and cold and sleepy and at times I wanted to stand up and scream— I turn myself in, take me back to camp for a shower, I'll be in Kinville tonight drinking jungle juice at Eddy's Sound Pub with a bar girl on my lap. But I kept on.

I'd been raised by a highly disciplinarian father. I understood unattainable expectations and failure and subsequent punishment. When I'd stood on those yellow footprints the first day at Marine Corps Recruit Depot, San Diego, I was fully equipped and wired for life as a marine. The Marine Corps environment is one of cause and effect, the first pragmatic principle we learn as children. When red, the stove is hot. When you fail, you disgrace yourself and others. When you succeed, be proud and others will be proud for you.

After six hours, I reached my objective. I aimed at one of the STA spotters sitting on the tailgate of a Humvee, and I shot a blank from my M16; I'd passed the stalking test. Four others completed the stalk with me: Collier, Vann, Vegh, and Kuehn.

At the conclusion of the indoc, after the oral and written exams and ten more times through the obstacle course, the only thing that mattered was having completed the stalk. The life of a STA marine is facedown in the dirt and the muck and the waste. The five grunts accepted for STA Platoon 2/7 were Collier, Vann, Vegh, Kuehn, and Swofford. We'd stay assigned to our line platoons during the next two months in Korea and the Philippines, and when back in Okinawa for the final month of the deployment, we'd join STA and begin our scout/sniper training.

It didn't matter that I was a line grunt for sixty more days, I thought of myself differently already, and so did my line platoon peers. Soon my training would exceed theirs, and I would learn how to kill better, and faster, with more precision, and if a war started, being a STA marine would increase the danger of my missions.

In May of 1990, when 2/7 returned to the States from the West-Pac, hundreds of our jarheads separated from the Marine Corps. Bottoms and Frontier asked for and received their discharges three months early so they could matriculate at Saddleback Community College for summer school, and Graycochea went to Hawaii and skipped the next eighteen months of his contract. Perhaps these three knew what was coming at the beginning of August; perhaps the salts' constant sense of impending doom had rung loudly enough that they listened.

The old salts—twenty-one or twenty-two years old—had seen it all: they'd been twice through Hondo and Fuji and the Northern Training Area, Pusan, Green Beach, Wake Island, Guam, Magsaysay

Street in the PI; they'd spent years of their meager salary on sex and maybe drugs and certainly alcohol; in Hondo they'd traded the chocolate from their MRE for ten blow jobs and a boot shine from the prostitute's little brother; in the PI they'd pounded fifteen Red Horse in fifteen minutes and received sample blow jobs from forty bar girls in one night, gone home with three bar girls for $20, caught fifteen cases of the clap, had their watch stolen off their wrist in the massage parlor/barbershop, been fired at by Muslim rebels. They'd floated on ships and ridden tired and exhausted through jungle and desert in hot, baking troop carriers, fired millions of rounds through the M16, the M60 machine gun, the M203 grenade launcher, detonated hundreds of Claymore mines, and thrown enough center-of-the-plate grenades to win ten Cy Young Awards, and they'd humped thousands of miles at a tactical pace, looking for nothing but other dumb jarheads in training. The salts were tired and mean and the last thing they needed was a war.

During our second trip from the Triangle to the rear-rear, in the middle of October, I become rather sick over the realization that the base we've been ordered to enjoy—showers, private toilets perfect for soothing masturbation, two bunks and an air conditioner per room, sidewalks, televisions, VCRs, chow hall, pogey-shack—is probably not, as we've been told, an abandoned oil company camp, but actually a military base that had sat vacant for years, waiting for the American protectors to arrive in the event of a regional conflict, protectors who'd be tolerated until they obliterated the threat and returned the region's massive oil reserves to their proper owners. We are soldiers for the vast fortunes of others. I realize this while sitting on a shitter and reading the English-language *Arab Times*. Secretary of Defense Dick Cheney is quoted as saying no limits exist for the number of U.S. forces deployable to the Gulf, and heavy mechanized units from eastern Europe have begun transport to the desert. Foot and mechanized infantry units, artillery battalions, and planes are integral to a defensive posture, but hundreds and even thousands of tanks mean an offensive operation is imminent. The paper reports on Palestinian-Israeli violence, and if I were apocalyptically inclined, I might well think that the end is nigh.

The intended effect of the barracks is to convince us that despite the hundreds of thousands of acres of desert that surround us, we are civilized men preparing to fight for the freedom of a civilized people. We are being cared for, the story goes. The Saudis are happy to host us in their country, we're told; in fact they're so happy, they've postponed certain drilling activities and removed their workers from the compound so that we may cool our sweat-soaked balls and brains.

So, as much as I should, I don't enjoy the rear. One STA team is still in the Triangle, and I ask Sergeant Dunn if I can arrange a ride to join them, because I'm tired of the air-conditioning and the $2 candy bars the Egyptians hawk in their pogey-shack. Dunn tells me no, that I have orders to enjoy myself, and he wonders aloud what my problem is:

"What the fuck problem do you have with air-conditioning?"

"I just don't like this place," I tell him. "It's spooky. Preordained. In the desert at least it doesn't look like they were waiting for us with a prefab red-carpet barracks."

"Stop thinking so hard. Jerk off and take a shower and sleep in the AC. Fucking relax, man. Who knows the next time you're gonna get a hot shower and a rack."

For most jarheads, such propaganda works. Any grunt in his right mind will do anything for a hot shower and a rack. The grunt is an addict; the rear-rear is his fix. You've been in the desert for six weeks. The colonel lied about the hot showers your platoon would receive after the MOPP-suit football game. You heard rumors that field units would receive ten pounds of ice per platoon per day. You've seen no ice. One day, because someone stole a case off a mail truck, you drank a warm soda. In the rear you may drink ten or twenty or thirty cold sodas in a day. And the word is that they're showing war movies in the rear-rear, *Platoon, Apocalypse Now, The Boys in Company C, Full Metal Jacket, Sands of Iwo Jima.* And the pleasure of the violent films is like the pleasure of cocaine or a good rough fuck.

I don't leave my small room for five days. I eat MREs and canned tuna and whatever else I scrounge from my platoon mates' care packages. Troy Collier is my roommate, and his mother has sent him ten pounds of caramel, and I eat half of it. My platoon mates urge me to *please shut up* about the place being rigged, about the Saudis wanting us to die for their oil. Everyone in STA but me enjoys the rear. Ten phones have been installed, and what the fuck is my problem, why don't I get on the phone to my girlfriend even if she is cheating on me, or my mom, who will love me no matter what. Make the best of the situation. Stop bringing everyone down with your negativity. Watch a couple of war movies and get pumped. Prepare yourself for killing.

One night I'm alone in the barracks, cleaning my M16, while the rest of the platoon watches movies at the Fox Company barracks. They're hoping for a replay of last night's showing. A Fox Company grunt's wife had sent him a video with his last care package. A homemade porn film had been spliced into a Vietnam flick. The barracks full of unsuspecting marines cheered a screen full of jungle carnage as the on-screen marines charged a VC bunker, then in midcinematic combat frenzy the barracks went silent when the screen turned from overwhelming firepower to the sleek power of sex. After a few seconds, the room erupted. The marines were elated that the amateur smut had made it past the censors, it was another coup! But the excitement only lasted until the marine whose wife had sent him the movie noticed something about the hooded woman, and what he noticed could have been a mole on her ass or the way she moaned or how she threw her head back as she came, but that coming woman was his wife, and the man was his neighbor, and he began to scream, "That's my wife! That's my wife fucking the neighbor, a goddamn squid!" At first the jarheads laughed, because they thought he was joking, but when he continued to scream and then began weeping, they knew that it really was his wife, and someone had the decency to turn the video off. But tonight they want a replay, because why not, the damage is done and when is the next time you'll be able to witness infidelity? And fuck that poor jarhead anyway. He's down at sick call on suicide watch, and as soon as the docs okay him, he'll be on an emergency-leave flight to the States, he'll be the fuck out of the desert.

I remove my firing pin from the bolt carrier and place it in my mouth like a toothpick, and with my tongue I dance the tip of the pin across my teeth. The sound is like a soft tapping against a fragile pane of glass.

The term *suicide watch* always makes me think of my older sister. I didn't know what suicide was until she tried to kill herself a few times. I was between the ages of twelve and fourteen at the time of her first attempts, and after a few sessions of family counseling and her extended stay in an institution (the place was called Serendipity, so it took me some time to realize that it was an institution), she was back living at home and the family situation, as the counselors say, was progressing normally. But, of course, my sister was not normal, and she'd spend the next many years trying to kill herself, and still now occasionally finds herself in the corner, with pills usually—so statistically we are supposed to understand she is not serious about ending her life but is only in the throes of a cry for help because she is a woman and she is in the corner trying pills, yet again—and then she stays at an institution with a dreamy, druggy name, such as Serendipity.

I liked visiting my sister in her institutions. Often they were in the foothills of the Sierra Nevada, slow-rolling foothills thick with trees and the various bent forks of snow-fed rivers. My mother and I would drive up the Sacramento Valley and exit the smoggy freeway for a slow and winding country route, where thick shadows cooled the asphalt and most sharp turns in the road yielded a stunning and steep view of one of the chilly rivers. By the time we arrived at the hospital, I'd have forgotten our destination.

We'd wait first in one waiting room and then in a more interior waiting room and finally an even more interior visiting room, and soon my sister would appear, in what I considered a robe, though the hospital I'm sure had a more appropriate name for the garment, and the three of us would visit. My brother would not visit because he was stationed somewhere with the army, and my parents didn't allow my younger sister to visit, fearing that the institution would frighten her, and my father didn't visit because he and my sister didn't get along, and often she blamed him for her mental condition, though as much as he was sometimes unfair to her, we all now know that it was the chemicals in my sister's brain and not her sometimes harsh father that caused her to open the bottle and swallow one hundred or however many pills. Incidentally, my father was never a bastard to me, and there are different theories as to why this is. I am a spitting image of my father, and I think that he wasn't a bastard to me because it would have been like being a bastard to himself, and he'd had enough of people being bastards to him while growing up.

The visits with my sister saddened me, but nonetheless they were comforting. My mother and I would offer my sister encouraging words and we'd all hold hands and cry, and also smile and occasionally laugh. We'd give my sister the family update so that she wouldn't feel so isolated, even though she was isolated. Sometimes her brain had recently been fried, as in electroshock therapy, though I believe they call it some other, better name these days, a name that sounds not unlike *serendipity*. If brain work had recently occurred, we'd barely talk, because my sister was incapable of responding other than with an occasional grunt or a flutter of her eyelids. We'd sit there, the three of us, holding hands and crying, and nearby usually another patient or two was busy visiting with family members.

Watching the other visitors react to the sickness in front of them, the related sickness, fascinated me. It is difficult for most people to face related sickness. I know this because through the many years of visiting my sick sister in institutions, I witnessed people related to sickness react poorly to the sick person and the sickness. I watched fathers berate daughters for hurting their mothers and brothers berate brothers for driving their parents mad, when everyone should've known the poor crazy person in lockdown couldn't help himself or herself. No matter the group counseling or the pills or the months or years of confinement, the crazy person nearly always returns to the island of their grief or madness. If you are on the outside, no matter how sick you might consider yourself, you are on the outside and cannot claim the lunacy or the malaise.

Throughout the years of visiting my sister in mental institutions, I also watched my mother react to my sister. My mother's reaction was a many-years-long sigh. As much as my mother loved her daughter, it was difficult for her to understand this related sickness, hard for her to comprehend that while she'd raised the daughter she loved, she was at the same time raising a sickness inside of the daughter, breast-feeding the sickness, driving the sickness to ballet lessons and clarinet lessons and softball practice, throwing birthday parties for the sickness, purchasing back-to-school clothes and new grade-appropriate dictionaries for the sickness.

The sigh is my mother's default setting for dealing with grief. While in Saudi Arabia, about to go to war, in the few letters my mother writes to me, I recognize the sigh blowing through her perfect script, and I feel as if I'm again in a visiting room with my mother, but this time I'm the patient, and the institution is not named Serendipity, the institution is named War.

I reassemble my weapon. I've been in the Marine Corps for less than two years, and I've probably performed this one act, assembling the M16, more than ten thousand times. I break it down again. I wonder if mothers worry because their marine sons live with high-powered rifles always within arm's reach.

Sometimes marines kill themselves when they've received bad news from home, from the woman they love, a wife or a girlfriend. This bad news often involves the genitals of the involved parties—in graphic detail the woman describes the other man's skills in bed, and particular acts the marine would never perform, such as with the mouth or the ass or even with innocent toys or easily acquired cooking oils. Even if not specified, these acts are always imagined by the marine.

Kristina, the woman I'm currently supposed to love, the woman who is supposed to love me, is having sex with someone else, a guy who works at a hotel with her, one of the clerks. Even though she has not described their sex in her letters, I know the sex is occurring because she has called him a good friend and a great listener. Also, a coworker and friend of hers, Katherine, who writes me honest letters, has referred to Kristina's "new friend." But I have a sense of humor. I recall Drill Instructor Sergeant Seats saying, "If I ever find out one of you goes and kills yourself over pussy, I'll chase you down into hell and kill your ignorant ass a second time."

When, a few weeks into this deployment, Kristina told me she'd found a job at a hotel, I imagined that soon she'd be sleeping with one of the clerks—during their breaks they'd use vacant rooms, the same vacant rooms that all of the other employees use, not even changing sheets between fornicators. My platoon mates talked me out of this scenario, insisting that I'd probably seen something similar on TV or in a movie, but that the likelihood of such a crime being perpetrated in real life was slim. I did not believe my mates, nor could they have believed themselves, but I appreciated their good-hearted attempts at soothing me.

I close my eyes and reassemble my weapon in seven seconds. I stand. I toss my rifle from hand to hand, marking a sharp cadence with the slap of my palms against the hard plastic hand guards.

Kristina's absurd insistence that we stay together in the midst of her infidelity is a result of her desire to be connected to the military, specifically the Marine Corps, and now, while I'm in a combat zone, receiving combat pay, she considers herself connected to combat. (During and after my various infidelities I never insisted we remain boyfriend and girlfriend, but somehow we would always be classified as such.) Combat must seem sexy to Kristina. I treat her military fetish with disdain because I know that the power of the fetish will not usurp the power of her simple desire to feel flesh, even the flesh of the lonely hotel clerk. I know that she takes pleasure in telling people that her boyfriend is a combat marine. I imagine her smiling as she tells the poor hotel clerk that the man whose girlfriend he's fucking is a marine. And I'm sure the hotel clerk likes telling his friends that the new girl he's stiffing is a dumb jarhead's girlfriend. Everyone loves to get over on the jarhead. Especially other jarheads.

I know that while I was in boot camp, Kristina slept with a marine recruiter. Some people might insist that this replacement lover signified her love for me, that by fornicating with the marine recruiter she included me in her infidelity, bringing herself closer to me because she could not touch me during the tortuous thirteen weeks of boot camp. In this version she'd shown me respect by choosing a marine rather than a civilian, and the recruiter was doing me a favor because while he fucked Kristina, he prepared her for the rough-and-tumble life of loving a jarhead.

But Kristina's various infidelities are not the reasons I'm standing in the middle of my small barracks room, placing the muzzle of my M16 in my mouth and tasting the cold rifle metal and the smoky residue of gunpowder. The reasons are hard to name. The history of my family and the species? The reports that the enemy to the north are elite fighters who learned how to throw grenades when I was barely off the tit? To move closer toward my sister? Cowardice? Fatigue? Boredom? Curiosity? It's not the suicide's job to *know*, only to *do*.

I have ammunition everywhere: hanging from my body, stored in metal boxes and wooden crates under my rack, packed thirty deep into magazines. It is hard to know why I've selected the M16 over the sniper rifle, the weapon with the larger caliber. The round the sniper rifle fires is much more advanced than the basic M16 projectile, precision versus ball. But the weapon I've locked and loaded is my M16. Though less powerful than the .308 round the sniper rifle fires, the 5.56mm M16 round has a lot of bounce and turn, and one hears countless stories concerning an M16 round entering a guy's neck and exiting through the tip of his left big toe, or going in the toe and exiting through the left eye socket. In the event of a proper head shot, the result is what we call pink mist. I've spent many hours of my life imagining what my bullets will do to the enemy.

The medulla oblongata shot is the most coveted shot, the epic shot. Entry through the mouth or the eyeball is also acceptable. The marine does not shoot to injure but only to kill. Sometimes my imagined enemy has been a Russian, sometimes a Chinese, sometimes an Arab, depending on world events and what version of those events I'm receiving or currently involved in.

I bend at the waist and place the buttstock of my rifle against the deck. My thumb rests on the trigger. I bite into the steel muzzle and feel my teeth reversing into my gums. With my tongue running between the slits of the flash suppressor, I imagine the trip my bullet will take, its movement through cerebrum, cerebellum, corpus callosum, pineal body, medulla oblongata. I think of a bullet traveling around my head and exiting through an eye socket or never exiting but rather spinning and spinning and ripping my brain to shreds until the momentum of ballistics is overpowered by fleshly resistance. Stop. Dead.

When you have the muzzle of a high-powered rifle in your mouth, there are many things to consider other than your despair.

Troy walks into our room and sees me. He stops. My trigger selector is on burst, so that rather than one bullet rounding my skull, there will be three, and this must have been the reason I chose the M16 over the sniper rifle. Burst.

Troy says, "What the fuck?"

And I might be only a half a second or many seconds, or even many years, from pulling the trigger, because who knows how many tries one is allowed until one gets it right, but Troy slaps me hard across the back of my head, and the muzzle plays around in my mouth, and I chip a tooth.

I look at him and say, "I was fucking around, I knew you were walking in the door."

He unloads my weapon, calls me various names, and throws my rifle on the rack with his.

He says, "They played it! That poor jarhead. Half the battalion plus assorted tanker assholes have watched his wife getting fucked, really getting fucked, by the neighbor. But I'd watch it again tomorrow. And *you* want to kill yourself? I need to go for a run. You coming?"

I put my boots on and we fill our two-quart canteens and strap them to our backs. Our side of the barracks, what looks like an extended double-wide trailer, is filling up with our platoon mates, and the story of the video is on all of their tongues. Kuehn asks us why the hell we're going for a run, and Fowler calls us suck-asses. Troy insults them both with numerous imaginative profanities involving farm animals and their mothers, and the two of us head into the hot night. We stretch outside of the barracks, and the whir of the hundreds of window-unit air conditioners sounds like one large motor idling at the start line, a motor without a body and without a driver, just pure power and fuel.

We run the perimeter of the base. It's absurd to be in the desert and at the same time confined. Marine MPs in Humvees are stationed every few hundred yards. I wonder if they know what they're looking for. If we scream, they might shoot us.

Troy says, "I really don't know what you were doing back there. If this is over Kristina, you need to pull yourself together. She ain't suicide-pretty."

"It's not about her. It's about the desert."

"The desert my ass! Motherfucker, I picked out and bought for you your first hooker in the PI. Don't try to jack me off! I don't give a fuck what it is, just don't pull the goddamn trigger!"

Troy had indeed bought me my first prostitute in the Philippines, and he considered that a blood bond. A year before our West-Pac he was stationed in the PI, and he knew the islands and the bars as though he'd been born in Manila rather than Greenville, Michigan. But on barracks duty in the PI he got busted from corporal to private for failing the marijuana portion of a piss test. He'd blown a choice assignment and been sent to the Fleet Marine Force, so he was particularly belligerent and disrespectful and thus great for morale. He was a terrible crying drunk, constantly moaning about a girl at home named Lisa who'd refused his advances since grade school.

Even before we both passed the STA indoc, Troy and I often drank together in Okinawa, and after taking in a few porn films and a $2 plate of *yakisoba,* we'd end up in my barracks, yelling profanities and asking for free beer. On Okinawa, it was easy to bum free beer. The Michelob semitruck pulled onto base every Wednesday at noon and sold cases of bottles for $5. There weren't enough refrigerators on the entire base to hold the beer all of those jarheads bought. After drinking a case of $5 Michelob, yelling at people for no apparent reason was rather common. It wasn't just drunkenness, it was stupidity and youth and forgetfulness. You must forget who you were before the Marine Corps. You must also forget the person you might be in the future, after leaving the Marine Corps, because when war comes, you might die and then all of your fantasies and predictions for the future will have become lies.

We run in silence. Troy is smaller and faster than me, but I can outdistance him. He tries to tire me out quickly, and I attempt to finish him off slowly. We run and run and the hours pass, and even though we're going in circles, I'm running away from whatever I left back in the barracks. I'm swirling around the thing until it becomes part of the swirl, and the swirl becomes part of me, and I'm still a part of that small sickness, and that sickness is still a small part of me, but it no longer has me bent over at the waist, chewing on the muzzle of my rifle. Maybe someday in the future I will revisit the sickness, but for now I'm done with it.

Troy snaps his fingers as he runs, a trick his high school track coach taught him to keep on pace. Our boots slap the sand with the sound of a theater curtain falling. And we are actors running around the stage. We are delivering our lines as we run. We are proving to the great theater director of All Time that we are ready for war or whatever. We can run all night, and we will run all night, through the sand, in circles around our fake encampment. The wagons are circling. We are the wagons. We have no reason to challenge one another this way, to prove anything to one another, there is nothing to prove, there is no challenge. We are the same body. We are nearly the same brain. We are running ourselves into the earth, literally; we run a path around the fence, like wild animals circling prey they don't yet know how to eat.

My shoulders hurt and my stomach aches and we have been running so long that even my fingertips hurt, but we continue. My crotch is raw, and Troy's is too, because he says to me, "I wish I had rubbed some petrol jelly in my crotch," and I affirm this desire. But

ANTHONY SWOFFORD

we will not stop. The sun rises. Reveille plays over the same speakers that call the Egyptians to prayer. We continue to run.

Perhaps I wouldn't have pulled the trigger. My despair is less despair than boredom and loneliness. Maybe Troy's good timing saved me. I think about my sister, this very minute living in an institution in California, and I consider myself a poor impostor, an actor speaking the wrong lines. I don't know what I want, but obviously I don't want badly enough to be dead. I think about Hemingway. What a shot. What despair. What courage. Some insist that the suicide is both a coward and a cheat, but I think the suicide is rather courageous. To look at one's life and decide that it's not worth living, then to go through with the horrible act. Millions of people live lives that aren't worth living. Many fewer people end their worthless lives. To look down the barrel of the gun or over the lip of the pill bottle and say, "That is what I want, that is the world that needs me, better than breath, better than banging my bones through the remainder of these sorry days"—there is the courageous man and woman, the suicide. But I don't own the courage to kill myself. I must return to the thing I know best, possibly the only thing I truly know: being a jarhead.

The mirage interferes, even long after the Gulf War. A few years later, after Troy might have saved me from killing myself, he is killed—now a civilian driving to work in Michigan one morning, at least hungover and possibly drunk, hitting a patch of black ice and then a tree and now he is dead.

Six of us traveled to Greenville, Michigan, for the funeral. Me, Atticus Larson, Roger Wagner, Sandor Vegh, Doc John Duncan, and Doug Welty. When we arrived at the Detroit airport, the five of them had been drinking for thirty-six hours and I'd been drinking for thirty (because I was late back to base after liberty and so found out about Troy's death six hours and five cases of beer after them), and since I was the closest to sober, I rented the car. The Michigan winter was brutal, and we'd left the high desert in a rush, bringing only our dress uniforms and one spare set of civilian clothes, and not one of us had brought a jacket, not even Atticus, a native of Wisconsin, who should've known better. It was 3 A.M. and we drove around Detroit for an hour before finding our way out.

We each had a bottle of liquor with us, and we passed the whiskey and schnapps and brandy and Scotch around, and this way we stayed warm and were able to continue a buzz, and I drove as the snow began to fall, and we didn't speak, other than the occasional *Fuck* or *What a motherfucking shitload of luck* or *Goddamn, goddamn.* We were all hurt badly, and ready to die, to join our friend. We wanted the pain to end and certainly the alcohol didn't help, and our good friend was dead, and we didn't give fuck-all about anything else.

The girl named Lisa, whom Troy had loved from afar for many years, had given us directions to the funeral home. Lisa and her parents were there and also Troy's fiancée, a girl he'd started writing to from the Desert when Lisa had finally made Troy understand she wanted only his friendship. Somehow Troy had convinced his future fiancée to join the Marines, and she'd done so while we were at war, and she had subsequently told Troy that the engagement wouldn't work, with him in Michigan now and her on the West Coast, but they should just wait and see. She was a nice woman, and smart and tough, and being grunts, we'd spent minimal time around women marines, and at first we weren't sure how to treat her, but eventually we treated her as a peer and the former fiancée of our dead friend.

The viewing lasted as long as we wanted and we were all still a bit buzzed but wearing down our drunks. Someone, I can't remember who, had said, "Let's stop drinking, you fuckers, we've got to carry Troy into the ground in a few hours."

We continued cussing during the viewing, profanity being as clear a trumpet of grief as any. Profanity and then silence. *Fuck fuck fuck* and then nothing. They'd done Troy up in his dress blues and shaved his mustache. His fiancée was angry they'd shaved him clean, but I didn't think it mattered. There might have been a few extra decorations on his chest, but I said nothing. He looked, as only Troy could, as happy in death as he'd been while alive.

We slept for a few hours at Lisa's parents' house, friendly people who'd prepared beds for us on couches and roll-aways and in guest rooms, but we thanked them and all slept together in the living room, on the floor, under a storm of blankets.

I affixed my expert pistol and rifle badges to my dress blues, along with the seven ribbons I rated, the red of my Combat Action

Ribbon in the superior position, red as in blood. I hated the feel of the uniform, but at the same time I knew that I looked good, I looked like one of their goddamn posters, I sounded like one of their commercials.

Troy's mother was some brand of born-again Christian, and I knew she was always unhappy with his drinking and swearing, and I also knew that, just like me, he believed in no God. But, of course, she had arranged his funeral, not he, and the preacher gave a windy eulogy full of Christ the King as God and on and on, and I grew bored with the whole thing. But I thought Troy might want it this way, that for all of his disagreements and fights with his mother, if she watched him enter the ground as a believer, he was probably fine with that, because it would help her and probably others. If while alive you hurt or disappoint people you love, there's no use continuing such behavior when you're dead.

At the graveside, three marines from a nearby reservist unit arrived to perform the gun salute and fold the flag for Troy's mother. Because of the weather—an inch or two of snow on the ground and a wind that chilled the temperature below zero—the burial lasted only a few minutes. The preacher offered more holy words, and the reservist marines fired their blank cartridges and folded the flag in that intricate and careful way that means death. We pallbearers slowly lowered Troy into the cold ground, his fiancée threw in a pair of her chevrons, and his brother kicked dirt and snow onto the casket.

Troy had wanted to stay in the Marines, he'd wanted to die a marine, but because he'd busted that piss test years before in the PI, they wouldn't let him re-up. One of the more annoying aspects of the Marine Corps was that rules constantly got in the way of sound decisions, and to allow Troy to reenlist would have been a sound decision, because he was a good marine and a great leader who loved and hated the Corps; he bled green, which, as they'd told us at boot camp, happens only to true Devil Dogs; he loved being a grunt, a cussed, dirty, foulmouthed and foul-minded grunt.

After his discharge, in November of 1991, he lived in the barracks with us for six weeks, and we brought him chow from the chow hall for every meal and let him clean his old weapon, and he trained a few of our new marines in optics and camouflage. He even went to the field with us once, a poor decision on my part, as I was the chief scout/sniper at this time and could've been sent to the brig if anything had gone wrong, but the operation ran smoothly and Troy got his last fix of humping the desert and firing rounds through the sniper rifle.

I watched Troy's mother being helped to the limousine, one of his boyhood friends at each of her elbows. She clutched the flag to her chest. Visiting Greenville, Michigan, helped me understand Troy's love of the Marines. The town had obviously been the site of a gross failure of industry. Largely white, the town was, I guessed, largely alcoholic and religious by the looks of the people we met. Nice people who were grieving for one of their own, and I couldn't announce that Troy had not been one of them for many years; it would've been callous for me not to let them grieve with that fiction.

After the burial, Troy's family held a dinner at a nearby Lions or Kiwanis Club. On the way over, we stopped at a liquor store and bought some beer and a few bottles of whiskey. We finished all of the alcohol before entering the hall. The older folks of the party were excited to have strapping young warriors among them, and they offered numerous compliments on our uniforms and bearing and the way we'd won that last war.

The reservists were also at the hall, and some tension started between us when their sergeant approached Atticus and questioned the validity of his ribbons.

"You look too young to have a Combat Action Ribbon, Lance Corporal. My bet is you were in boot camp during Saudi. You know that's a punishable offense, wearing ribbons you don't rate?"

Atticus said, "Get the fuck off my CAR, man. I don't see any war on your chest. You were sucking dick over at the reserve center while I was ass out of luck in the Desert."

"I'll look you up at headquarters, marine, and I don't care if you're active duty, I'm a sergeant and you're a nonrate. You show me respect."

"I'll respect my fist up your ass."

Roger, our ranking member, himself a sergeant, backed us down and told the nice reservist that unless he wanted a serious ass-kicking in his hometown, he and his boys should probably DT the fuck out of there. They each grabbed a slice of cake and exited through the rear of the building.

After the funeral dinner we returned to Lisa's parents' house for a party with Troy's friends from high school. They were nice people, the same age as most of us, sad over seeing a friend they'd known for many years return briefly only to die. We knew their names because even though Troy didn't like Greenville, he liked his friends, and other than shoot rifles, the thing grunts spend most of their time doing is telling stories about the civilian world they left behind, even though they should be forgetting it.

During the few months Troy had been back home, he'd told his friends about us, and so we quickly eased into the conversation as though we'd all known each other for many years. They embarrassed us with great thanks for having served overseas. They recounted combat events Troy had told them, and we realized by the context of their stories that Troy had made us heroes for his friends because we'd been heroes to him. At this point I was the saddest I'd yet been over Troy's passing, because the true friend from war is the friend who obliterates his own story by telling the stories of others. Through briefing his hometown friends about the rest of the platoon, Troy had effectively diminished his own role; he'd become the tale teller and removed himself from the tale. If at any point during my marine experience I was proud of my service, it was then, because whatever the Marines and the Gulf War meant to me, my friend Troy had served with honor, proudly, and he'd returned a happy man, quite possibly a better man for having gone to war, and I felt joy knowing my friend had died happily, a warrior with a Combat Action Ribbon and a few campaign ribbons and useless murderous skills that filled him with pride.

Troy's friends left and Atticus suggested we go to the bar they'd mentioned as Troy's favorite drinking establishment, where many of them had been drinking with Troy a few hours before he died.

The bar was in the basement of an antique shop. Roger bought a bottle of whiskey and we finished it in one pass. Atticus sat at the bar and told the bartender how pretty he thought she was, and that if she could get him so fucked up that he forgot Troy was dead, he'd give her $100. Sandor shoved four shots of something in front of me, and I took the drinks in quick bursts and the liquor burned down my throat and I knew that before the night came to an end we would cause trouble in this bar.

None of the locals in the bar were Troy's friends. Most of the men had long hair and wore heavy-metal T-shirts and ripped jeans and Converse tennis shoes. The women ranged from hard-luck drunk to recent high school beauty queen on her way down. A few of us danced to industrial music on the small dance floor, Nitzer Ebb, I believe, and because of our thrashing and beating against each other's bodies, none of the locals could fit on the floor. We head-butted each other, and Doug and Sandor exchanged blows to the face. Roger bought another bottle and we passed it around and Atticus threw it against the wall when he emptied it. None of the citizens seemed to notice or care to react. We finished more bottles, and the bartender made us drinks she called Troy Colliers, pint glasses filled with God knows what, and we each emptied a few of those.

The music turned to country, an obvious attempt to allow the older locals some time on their own floor, and we returned to our table. Atticus joined the bartender behind the bar, and she made him another Troy Collier before sending him to the bathroom to vomit. He returned and sat at the bar, passed out with his head in his hands. This is when a local boy made a mistake. He grabbed the little bit of hair on top of Atticus's head, pulled back his head, and said, "Hey, jarhead, don't you think you need a haircut, just like your fucking dead friend?" and he shoved Atticus's head into the bar. I made it to the guy first, and I picked him up and threw him behind the bar and he fell to the floor in a clatter of broken bottles. The bartender screamed and ran through the back door. The locals charged us from all corners, and there were six of us against ten or twelve of them, and we beat them thoroughly and ruthlessly for what must have been ten minutes. We broke chairs and bottles of liquor over their heads, we broke bones and skulls and some of our own fingers, but we beat them as we'd never beat anyone before, and when they connected, rarely, we felt nothing because their blows were soft and could not damage us, and they called us dumb jarheads and told us they were happy our friend was dead, our shithead jarhead friend who came home from war thinking he was a badass, and we beat them and beat these words out of their mouths, and we cried as we beat them, we called them sons of bitches and civilian fucks and motherfucking whores and we didn't stop until the police arrived.

We had nowhere to run, because everyone knew who we were and where we were staying. The cops took us outside and put us in their cars. They told us we'd beat up some of the biggest shitbags in their town, and they were sorry our war buddy had died, and how about if they took us back to where we were staying so we could get some sleep before leaving town early in the morning?

I felt somewhat sorry for the men we'd beaten. They had good reason not to want us in their bar—they'd recognized us as foreigners, just as they'd recognized Troy as no longer belonging to Greenville. Those men had actually shown Troy more respect than his family or his friends, because the family and the friends had loved Troy and with their selfishness and love had wanted him to again be a part of their world, but the men we'd fought were willing to tell Troy that he didn't belong.

The next morning, Troy's mother showed up at Lisa's parents' house. I was half-asleep, but I heard her yelling at Doc John about the great disrespect we'd done her dead son, that our drunken and violent behavior had permanently tarnished his death. And I felt sorry for his mother, because although I understood that from her perspective we'd certainly disgraced Troy's memory, I knew that if Troy had had any choice in the matter, he'd have wanted us spending the evening of his funeral drunk and at combat.

We stayed drunk for many months. There was the problem of cause. Why was our friend dead? In the PI he'd been on hot jungle patrols against Islamic rebels. He'd lived through the Gulf War with us. We blamed the Marine Corps at first: if they'd allowed him to reenlist, he'd never have been driving down that cold road. We blamed the economy and the failing town of Greenville: if the nearest worthwhile job wasn't thirty miles away, he wouldn't have been driving down that cold road. We blamed his fiancée: if she hadn't postponed the marriage, he would've been living near San Diego, where there is no such thing as black ice on cold roads. And then there is the realization that the cause of a death like Troy's is ineffable, everywhere and nowhere at once, unknowable, like the mirage. I'd been prepared to watch many of my friends die in combat. Just before we engaged the Iraqis, I'd decided that I would soon die and this was okay, and I went forward into battle with the dumb death stare of the dead walking. But after the war I was shocked back to life, and to the glory of my friends still living, and so I was unable to comprehend that one of us was dead. The problem with living through war is the false sense that after combat you are untouchable. We stayed drunk for many months.

It's late October, the Saudi desert is bursting with over three hundred thousand U.S. troops, and STA Platoon is a few men short, depending on whom you ask. Some people insist a STA Platoon requires sixteen men, some say twenty-one, and others say twenty-six. I've heard all of the arguments over the years for the different platoon strengths, and not one of them is any better than the others. The people who want sixteen seem to be of the mind: the smaller, the more elite. The twenty-ones follow published Marine Corps doctrine. The twenty-sixes declare: the more bodies around, the smaller the chance the rockets and grenades will find me. We are running a platoon of fourteen, and no matter your preferred number, with the expected heavy casualty toll from offensive operations, STA needs more men. Because we consider ourselves highly trained and our talents indispensable, the concept of counting bodies is contrary to our idea of STA: we aren't the line platoons you might fill with any old grunt fresh out of the School of Infantry. However, the line companies in the Triangle are full of just that—boots, real greenies five days out of Camp Pendleton, their rucks still smelling like the Pacific Ocean. STA wants grunts who've deployed at least once, men who have a little of the PI jungle and Okinawa training areas in them. We prepare an indoc because no one has ever heard of marines simply being assigned to STA Platoon. We plan the land-navigation course, the classes we'll give the indocees in such areas as marksmanship and nuclear/biological/chemical defense, and we scout possible areas for a thousand-yard stalking exercise. Johnny Rotten and Combs and Dickerson, the three senior corporals, talk to Siek about recruiting for the indoc. He tells them to fuck off, that he'll decide who's in STA Platoon, and maybe he should run all of us through his own indoc to see if we're actually as balls hard as we insist. Staff Sergeant Siek doesn't care what has and has not occurred in STA Platoon. We know this all too well.

Siek hadn't trained as a scout or sniper, but for five years before joining our platoon he'd been running officer candidates through the gauntlet at Quantico. He was a real spit-shine guy, a classic lifer, thin and strong and mean with a torturer's smile, the smile that says, "I am enjoying this, I am enjoying every second of fucking you." He looked a little like Daffy Duck with a tan and sinewy muscles and a devil's streak. He wore the tightest of high-and-tight haircuts.

We knew he didn't like us because he'd made that clear a few hours after Captain Thola had introduced him in June. We'd come off a month of leave after our West-Pac, and none of us was very interested in training other than a morning run and three thousand or so yards at the pool. We were at Twentynine Palms, the new permanent duty station of the Seventh Marines. The regiment had moved from Camp Pendleton in north San Diego County to the Mojave Desert. We'd been violently screwed with the Green-Weenie, the famous Marine Corps brand of screwing. The town of Twentynine Palms had about fifteen bars, one grocery, two army/navy stores, and one Chinese restaurant run by an Anglo family. We spent more money on gas, driving to L.A. or San Diego on weekends, and even on a few desperate weeknights, than we did on beer and liquor.

We sat in a lazy school circle in our platoon ops room, a barracks room we'd convinced the billeting sergeant we needed to store our ghillie suits and optics but that we'd actually converted into our private rec room, with TV and VCR, porn magazines and videos, a blowup doll, a refrigerator full of beer, and a respectable wet bar. We were on the third floor of the barracks, with a nice view of the Bullion Mountains.

After Captain Thola left, Siek said, "I know you assholes think STA stands for Sun Tan Association. Or Steal, Take, and Acquire."

A few of us let out chuckles.

"I know you think you're the shit because you run around wearing underwater demolition trunks just like the SEALs and Force Recon. And you make your own training schedule and shoot your own rifles. I'm not here to contest your tactics or tell you you aren't the best shooters in the battalion. I am here to tell you that you marines are considered an undisciplined group of showboats. Being a marine means more than one-shot, one-kill. It means discipline in the rear, squared-away uniforms, and respectable behavior while on leave and liberty. I know you underage marines aren't drinking in the barracks, right? I know you underage marines never drink, because it is illegal in the U.S. of A. to drink alcoholic beverages unless you're twenty-one years of age. You are no longer on a West-Pac. And don't try the old crap story 'I'm old enough to catch a bullet, I should be old enough to drink.' Bullshit! I'm bringing you jarheads back to basics! Charlie Uniform inspection tomorrow morning at zero six. Ribbons and badges."

"What the fuck, Staff Sergeant," Kuehn said. "Tomorrow is Saturday. I'm going out of town with my wife. That's my time off. You can't take my family time away from me."

"I can take whatever I want. I'm an E-6. You're an E-3. Do the motherfucking math! For a few years now I've been hearing funny rumors running around the Marine Corps, the idea that the marine's family is more important than the Marine Corps. The ballsacks who say that are liars and possibly Communists."

Siek ordered Kuehn to empty the shitcans in all three of the battalion barracks, about thirty shitcans in all.

Kuehn didn't move until Siek said, "Or, I could take a stripe right here."

As Kuehn ran from catwalk to catwalk, emptying the battalion's garbage, Siek ordered us to take off our blouses, and he ran us to the first slow rise of the Bullions, and he began to put us through the traditional Marine Corps Daily Seven, the same calisthenics that the line companies did, the same calisthenics we'd performed during boot camp. We laughed through the exercises. The Daily Seven was to STA what a frog dissection was to a brain surgeon.

Combs said, "Staff Sergeant, our time might be better spent playing bridge."

Siek didn't like this, and he increased the intensity and velocity of the exercises, but still no one labored. Kuehn joined us, having emptied the battalion's garbage. Siek exercised us for many hours in the way of infantry line companies and Officer Candidate School, and throughout the ordeal we were never physically challenged, but we knew the face of our platoon had changed. Siek continually insulted us and our training and told us that what he knew of STA was that the platoon was full of cocky marines who had passed an indoc and then thought they were the top of the battalion and this to the discredit of the basic infantryman. Officers and senior enlisted had allowed the STA lie to pollute the very heart of the Marine Corps infantry battalion, and he'd joined our platoon to reverse that terrible trend.

At the time, because he was busy busting my ass, I didn't recognize Siek's self-interest in breaking us down and rebuilding us his way, or at least what he considered a better way. He had a family and a career, and we were, for the most part, under twenty years of age and deeply concerned with where the next lay would come from and when the next night of drinking and fighting would occur, well trained but casual in our commitment to the skills and especially the discipline that would save not only our lives, but Siek's. Standing in front of Siek was not a platoon of elite fighters, but a platoon of young assholes, and his safety and welfare, his life, depended entirely on the combat performance of those young assholes.

*   *   *

In Saudi, we know that Siek is conspiring to fill the platoon with people not to our liking—this means anyone given the honor of joining STA without first being tested by the platoon in the same ruthless fashion we were once tested by men who'd been tested by the prior generation, and on down the line, through the wars, back to 1775.

On the first of November, we bivouac at regimental headquarters for a five-day stay. One afternoon Siek tells Johnny that he's going to the rear-rear and then drives off alone in a Humvee without offering any other details. We're happy he's gone, we don't care why. Probably he'll pick up ammunition and maps and maybe a week or two of the *New York* or *Arab Times*. He should be gone at least a day.

Regiment runs out of a semipermanent tent city that isn't actually the rear-rear, but it offers some amenities, such as showers, though not hot showers but only lukewarm. I don't have as much trouble here as I do with the rear-rear, the prefab bases. A tent city can crop up anywhere, a sign of the mobile Marine Corps, the quick and lethal movement of troops, the coming desecration of the enemy.

We sleep on cots, and hot chow is guaranteed at least once a day, the mail arrives fairly regularly, and most important, Kuehn knows a guy from regimental S-2 who sells from his rather potent supply of Ho'made Desert Hooch, as he calls it. I've seen the guy around since I joined the regiment in 1989—a tall, slope-shouldered kid who is probably smarter than any officer in the battalion; probably he should be studying astrophysics at Harvard or MIT but his parents couldn't afford it or he broke the law and lost his scholarship and so he joined the Suck.

Minutes after Siek departs we track down the S-2 guy. His glasses sit crooked on his nose, and when he speaks, he talks into his left shoulder. His uniform holds as many draws and crevices as a topographical map, and he calls everyone a goddamn something, especially the officers. He tells us about the love letters he writes for his major and that after a few months he feels like he's been fucking the major's wife, how writing *Dear sweet Gloria, I wish I were up in you now with a finger in your ass* is as natural as greeting the major every morning with a crisp salute as the major exits the shitter, headed for the ops shack. The S-2 marine charges us $40 for a five-gallon water jug of his Ho'made. I think his story about the major is bullshit and that he considers us goddamn bastards with the rest of them, but that's fine, we have our drink.

We stay in our tent and drink, ignoring the list of classes and maintenance tasks Siek assigned us to complete during his absence. We drink the Ho'made with our canteen cups, and the liquor tastes like the metal cups, with a splash of grape juice. After a few drinks each we are getting drunk. Kuehn tops his hooch off with a shot from his bottle of Jack, and after an hour he swears he's hallucinating, something about Dallas Cowboy Cheerleaders.

Troy, after having failed miserably for years on the page, tries to record a love tape for Lisa, back in Greenville, but mostly he sobs. (The tape recorder and blank tapes are a gift from the Red Cross.) Dickerson performs push-ups in the corner and between sets he looks at himself in his field mirror and repeats what a bad motherfucker he is, that soon he'll fulfill his destiny, kill legions of ragheads, be a war hero just like his papa and his papa's papa. Dickerson is one of the best marines in the platoon. He's an expert at every aspect of scouting and sniping, but I've never trusted him, probably because he knows he's one of the best marines in the platoon and that no one can challenge him, and he exploits others with his knowledge as often as he shares it.

Combs is talking to no one in particular about Oklahoma, about how all those stupid Texans never know what they're missing. Kuehn yells toward Combs's general direction that the only thing Texans go to Oklahoma for is to screw the loose women. Johnny Rotten has taken apart and put back together his Walkman three times, and he swears he's improved the sound and it's better than sitting in a concert hall. I'm attempting to read *The Stranger* but I'm so drunk my eyes feel as if they've been twisted around my skull, as if my right eye is located in the general vicinity of my left ear.

JARHEAD

I abandon *The Stranger* and pull from my ruck the letters I've received from Kristina and I begin to burn them. No one seems to notice. Kristina had gone to a card store in a shopping mall and ordered personalized stationery. In the lower right corner of her letters, two imp-like creatures are holding hands under a palm tree, with a caption floating in the clouds that reads "Tony and Kristina Forever." The stationery makes me ill, or rather, the caption's fraudulent and even dangerous sentiment makes me ill. Nothing is forever, and certainly not a cheap relationship fabricated on personalized paper, and I'm about to die or not and kill or not, but no matter what occurs I will never be the same, and that is the only thing that might last forever—exile, change, change the only sustenance I know, today is only today and tomorrow is tomorrow and a far ways away and then you might die or walk farther with your heavy rucksack and your weapons.

I've received hours of ridicule from the platoon because of Kristina's stationery. I'm angry. I try to read her lies through the folding, burning imps, but I can't make out the words, though certainly I know her lies by heart. I dig deeper into my ruck and remove a stack of laminated photos. Three are of Kristina in various seminude positions, the only piece of cloth covering her being my dress-blue blouse. I attempt to hold an auction. Troy once offered me $20 for one of the photos, and Kuehn is known to have paid $30 for a photo torn from a German hard-core magazine, but he says, "I need penetration," thus refusing Kristina.

"That bitch is damaged goods," Troy says. "Right now she's dorking some hotel clerk. Unfaithful is unfaithful. I don't want her photo. I got better jerking material in my head."

Near the regimental mess there is a Wall of Shame, where jarheads post photos of unfaithful women, women who've gone bad on debts or stolen some poor jarhead's car and all of his clothes or simply informed him that the ride has ended.

The truth about cheating jarheads is for the women to tell, and I've never heard those stories, told in America while the jarhead floats at sea or walks the Desert. But the players and the game are

91

always the same: the jarhead cheats, the wife or girlfriend cheats; the wife or girlfriend cheats, the jarhead cheats. Often, back at home, old, grungy jarheads years out of the uniform, the woman's drunkard uncle or her father's poker buddy, will fan the flames of jealousy and mistrust with comments like "I know when I was in the Corps, I never knew a faithful jarhead, other than myself. The problem is, they give the stuff away on the street corners, and you can't blame the kid for partaking. That's why he's not writing. He feels guilty over screwing fifteen-year-old prostitutes on the streets of the PI."

In sexless Saudi we're carrying on our backs the overseas sins of generations of fighting American GIs—gang rapes in Vietnamese jungles, the same in Seoul and Pusan, pregnant Englishwomen abandoned after World War II, Japanese women raped and impregnated and abandoned during the Occupation, thousands of French whores filled with syphilitic cocks while the Great War raged on.

Forty or more photos are affixed with duct tape to the Wall of Shame, actually a six-foot-tall post that looks like a third of a telephone pole. From a distance it might appear as though a suburban American neighborhood has been afflicted with a series of suspicious pet disappearances. Most of the women are young, eighteen to twenty, with an equal distribution of wives and girlfriends and unwisely sustained cheap fucks. On the duct tape jarheads have written various messages—*This bitch fucked my brother*—*Jones from 2/5 is now with her, used to be my girlfriend and best friend*—*She's my wife and lives with my mother and my mother loves her more than me, they told me to go somewhere else if I leave over this shithole desert*—*Stay away from her, she'll take all yer money, she hangs out at the Whale Club in Oceanside*—*She fucks all the men she wants and all I get is more masturbation.* I tape the three dress-blues photos of Kristina to the pole, and I write—*I don't know but I've been told she's seeing someone new.* I look at more of the pictures and I think of the poor jarheads who've left their platoon tents and walked the slow desert walk to the chow hall, but rather than receiving hot chow they've proudly displayed the narrative of their cuckoldry. It is not necessarily a bad thing to be able to tell the story of your woman's betrayal.

I recognize two of the women on the Wall of Shame. Before my first deployment to Okinawa, while we sat mustered at Camp Pendleton with our gear on the deck and wives nearby kissing their husbands good-bye, a scuffle started between two grunts from Fox Company. A tall and pretty blonde stood between the grunts, screaming at them both, and eventually a staff sergeant and a gunny escorted the woman out of the muster area, she cussing the entire way, cussing the staff and the gunny, cussing the Marine Corps and every dumb jarhead in the bastard.

When I asked, my squad leader told me that the man she'd been saying good-bye to was her boyfriend, and the man who'd started the altercation was her husband's best friend, and in an hour when the planes landed from Okinawa, full of First Battalion marines returning from a West-Pac, her husband would exit the rear of the plane and her boyfriend would enter the front.

The other Wall of Shame woman I've seen before was once the wife of a grunt I met in a club on Okinawa. He was walking from club to club, showing his wedding picture to every drunken jarhead he could corner and telling his sorry story. He'd just been on base at the NCO club, drinking with a group of marines from another unit, a tank unit if he remembered correctly, and they were sharing sex stories, the craziest fuck ever, the craziest place ever, the most dangerous fornication, et cetera, having a grand old time, and he hadn't yet had a chance to tell his story when the guy next to him, new to the island by about five days, began describing a woman who sounded a lot like the grunt's wife—dark brown hair, strong nose, nice chest, runner's legs, Southern twang, ass as hard as a stack of bricks, hips that billowed like a flag, lips that sang like an exotic bird, et cetera, the tanker said. And then the tanker mentioned that the woman was married to some dumb grunt—and that's a quote from her, dumb-as-a-board grunt—and how the dumb grunt had bought the woman a new convertible before his West-Pac. The tanker said that all he did his last three days in the States was fuck this broad, this poor dumb grunt's wife, in her new sky-blue convertible, parked at the beaches at Oceanside and San Clemente and Dana Point, and God bless America and the cheap sluts who guard her holy shores, the tanker said. And that's when the cuckolded grunt began to beat severely on the tanker, and he didn't say a word, he just beat the tanker to the ground, probably broke a few teeth, maybe the soft jaw, certainly the nose. And then he wept his way through Kinville, from bar to bar, while the MPs looked for him on base, he wept in the drinks and the laps of former and future and currently cuckolded jarheads, and I was one of them.

Siek arrives from the rear-rear at 2300 or so. We've been passed out for many hours. Someone is supposed to be on firewatch, no one knows who, and when Siek realizes we're passed-out drunk, he curses and screams in the way of the Old Corps. He tips Dickerson and Johnny Rotten and Combs out of their racks and tells them to report outside at once. We don't know yet, but standing at the top of the berm are six new members of STA Platoon, handpicked by Siek and Captain Thola. Siek couldn't have asked for a better way to introduce the new marines—by thrashing his senior NCOs he's sending the message that anyone can make a mistake, and when he does, he pays. The lantern is burning to flickering ash, and three or four of us poke our heads from out of the hootch and watch our leaders being thrashed. The six guys at the top of the berm look frightened and fascinated. Kuehn yells at them to go get their sick kicks somewhere else, and Siek says, "They are now in STA Platoon, fucknuts."

They're all boots except Martinez, who may as well be a boot after twenty-four months of guard duty on Diego Garcia Island in the Indian Ocean. He recently got busted for something. He looks like a sleeper, as if he were caught just as we'd been. But rather than sleeping while he should've been watching over his drunk buddies, he probably nodded off in a dark corner of the head while the sergeant of the guard expected him to be walking port arms in front of a docked nuclear sub.

The thing about getting busted is, you never want it to happen to you, but when it happens to others, you want to hear the story, you want to know how they almost got over on the Suck, and more important you want to know how they got caught, so if you ever pull the same trick, you'll slip under the wires.

Martinez won't tell us anything of value. He smiles and says, "I never got busted and then I did this once and they put me on the boat straight up the ocean. Two nights ago I was in a bar with a woman on my lap and ten empties on the table. This Siek guy sounds like a real hard-dicked bitch. What is this STA Platoon shit, anyway? I lied and told him I knew how to hunt. I figured it had to be better than the line companies."

Crocket, from Auburn, Alabama, looks like he stepped down from his daddy's tractor about fifteen minutes ago. On his upper lip he has something he wants to call a mustache, and Combs lets him know promptly that STA marines don't grow mustaches. Crocket is thick, though. Pure ripped Alabama muscle.

Dettmann is from North Dakota, and when Dickerson tells him to show us a picture of his girlfriend, he pulls out a five-by-seven of his Harley-Davidson. Dickerson asks him how many holes she takes it in. Dettmann will not remain Dettmann for long. He proudly demonstrates his double-jointed elbows, and there's something sweet in his desire to show us this, his attempt at proving his worth. Kuehn christens him Ellie Bows and decides that with a mop on his head, Dettmann with his thick lips will look a lot like a streetwalker, and we spend a few hours amusing ourselves by threatening Ellie Bows with searching out a mop head and having our way with our new favorite woman.

Larson is as big as Crocket, but smarter. Atticus is his first name and he quickly becomes Addie. Addie misses Wisconsin, snow-mobiles, and drinking Pabst out of the keg he and his friends installed in an ice-fishing hut in the middle of the lake.

Andy Goerke looks like Billy Joel, and he becomes Billy Goerke or Andy Joel. His girlfriend is forty-something and she left her husband and three or so kids for young Andy. She likes baby oil and shower curtains, but that's all he'll tell us, at least right away.

Meyers is one of those guys you'll forget unless he's standing in front of you. The jarhead you're looking for when the head count doesn't jibe but no one can remember who the hell is missing. He's from the Chicago suburbs, and his father or grandfather is a captain of a dying industry. I know already that he'll do everything he's told exactly as he's told, and that if he lives through the war, shortly after we return to the States he'll ask to leave the platoon for a line company and I'll never see him again. He is a marine but he's not a STA marine.

These are the new guys, the men we must bring up to sniper speed in weeks or maybe even days because we have no idea *when* the war will begin, only that it *will begin*.

By mid-November we know that we're in-country for the duration. There's been talk of rotating units to the Mediterranean for a week of rest and relaxation, but two-thirds of the Marine Corps is in Saudi Arabia, and that means no replacements. Through our mirage of news sources—the *Stars & Stripes,* the *Arab Times,* an occasional BBC broadcast caught on a shortwave radio borrowed from Comm, letters from parents and siblings and friends—we know that by the end of the month the total U.S. troop count will top 450,000.

As the United States pours more troops into the Saudi desert, Saddam Hussein continues to mass men and weapons at the Saudi-Kuwaiti border. The UN has passed ten resolutions condemning the Iraqi occupation of Kuwait. Saddam regularly heckles George Bush, insisting that the blood of the Americans will flow like a great bursting river, and hinting that he'll use gas.

We're in a war zone, receiving combat pay, an extra $120 a month, even though no rounds have come downrange yet, and I wonder about this, how they justify combat pay, how the abrogation of our taxes has been approved before suffering a single American casualty. But despite or maybe because of the moniker theater of war, in the rear-rear we must shine our boots and shave our faces and salute officers and wear a relatively clean uniform, and we've been ordered to refrain from profanity in conversation and also cadence—the sentiments in our cadence calls must be patriotic and loyal to the Corps.

Meanwhile, we've been attempting to line up a long-distance range, and it finally comes through. We plan to depart our bivouac at 0500 and start putting rounds downrange at 0600. Dettmann is firewatch and he's supposed to call reveille at 0400. Dettmann is in my team, and Johnny Rotten, my team leader, has been in the rear for a few days taking care of gear acquisition and attempting to track down aerial photos of the border, and he will meet us at the range. So, as the ranking member of the team, I'll be responsible when someone fucks up, and Dettmann does just that.

The first person to wake up is Staff Sergeant Siek, at about 0630. Hell comes apart at the seams as Siek screams and curses, and he calls me over and asks if there's any way on earth his watch is two and a half hours fast and he's actually having a bad dream and the so-called elite scout/sniper platoon hasn't just missed their first chance at rifle time in three months. He hopes to high hell I'll tell him a sweet story about screwing so he'll fall asleep for a few more minutes until one of my idiots calls reveille.

Of course, I can do no such thing, because it's 0630 and we have missed our shoot, and I have no idea *where* Dettmann is but I know *what* he is—asleep. If we were closer to the border, and if combat were closer to our hearts, my first thought would be that poor Ellie Bows had been captured by an elite force of Iraqi fighters, and I'd order my team into search-and-rescue mode, and using our highly efficient tracking skills, we'd find Dettmann and the dirty rag-heads who'd abducted him, and we'd lay down some serious hell-fire, killing every last one of the unlucky bastards and taking Ellie Bows home like a Best Butter trophy from the North Dakota State Fair. But I know that Ellie Bows is somewhere nearby, snoring.

I find him a few hundred yards from our hootch, leaning against the major's Humvee, sleeping, a half-eaten peanut-butter cracker, from the first care package his mother has sent him, in one hand, his Walkman in the other, playing a loop of his Harley-Davidson idling in his parents' garage. I kick Dettmann in the stomach, and he coughs up cracker and peanut butter and drops his Walkman and asks me what's my problem. The sun meets the horizon from below. I ask him what time he thinks it might be, and he says, "Sorry, Swoff, I didn't mean to fuck you."

Siek thrashes me for a few hours. Not since boot camp have I received such a complete and ruthless thrashing. He uses water, forcing me to drink three canteens and then running me around the perimeter of our position, until I vomit the water, and then more water, and more running, and more push-ups and sit-ups and bends-and-thrusts and more vomiting. Commanding the team for a few days was my first try at small-unit leadership, and I've failed quite perfectly, confirming for Siek that I deserve the sad rank of lance corporal.

But my punishment is not over. Not with shitters nearby. The shitters in the rear vary in size and design, and while it would make sense for the number of shitters to correlate to the number of marines in the rear, you rarely discover such logic employed. A rear area with five hundred marines might have one three-holer or ten three-holers, depending on various tactical factors such as how far the colonel is willing to walk from any point on the perimeter to a shitter.

The shell is usually made of plywood. If the engineer acquired enough wood or was for whatever reason feeling creative that day, the shitter might be fully enclosed with two side entries and a pitched ceiling, three or four steps from the ground to the shitter proper, an actual seat rather than a hover hole, handles on either side of the seat, shit-paper holders, screens, magazine and newspaper racks, a bookshelf, even a solar-powered radio. The depository is always half of a fifty-gallon oil barrel. If the engineer was in a foul mood because he had once again been ordered to build a shitter for the lousy grunt regiments, the shitter will be a piece of plywood with a jagged hole cut into the center, placed unsteadily on top of the half oil barrel.

A marine on shitter detail doesn't care what the shitter looks like. His only concern is the barrel. If he's lucky, he'll be on detail with a platoon mate so that the two men can complain to one another and feel good even though they know the rest of their platoon is at that same moment either doing nothing at all or performing an easy task such as stacking heavy boxes of ammunition.

The jarheads burning the shitters wish they were stacking ammunition, but the jarheads stacking ammunition never wish they were burning the shitters.

If you are a sergeant in the grunts and you want to take care of your jarheads and keep them out of shitter detail and pure hell misery, you do the best job you can at sucking up to the S-4 marines because ultimately they decide who cleans the shitters and who loads the chow, water, and ammunition, who rakes the sand in front of the colonel's GP tent, who puts the Armor All on the colonel's Humvee tires, et cetera. The S-4 keeps two lists. One list is official, written on paper, and if you were to examine the list, you'd have to admit that the S-4 hands out work party duties fairly. The problem is, the other list exists in the collective brain trust of the S-4. This is the real list.

If your sergeant is not an ass-kisser, if he foolishly believes he exists on a plane above ass-kissing, you will experience bad luck. Your sergeant can afford not to kiss ass because he will never be ordered to burn the shitters, and even if back in the days when he was a nonrate he had to burn the shitters, he has forgotten those horrible hours. Or your sergeant might be a perfectly capable ass-kisser, and not only capable but quite happy to kiss, he might even enjoy it, he might be proud that his platoon never suffers shitter detail, and if this is the case, you are a lucky and blessed bastard. It's most desirable to serve under the number one ass-kissing sergeant.

But you might receive shitter detail by pissing off your sergeant so that he requests the dirty duty for your platoon, or even worse, for you *personally,* by *name* and *rank,* as though shitter detail were an award or a promotion and not an extreme injury to your health, morale, and welfare.

So Siek furthers the punishment of my poor leadership; I receive one week of solo shitter detail because of Dettmann's failure on firewatch.

I've been double possum-fucked—fucked twice by the same two-peckered possum. The rear is equipped with four three-holers, and that's a lot of filthy work for one man. This seems like a gross failure of justice, and I tell Johnny this, but he only manages one of his half-wry smiles and what sounds like a blatant lie: "I'll see what I can do."

The burner must report to S-4 and retrieve the tools of his trade: a metal fence post, welder's gloves and tongs, five gallons of diesel fuel, and a box of matches. The marine handing out these items acts as though he's sorry you happen to be standing in front of him, as though he knows a mistake has occurred and as soon as he's able he'll straighten things out. He wisely affects this pose so as not to be stabbed through the heart with a metal fence post covered with burning human waste.

Though it's not an officially endorsed practice, most men on shitter detail will sign their name or at least their unit moniker somewhere on the shitter, usually with a grease pencil but sometimes with spray paint.

The structures assigned to me have been in-country since the beginning of the deployment, and it comforts me to read the names of three marines I went to boot camp with. But I don't sign my name or unit.

These are rather deluxe shitters, not the simple barrel-and-hole variety, so that the depositories are housed behind a hinged door. I use the welder's tongs to remove all three barrels and I pour diesel over the waste, and I'm prepared to start the fires when a major approaches and orders me to replace one of the barrels so that he can shit. He's not going to walk to the other side of the perimeter for his morning glory, as he calls it. I explain that I've already poured fuel into all of the barrels, but he insists. So I do as ordered, and I sit ten feet away in the sand while the major shits. I consider lighting the tinder under the major's ass, and thus lighting the major's ass itself, but I refrain. When he's finished, I remove the barrel, light all three, and commence with the worst part of the job, stirring the burning waste.

The smell is atrocious, vomitous, bilious. I stir the burning shit and I wonder if somewhere in Kuwait or Iraq my peer enemy might at this moment be stirring the burning shit of his regiment. Maybe he's allowed a subordinate to fall asleep on duty or otherwise discredit and shame his unit, thus being assigned shitter detail. I wonder what the Arabic term for shitter detail is, if they use diesel and a metal fence post that could also be used to build burning obstacles around a mine-field, directing the enemy, me, toward my death. And I'm sure the poor man, my brother in arms at the moment, is also feeling sick to his stomach, about to vomit. And I vomit into the burning waste of my regiment, the shitblack smoke covering my face.

Two marines I don't know walk by and laugh at me, and I know they are pogues, probably from the S-4, because a fellow grunt would never laugh like that.

I finish the nine other barrels at the three other shitters without incident. Maybe I needed to get that first shipment of bile out of my body and now I can burn shitters for the rest of my life.

Back at the STA hootch my mates are cleaning their rifles, writing letters, playing cards, and sleeping. The first and only STA marine to receive shitter detail in the Desert, I will never live it down—Combat Action Ribbon, all of the other ribbons and medals I'll rate with the platoon, Airborne School, Meritorious Corporal, epic bar fights, sexpot girlfriends in Palm Springs and Hollywood, none of it will matter as much as my shitter detail—for the next two years barely a week will pass without someone crying, "Hey, remember when Swoffie had to burn those shitters over in the Desert!"

Later in the evening Johnny calls me outside and says, "I heard of a PFC in Combat Engineers who will burn the shitters for twenty bucks a day. He'll only take cash, no IOUs or porno or booze."

I've been receiving a bimonthly disbursal of $40 cash, with no way to spend it other than buying cookies at the PX or candy bars from the Egyptians, so I find the private first class and pay him the six twenties, and I'll kiss his goddamn feet if he insists.

The PFC is a pasty-looking guy who blows up bridges and minefields for a living, and I can't imagine what drives him to burn the shitters, it can't *only* be the money, but whatever sickness seethes through him, for $120 I've relieved myself of a great misery.

A few days later, in the barracks in the rear-rear, I hold my locked and loaded M16 against Dettmann's left temple. Meyers sits on his rack and pretends not to notice. I haven't planned on threatening to kill Dettmann. I've been cleaning my weapons, first my sniper rifle and then my M16. Dettmann and I have been competing in a weapons assembly race with our M16s, sitting cross-legged and facing each other. I've beaten him thirty times in a row, by two or three seconds each try, and I've become tired of the routine, and this last time after I yell *Done,* I simply lock and load a thirty-round magazine, rub the muzzle against Dettmann's temple, and ask, "What would you say if I told you I was going to kill you for fucking me like that?"

I know this is crazy and reckless, but I think Dettmann might learn something, I don't know what. And I know that if in a second I say *Fuck it* and pull the trigger, I'll be able to lie my way through an accidental discharge, and the Dettmanns in North Dakota will be sad, and I'll probably spend some time in the brig, maybe even years, but I'll be the fuck out of Saudi Arabia and the endless waiting and the various other forms of mental and physical waste, and also, I'll finally know what it feels like to kill a man.

I say, "Ellie Bows, I am in the firing position known as the sitting position. After the prone position it is considered the most stable shooting platform for the M16. In other words, the platform most likely to enable the marine to effectively kill his target, his target being a human, generally an enemy, but sometimes, by mistake, a friend, or friendly. We call this friendly fire, or friendly fucking, or getting friendly fucked. Sounds like finger-fuck, but it feels much different, I'm sure."

ANTHONY SWOFFORD

Dettmann apologizes for falling asleep on watch. He thinks that my killing him is a severe reaction. He says, "Come on, Swoff. I'm sorry. I don't think you'll pull the trigger. You're just fucking with me."

I say to Meyers, "What do you think, Meyers? Do you think I'll kill your homeboy from boot camp?"

"Sure you'll kill him."

It excites me to know that Meyers believes I'll kill his friend.

"You two have known each other almost five months now. You're some salty motherfuckers. That's why Ellie Bows can fall asleep on firewatch. She's so damn salty she doesn't have to do what her team leader tells her. Meyers, you don't see shit, right?"

"I'm not here. This isn't even my room."

"Ellie Bows," I say, "after I put this bullet in your head I'm going to drag you over to Kuehn's room and let him throw that mop head on you, let him go to town. How's that sound?"

"Come on, Swoff! I'm sorry! I really screwed up! I was just sitting there bored as fuck, thinking about home. I'm tired of this shit! Just like you!"

"You're tired? You've been here three weeks!" I work the muzzle around his ear. "Let me get that wax. You didn't learn to clean your ears in boot camp, did you? Don't you know that hygiene is the second most important thing to bullets on the battlefield? This 5.56 will clean your dirty ear."

I don't know who is more nervous, me or Dettmann, but I continue to talk, and as I talk, I soothe myself and come closer to believing that I can finish this reckless act. I am, after all, a trained killer, and my heart has been hardened so as to allow death to enter. I don't know Dettmann and I don't like Dettmann, he's a goddamn boot who was eating corn and pig and praying at the farmhouse table when I deployed to Saudi. I have more in common with the Iraqi soldiers at the Kuwaiti border, men who dug in a few days before I landed at Riyadh, than I do with Dettmann. The loss of Dettmann won't be a loss, but an inconvenience, a little bloody mess.

I alternate my muzzle between his ear and his pulsing temple.

104

We discuss the ballistic possibilities, depending on the bullet's point of entry, and the technical specifics of the M16 rifle.

I tell Dettmann to repeat after me:

"The M16A2 service rifle is an air-assisted gas rifle that fires a 5.56-millimeter ball projectile."

"Maximum range, 3,534 feet."

"Maximum effective range for the point target is 550 meters."

"Maximum effective range for the area target is 800 meters."

"Cyclic rate of fire, eight hundred rounds per minute."

"Average rate of fire, ten to twelve rounds per minute."

"Sustained rate of fire, twelve to fifteen rounds per minute."

"Muzzle velocity, 3,100 feet per second."

Dettmann's ears are bloodred, and he's weeping, his eyes shut tight like a cornhusk so the tears must force their way out, one drop at a time.

"Rifle weight, 7.78 pounds, 8.79 pounds fully loaded with a thirty-round magazine."

"Rifle length, 39.62 inches, 44.87 inches with fixed bayonet."

"The bayonet weighs .60 pounds."

"The rifle cleaning kit and cleaning/lubricant/protectant are stored in the buttstock of the rifle."

"The key to a properly functioning M16A2 is weapons maintenance and love."

Dettmann is shaking his head no as he speaks. Snot runs from his nose.

"This is my rifle."

"There are many like it, but this one is mine."

"My rifle is my best friend."

"Without me, my rifle is nothing."

"Without my rifle, I am nothing."

Dettmann opens his eyes wide. He looks as though he's experienced a religious epiphany. He's moving his lips, but I can't understand what he's saying. He's spitting as he tries to speak. His ears have turned an even deeper red and his cheeks are flushed, and he's sobbing violently, his head bobbing like a barque on a rough sea.

I push the magazine release button and my magazine clanks against the deck, and I discharge the round from the chamber and force the round into Dettmann's mouth, like a dentist forcing a painful tool through the tight lips of a child. It stays there. I throw my rifle onto the deck, and the sound of the hard plastic hand guards and the rifle metal bouncing against the concrete is not unlike the mad clatter of a New Orleans funeral march returning to the city from the grave.

War is coming, and so more men arrive. Fountain and Cortes are the next and final Siek-appointed members of STA to join us in Saudi. We begin to think Siek travels to the rear-rear and holds up a sign not unlike a beggar's, asking for assistance of whatever kind and value. Fountain and Cortes look like a Latino Abbott and Costello. Cortes is a boot and about thirty pounds overweight, and Fountain must weigh an ounce or two above the minimum acceptable weight. Fountain is Cuban-American and Cortes is Mexican-American, and they argue over who has the better Spanish, and whose mother cooks the better food. I prefer this argument to the Texas versus Oklahoma barn burners that occur between Kuehn and Combs, if only because the Cuban-American versus Mexican-American argument is newer and nominally different.

Cortes acts like a boot, wears his gear like a boot, and asks boot questions. He falls behind on humps, complains about the lack of hot chow, tries to hide porn mags, and swears he doesn't masturbate and that he'll never go down on a woman. Standard boot fare.

Fountain had been in the Army Rangers before joining the Corps. Prior-service guys from other branches are always looked on with at least a bit of disgust and certainly suspicion. You know he joined the Corps because throughout the many sorry years he spent in the other, lowly service he walked around—and the other services don't march, they walk—wishing he'd had the wisdom to enter the marine recruiter's door, not the army doggy's or squid's or flyboy's.

So Fountain can't be trusted. His stories are too good. One day he pulls out a Ranger patch that he thinks he might be able to sew to his uniform, and we inform him that while the other services want to look like Boy Scouts, the Marines are damn happy looking like warriors. So, no patches. Army boots leave boot camp with three ribbons: one for showing up, one for throwing a grenade, and one for finishing. It takes a marine at least a year in the Fleet to rate a ribbon.

Combs says to Fountain, "A Marine Corps cook could skip and whistle through Ranger school while stewing together twenty vats of the best damn chili-mac any side of Riyadh."

Fountain speaks vaguely about action in South America; he won't name a country or a year. We know the Rangers are high speed, but they aren't high speed enough to keep a major mission quiet. The CIA, sure, the SEALs, sure, maybe the Green Berets, but not the Rangers. And the fact is, when you're about to go to war and a new guy drops into your hootch one day and he boasts about the Shit, you can't believe him. You want to believe him, because if it's true, here's a live, wiseass reason that it's okay to charge across the border to fight the elite Red Legion or Red Guard or whatever the *Arab Times* calls them and shoot the place to oblivion, because if a guy like Fountain can make it through with the Army Rangers in an unnamed South American country, then probably combat is not so bad and you will also make it out alive.

Other than the mystery missions in South America, Fountain has even more troubling stories, and not about a foreign country, though they do concern a kind of battle: Fountain spent a few weeks after the School of Infantry in Twentynine Palms waiting for his orders to Saudi. He slowly offers information about the state of affairs back home, and for any married guy who has a wife living in Twentynine Palms base housing, all signs point to piss poor.

Because many houses were abandoned when the husbands

deployed, wives with children in tow scattering back to their parents in Whitehall and Four Forks and Baltimore, Lance Corporal Fountain arranged a sweet deal, he tells us. Despite being a boot and a nonrate, he set his wife up in base housing and not only in base housing but in NCO base housing, structures that were newer than the nonrate structures by a good half century. Fountain tells the story of how none of the remaining war wives, home alone with the kids and the checkbook and the car, were interested in becoming friendly with him or his wife, and at first they tossed it off as jealousy and fear and simple Enlisted Wife Bullshit, but soon, after only a few nights of sipping drinks together on the porch and sleeping under the stars, in the front yard, because the desert was still warm at night, he and his wife noticed the mysterious movement of POVs, personally owned vehicles, into the driveways of the war wives late at night and out of the driveways in the early morning. Fountain says he doesn't want to be the guy throwing the bucket of shit on the war parade, but as far as he knows, there's a regular fuckfest going on back at the Palms, and since the base is full mostly of boots at communications school, it must hurt that much more to know that not only a boot but a comm boot not even out of school is probably doing your old lady every night, appearing and disappearing like a ghostpecker on wheels.

We look around the hootch at one another, and after quick memory runs through marital status and just where so-and-so's wife is, we realize that no STA wives are living in Twentynine Palms. And so we all breathe easy.

Kuehn says, "Don't make a fuck anyway. STA wives don't fuck around."

I feel oddly proud of the term *STA wife,* and I'm happy for my friends who have wives that fit that description, and I'm glad to hear Kuehn's clear and incontrovertible statement concerning the fidelity of the STA wife.

Troy says, "Hey, Tone, too bad we can't say the same for the STA girlfriends, eh? Those bitches."

I say, "I'm not sure anymore that they're bitches. They're on the other side of the pond. It's all fucked up here and not there and so why should they swim this way?"

Dickerson says, "Hey, you sound like a goddamn poet or some shit, but if my old lady fucks around on me, she fucks around on me. Two plus two is still motherfucking four, no matter what the fuck war is going on. A bitch is a bitch, a lady is a lady."

"Dickerson, you're our own personal Dr. Ruth," Troy says. "Next time I can't get wood, I'm coming to you for advice. Do you include a reach-around or is it gonna cost me extra?"

"The only women you've ever had you paid for in the PI, so don't go talking shit to me. You almost married a bar whore! You don't need a reach-around. You need me to slap you across your face."

I say, "Let's all make up happy and remember that in the morning we get the range that Ellie Bows fucked us out of."

Troy says, "Fountain, what's a ghostpecker?"

"It's a pecker that's fucked your old lady, but you'll never know."

We make our way back to our respective corners of our little desert outpost and talk in groups of two or three or five. Despite our various disagreements on anything from religion to sports teams to poker rules to the best measurements for breasts, waists, and hips, we are a tight platoon, and it doesn't matter whom you train with every day in your team or whether you shat on the same shitter as the famous Vietnam sniper Carlos Hathcock after he delivered the speech at your sniper school graduation, you can look anywhere and you always have a friend. And if need be, because of your stupidity or vanity or selfishness, you also have someone near who will slap you or field-fuck you or spend a few days telling you what a worthless piece of shit you are, until you realize that whatever bug you have up your ass is about a week late in being removed. It's not original to say that the combat unit works like a family—but the best combat unit works like a dysfunctional family, and the ways and means of dysfunction are also the ways and means of survival.

We called Fergus Rocker because he wanted to become a rock star or a singing actor. His father, already in his seventies, had been a Protestant preacher, and Fergus's aging mother was the choir director of all his father's congregations. Fergus sang rock lyrics to the tune of "Amazing Grace." He had an okay voice, but hard-metal tunes sung toward phantom church balconies are hard on the ear. Fergus had dusty brown hair, a receding hairline, and a round face, and he *looked* like the young son of septuagenarians, as though he'd been on a shelf for many years before being born.

Fergus hadn't actually passed the indoc he took, but I'd told Sergeant Dunn I would train Fergus personally, and if he failed, it would be my failure. I knew Fergus was smart. He'd placed last in one or two of the physical endurance tests but passed with high marks everywhere else. I saw some of my same complaints against the Corps in his face. He became a good STA marine, though he required much of my time and attention.

After we returned from war, while most of us concentrated on drinking, partying, and inadvisable sex, Fergus took voice and acting lessons at a community theater in Yucca Valley, twenty miles west of base. One Saturday evening I watched Fergus deliver a strong performance in the title role of Chekhov's *Uncle Vanya*. Afterward the cast and friends went to a café in Joshua Tree, near the national park. The café was a great find for Fergus and me. There wasn't a single jarhead in the place, and contrary to custom for businesses within missile range of a military establishment, the café's walls weren't covered with pictures of nearby units and weapons and munitions and dumb, smiling GIs giving you the bird.

Fergus and I began hanging out at the café, and we received a coffee education from the owner, and he was happy to talk to us about Camus and Céline and Chekhov. A former massage therapist to the stars, he'd recently escaped L.A. and was pleased with the pace of the high desert. He had pictures of former clients taped to the counter, and he claimed to know where Cyndi Lauper had recently bought a home in Joshua Tree. We were of course not at all interested in the location of Cyndi Lauper, but his café offered a sober alternative to the bars in Palm Springs and San Diego—dollar shots until 10 P.M. and jarheads brawling in the street with college kids.

When winter arrived and so too the European mountaineers, mostly Germans, to climb and camp in Joshua Tree National Park, the café became crowded with the foreigners.

Fergus and I occasionally slept in the park over the weekends, spending the days climbing and rappelling with our STA-issue gear. Our equipment wasn't as high speed as the Europeans'; but we could beat most of them up and down the great boulders. Our plan was to befriend some of the Germans and leave open the door for an invite overseas.

The Germans weren't interested in talking to us. They seemed sophisticated—we were fooled into believing that accent equaled erudition and good taste. My older brother was currently in the army, stationed in Germany, and spending time among the Germans would, I hoped, bring me closer to my brother, distant now for many years. But I could see in the eyes of the Germans that they considered Fergus and me crude specimens from a crude culture and that we would make no inroads. I knew that their government had joined the coalition to defeat Iraq, and I also knew that these people had probably been against the action. I wanted to tell them that I too had been against the action, but this would've been a simplification of my complex feelings surrounding the war, and a lie, and any attempt to make the Germans believe me would've instantly been recognized as deliberate obfuscation. Many nights I backed myself into a corner of the café with a copy of *The Myth of Sisyphus* or *Death on the Installment Plan,* content to read and reread and attempt to understand. Fergus worked his way through the complete works of Chekhov, and we hoped that a pair of young and pretty German girls would chat us up.

One evening, two German women in their midtwenties asked if we knew the way to Amboy. We did, and we also knew that they wanted to go to the desolate desert town to say they'd been somewhere Charles Manson had called home. They asked us to escort them in their orange VW bus.

There was a quarry outside of Amboy, and the yellow lights from the quarry burned all night, and when greenies made their first training mission in the Palms, the salts would tell stories about marines being abducted and cooked in a stew that burned night and day, fueled by the hate and madness of Manson children. We drove toward the yellow lights and told the German women the same stories that salts had been telling boots for twenty years. The women seemed to believe us, and I saw, in the rearview mirror, both fear and pleasure in the driver's face.

I don't recall their names, only that they weren't especially pretty and were extraordinarily muscular rather than lithe like many female climbers, and that neither had showered for a few days.

The women were rather disappointed when they realized the menacing yellow light burned from the border of the quarry and that no monuments or statues honored Manson. Amboy had one gas station and two diners, one of which had a hand-painted sign in the window that read: IF YOU'RE LOOKING FOR CHARLIE MANSON YOU'RE ALREADY DEAD.

On the return drive the women abused us verbally for being U.S. marines. The passenger laughed that we would dare to call Desert Storm a war, and she told us her uncle had helped burn thousands of Jews before escaping to South America, and no matter what side a person had fought for in World War II, *that* was a war, not an "operation" with boys returning home complaining of false ailments because they hadn't fought long or hard enough.

I told her quite confidently that our war was important not because of duration or the number of dead and tortured and burned, but simply because we'd been there and only so many men know the horror of war and the fear, and they must suffer it, no matter the war's suspected atrociousness, because societies are made, in part, by the men who have fought. I told her that the importance of a war is never decided within years and certainly not within months, but rather in decades, or even centuries. After V Day the vision of the victors is obscured by champagne and skirts and parades, increased profit, decreased loss, and joy, for the war is over and the enemy dead. The war is over and the enemy dead. I said, "The value of every war is negligible."

She thought I was full of shit, and she told me so: "You are fucking full of shit. You go to Germany and then tell me about valueless war."

I told her that the problem with believing your country's battle monuments and deaths are more important than those of other nations is that the enemy disappears, and it becomes as though the enemy never existed, that those names of dead men proudly carved on granite monuments cause a forgetting of the enemy, of the humans who died and fought in other cottons, and the received understanding of war changes so that the heroes from one's own country are no longer believed to have fought *against* a national enemy but simply *with* other heroes, and the war scar is no longer a scar, but a trophy. The warrior becomes the hero, and the society celebrates the death and destruction of war, two things the warrior never celebrates. The warrior celebrates the fact of having survived, not of killing Japs or Krauts or gooks or Russkies or ragheads. That large and complex emotional mess called national victory holds no sway for the warrior. It is necessary to remind civilians of this fact, to make them hear the voice of the warrior.

These are the things I told the German women.

Back inside the café the women joined other German climbers who were sitting in a circle on the floor, and the Germans talked about us and laughed, and I heard them call us *jah-heads* and throughout the night I considered fighting the laughing Germans, the women too, beating them all severely. But I read my book and kept my fists to myself. Fergus and I drank coffee and read late into the night but didn't speak, and later, as we arrived at the barracks, he said, "What was their problem?"

Two years after I left the Marine Corps I received a call from Fergus. He'd been living in Seattle, trying to catch the grunge music tide but failing. He wanted to visit me in Sacramento. I hadn't spoken to any of my former STA Platoon mates since leaving the Corps. As well as I'd known Fergus while we were in and would even have called him a friend, when I discharged, I abandoned the Corps and all personal links to the institution, and his call brought me into contact with emotions and events I'd buried.

My girlfriend knew little about my time in the Corps, and I'd only talked once about STA Platoon, when at the state fair I'd won a six-foot stuffed pink gorilla at a BB shooting contest that no one had won for three months. The carnies wanted me to sign the target, and I did, with my name and *USMC scout/sniper*. One of the carnies yelled, "No fucking wonder! Boss is gonna be pissed, the goddamn pink gorilla is gone to a jarhead."

(The gorilla sat in the corner of my girlfriend's room for many months, until one night, drunk and angry with me for having accepted the free drinks a female bartender had offered, she told me to leave her house and to take the gorilla too. I walked three or four blocks in the rain toward my car, the pink gorilla beneath my left arm.)

Fergus met me and my girlfriend and a few of our friends at a bar downtown, two blocks from my apartment. If it ended up that he was wasted and crazy, I'd ditch him and never hear from him again.

His hair was much longer than mine, nearly to his ass, while mine hit past my shoulders. His beard was not as thick as mine, but less tame. We laughed at the predictable fact that we both wore long hair and beards. It was October, and only as cold as Sacramento might ever turn at night in October, the midforties. Fergus wore cutoff camouflage trousers, combat boots with olive drab socks pulled to his knees, and an olive drab, wool field shirt half-unbuttoned with no skivvy shirt beneath. He worried me. I introduced him to my girl-friend and friends, who seemed less interested than before in meet-ing Fergus, and they stood back from us as though they were scientists looking into the mystery of space and time. I bought a round, and my friends and girlfriend peeled off and left the two of us to reacquaint.

Fergus had been working a series of low-paying jobs and sleeping with a series of low-life women. He was sure that one of the women, or a neighbor, had been entering his apartment at night and moving his furniture, not moving it far, but just enough so that over a few days he'd notice. I'm not sure why I didn't recognize this as paranoia. But it's always possible that a former lover would show up at your apartment and mess with your furniture, mess with your head, and he did tell me that he'd once pulled his pistol on the neighbor, down in the laundry room when Fergus wasn't expecting anyone else to walk in at 3 A.M.

He wrote the lyrics to a few of his new songs on a napkin, and the lyrics were poor, and I couldn't get the tune of "Amazing Grace" out of my head. The songs were about smoking pot and screwing peace-ful hippie girls, flowers by God in their hair, and I told him that the work sounded familiar, that he might try some new themes. He asked me what I knew about writing songs, and I told him nothing. He asked me no questions about my life or work.

In the past, we'd been tempering agents for one another, and of my many hundreds of insane drunken evenings while in the Corps, none of them had occurred with Fergus. But our restraint disappeared, and over a few hours, as my girlfriend and friends watched from the bar, Fergus and I shared eight pitchers of beer. When the bar closed, we were drunk, and my girlfriend urged us to go for breakfast. I declined the invite, and I told my girlfriend I'd speak to her in a few days. Fergus and I walked to my apartment and continued drinking, a bottle of wine, and shots of whiskey, and eventually he convinced me to pull out my ruck and change over into my desert camouflage. At this time, my body was still tight enough to fit the uniform.

I dressed, and we began singing cadence and slapping each other across the face, and head-butting one another, and we eventually ran into the street. We were blind drunk, and angry at one another for changing, for slipping. We went on a loud cadence run through the streets of downtown Sacramento. We sang our favorites, the ones about raping and burning and killing and pillaging, and one-shot/one-kill. We drank and sang and ran and beat on each other the entire next day, Sunday.

Monday morning I awoke in a park ten blocks from my apartment, Capitol Park, and as I opened my eyes, the sun hit the state capitol rotunda, and I recalled visits to the building in grade school. But this visit was different. The gear from my ruck was strewn all around me and I had no clothes on. I couldn't find Fergus, and he wasn't at my apartment when I returned.

I heard from Fergus two more times. A year or so later he called one morning at four. He said he was on his cell phone, inside the U-Haul he'd loaded that afternoon in the Queen Anne neighborhood of Seattle. He was skipping out on his rent and moving to Colorado to hook up with Smith, another former STA marine. He had all of his belongings and his motorcycle loaded, and he planned to sleep in the U-Haul overnight so that his entire life couldn't be stolen from him.

"Why're you calling me?" I asked.

He'd been drinking at his favorite nearby bar, he said, hoping to hook up with the bartender one last time—her blue eyes and blond hair were amazing—when finally he'd stopped trying after last call. On his walk up the hill he'd come upon two guys beating on a middle-aged gay man across the street, and he yelled two or three times for the men to stop, and they wouldn't, so finally he pulled his pistol and shot at the men. He didn't care whom he hit as long as the attack stopped, and he was sure he'd scored a hit because one of the assailants fell and the gay man ran away, and the other attacker began screaming over the body of his friend.

After Fergus had fired the shot, he'd shit his pants. He'd heard sirens and people yelling from apartment windows. Then he'd run.

I told him to bury his gun in one of the packing boxes and get in the cab of the truck and drive away, to drive to Portland and pull over downtown and sleep, to clean his weapon Marine Corps style the next morning and then toss it over one of the bridges, and to never call me again and never tell anyone what had happened.

He called collect a few months later, from a phone booth in Durango, Colorado. He and Smith had been getting in fistfights with each other. After a few weeks he'd moved into an abandoned building, an old bank, he told me, and he had his Marine Corps–issue cot set up in the basement vault, and through a contraption of hoses and buckets and gravity he'd assembled sort of a field shower, not a shower really but more like being pissed on from above. He felt good about the future, he liked his surroundings, and he felt certain he'd take a few theater classes at the community college next semester. I asked him if maybe he should talk to someone at the Veterans Administration hospital, and he declined, insisting that they could not tell him anything he didn't already know. Before we hung up, he said, "We fired the same rifle. You have the same problems as me."

Fergus knew we would always be jarheads. The sad truth is that when you're a jarhead, you're incapable of *not* being a jarhead, you are a symbol, so that in a city like San Diego, where there are more jarheads than windows and the jarheads are embarrassing because of their behavior and dress and you want more than anything not to be associated with the Eagle, Globe, and Anchor, you still are one, one of those things, marine, jarhead, and thus associated with the bad behavior and offensive style of dress of every jarhead walking the boardwalk, drinking excessively, starting fights. Though you might be an individual, first you are a symbol, or part of a larger symbol that some people believe stands for liberty and honor and valor, God and country and Corps. Sometimes this is correct, sometimes this is foolish. But either way, you are part of the goddamn thing.

That jarhead, with the high and tight haircut, the Disneyland T-shirt, acid-wash jeans, farmer's tan, poor grammar, and plain stupid look on his face, he is you. And that one, with the silly regulation mustachio, the overweight wife from his hometown of Bumfuck, with three kids in tow, three kids covered with sticky boardwalk foods and wet sand, one of them crying because he has to pee and the older sister just punched him in the face, he is you. And that jarhead is you, the one with the wife just twenty-four hours out of a bar in the PI, the both of them deeply in love with each other and all things American—you can tell this by the U.S. flag miniskirt she's wearing and her red, white, and blue high heels, and the ocean-wide patriotic grin on his face—goddamn, he is you. And the two jarheads drunk-stumbling out of the bar on the corner, into the fierce noon ocean sunlight, chasing the private-college frat boys, now catching the frat boys from the private college, now beating severely the frat boys who screamed *Fuck all dumb bastard jarheads in the ass* before trying to run free from the bar, those two jarheads beating the frat boys and having the time of their lives, they are you. And when the jarheads pick the bloody frat boys up and say *You dumb fuckers, you dumb fucking frat boys, let's go catch a beer,* then too the jarheads are you. And the jarheads fighting and warring and cussing and killing in every filthy corner of the godforsaken globe, from 1775 until now, they are you.

This is troubling and difficult to admit, and it causes you unending anguish, and you attempt to deny it, but it's true. Even now.

CARE AND CLEANING
OF THE M40A1 RIFLE SYSTEM AND OPTICS

1. Tools and materials authorized
   A. Patches
   B. Camel-hair brush
   C. Bore brush, .30 cal
   D. Bore brush, .45 cal
   E. Bore cleaner
   F. Cleaning/lubricant/protectant
   G. Lubricant, medium
   H. Lubricant, light
   I. All-purpose brush
   J. Lens paper
   K. Antifog spray
   L. Brass rod
2. When to clean the rifle
   A. Before firing
   B. After firing
   C. Cold climate
   D. Hot, humid climate

    E. Saltwater exposure

    F. Desert operations

3. Optics

    A. Camel-hair brush

    B. Forced air

    C. The armorer is the only person authorized to break down the scope

4. Optics operations in cold climate

    A. Condensation—avoid condensation

    B. Frost—avoid frost

5. Optics operations in hot, humid climate and saltwater atmosphere

    A. Direct sunlight—avoid direct sunlight

    B. Humidity and salt air—avoid humidity and salt air

    C. Perspiration—avoid perspiration

The man fires a rifle for many years, and he goes to war, and afterward he turns the rifle in at the armory and he believes he's finished with the rifle. But no matter what else he might do with his hands—love a woman, build a house, change his son's diaper—his hands remember the rifle and the power the rifle proffered. The cold weight, the buttstock in the shoulder, the sexy slope and fall of the trigger guard. Where do rifles come from? the man's son asks.

The rifle stinks like wet earth, like from where it came before being melted and molded into that sticklike form. And when you run out of ammunition and you're lucky that the enemy has run out at the same moment, you can beat the enemy with your rifle, as though the rifle were a baton, or a branch from a thick oak. The man remembers this: there are many different ways to fight and kill with the rifle.

Supposedly, and according to tradition and lore, the sniper needs only one bullet per kill. This is incorrect. The sniper requires thousands of bullets and thousands of hours of training per kill; he needs senior snipers on the deck beside him at the rifle range, telling him why he is not producing a dime group from a grand out. (A dime group is three shots that, when inspected on the target, can be covered with a dime.) There are reasons you're not hitting a dime group at a grand. Your spotter called the wind at five to eight but the wind is an eight to eleven. You hadn't completely expelled your breath when you shot. You are afraid of the rifle. Your spotter gave you the correct dope but you dialed the scope incorrectly. You are tired. You are stupid. You are bored. You are a bad shot. You drank the night before. You drank excessively the night before. You are worried about Suzi Rottencrotch and her man Jody back home, in the hay or in the alley or in a hotel bed. These are all unacceptable reasons for not achieving a dime group at a grand. A nickel group is occasionally acceptable. A quarter group and you are dead. You have missed the target but the target hasn't missed you. You must remember that you are always a target. Someone wants to kill you and their reasons are as sound as yours are for killing them. This is why you must know the dime group like you once knew your mother's nipples. Quarters are cheap. On your corpse no one will check the group, not even your mother. Your enemy will be the last person to witness you as a living thing. He'll acquire you through his optics and he will not pause before pulling the trigger.

The dream starts in November, after I read an article in the *Arab Times* about the Iraqi Republican Guard snipers.

I'm a boy again, wearing the glasses I had as a boy, and I'm on a quest, for what I don't know, in a land vaguely familiar that sometimes resembles the alleys of Tokyo and sometimes my grammar school. I might be looking for the denim jacket I lost on the playground in fifth grade. I might be looking for the candy store. Women walk through the alleys wearing red tights. Sometimes I try to sleep with them, and though I'm hard, the tights keep me from penetrating, but I come on their tights. Money changes hands. There's no logic for why I choose one woman over another, or why any particular woman allows me to choose her. Once, the nonact is consummated on a toilet. In the dream, no one speaks. Diseased dogs roam the alleys, and addicts of either pills or drink or dope float above the alleys as they take their preferred drug. I never find what I'm looking for. I sweat throughout the dream. Eventually, I turn a

124

corner out of the alley, and a sniper shoots me in the left eye. The shot doesn't hurt, and I return to the alley, and though my eye has been blown away, I still maintain vision through the socket. I can see the hole that the projectile made in the glasses lens. I begin coughing up pieces of shattered glass, but no blood issues from my mouth, though as I cough the glass into the dirty alley, I know my belly is stuffed with glass and that it might take me years to expel all of it. As the clean glass hits the ground, I hear the sound of chimes marking time, though I can never figure the hour.

This dream recurs every night, until the Scud missile drills begin, and after that I'm unable to complete a full evening of sleep.

Before joining the Marine Corps I'd fired two weapons—a bow and arrow and a .22-caliber rifle, both at Boy Scout camp, at the age of twelve. If I hadn't requested to leave camp a week early, I would've also fired a shotgun and a larger-caliber rifle, but I missed my mother, I had no friends at camp, the food was lousy, I was afraid of showering in public—actually, in the forest, the shower not a shower but half a dozen garden hoses draped over the lowest branches of a pine—and the leader of the camp was grouchy and probably a drunk. Because I cried-out a week early, and my parents lost the non-refundable fee, I had to repay the money for the aborted second week. My mother supported me and my sweet reasoning behind quitting camp (that I missed her), but my father insisted I repay the money—my Boy Scout camp fees came from general family vacation funds, and to be fair to the rest of the family, members of the tribe who stayed the duration at their camps of choice, I had to reimburse my parents for the lost week. I don't remember if I ever repaid this money, but I did miss the larger weapons, and for many years I felt inferior for never having fired a shotgun or large-caliber rifle.

Two years later, in 1984, I was fourteen when the marine barracks in Lebanon was bombed, killing 241 U.S. servicemen, mostly marines. The number of dead was burned into my consciousness.

As I folded my newspapers each morning, staring at the front-page images of the marines, the carnage crept into my brain, and also the sense that my country had been harmed and that I was responsible for some of the healing, the revenge. My country had been attacked, and I was a part of my country. Before me my father had gone to war and also my grandfather, and because of my unalterable genetic stain I was linked to the warrior line. I knew at this early age that despite what some politicians and philosophers and human rights advocates and priests insist, war is about revenge, war is about killing others who have killed and maimed you. After war there might be peace, but not during.

In the afternoons I watched the news bulletins, this being long before the sedating nonstop news loops of the cable stations, and as the marine bodies were carried from the rubble, I stood at attention and hummed the national anthem as the rough-hewn jarheads, some in bloody skivvy shirts, carried their comrades from the rubble. The marines were all sizes and all colors, all dirty and exhausted and hurt, and they were men, and I was a boy falling in love with manhood. I understood that manhood had to do with war, and war with manhood, and to no longer be just a son, I needed someday to fight. I thought of the marines constantly; my schoolwork, normally failing, failed even more spectacularly. Yes, I thought of the marines constantly, and I was engaged by woodshop and wrestling practice, but I sat dazed through my other classes.

While delivering my paper route, I wore my father's jungle camouflage boonie cover from Vietnam. He'd given it to me. Each morning I threw my ninety papers, with expertise, using the same aiming technique that would later help me while tossing grenades, and as the papers spun through the air toward my customers' porches, I saw—in the front-page photos of the bombed marine barracks—the kaleidoscopic trajectory of my future. The two other kids whose routes adjoined mine thought I was crazy and that with my camouflage hat and talk of war and retribution I might kill someone or myself.

They were my best friends and the three of us would, on Sunday mornings, finish our routes as quickly as possible and meet at the local donut shop and buy a dozen donuts each. One of the prettier older girls from school worked there, a girl who was probably poor and trashy but looked, through my eyes, attractive. I'd offer her a donut and she'd thank me and take a French crueller or an old-fashioned from my box, and I felt that this too was part of manhood, offering a woman a piece of something you owned, however small and possibly worthless. And she obviously already knew some of the magic of womanhood, allowing the man to think he has given you something you might not otherwise acquire, or that beforehand you didn't even know you needed. She saw my inability to meet her eyes—that I would pretend to check my watch before looking at her, before stuttering out my incomplete sentences—and she often went out of her way to be friendly toward me.

The donut shop is now gone, replaced by a megasupermarket. I believe the donut girl's name was Heather—years ago I heard she'd become pregnant a few times by various men, but still I remember fondly those Sunday mornings when I offered her donuts and grieved over the dead marines in Lebanon.

Shortly after the bombing I ordered a USMC iron-on from a recruitment ad in *Sports Illustrated*. One evening my mother ironed the Eagle, Globe, and Anchor onto a white T-shirt. Our kitchen was rather long and narrow, and my mother opened her ironing board in that space, and I sat at one end of the kitchen on a step stool while at the other end she applied my future to the shirt. She carefully cut the Eagle, Globe, and Anchor from the larger sheet of material, and I watched her steady hand with wonder, my mother always an expert at matters of craft and penmanship and the like. I felt the heat from the iron radiating throughout the room. The steam rose, the old iron coughed and spit, and my mother ran the iron across the shirt in smooth strokes, with the same rhythm as one might use to rock a baby.

I wonder now if she wanted to mar the job, to blur the ink or burn the shirt, desecrate the God-holy icon of the Corps. Or if she didn't, why not? Maybe if she had, I wouldn't have gone on to join the

Marines because I'd never have worn the shirt, but she prepared the iron-on perfectly. Before she removed the backing, my mother half-heartedly counseled me against joining the military, especially the Marines.

"You should go to college before you decide to run off in the military. I missed college because I married your father, and the next fall when I should've been at the university, I was in Seville. Spain was nice, but college would've been better.

"You don't want to run away to dirty foreign countries. Every marine we ever met complained about the Marine Corps. They get paid less than anyone else and the food is supposed to be the worst." She looked away from me. "And the women near the bases have diseases. And remember your uncle."

My father's brother had been a marine, an embassy guard in Denmark, and he'd died one night on duty after ingesting, with his daily half gallon of milk, an avian disease. I'd heard the story once before, told by my father one night when he might have been drunk or lonely. My mother retold the story. I wasn't sure what it had to do with the local women having diseases, but I didn't interrupt her.

My father had received the news of his brother's sickness and rushed to Denmark from Spain and stayed at his brother's side until my grandparents arrived, and my uncle was medevacked to the States—the story goes my grandfather pumped a bellows to fill my uncle's lungs the entire flight over the Atlantic, and my uncle died minutes after touching down in Maryland. *It is best to die in America if you can.* My mother was sad over Uncle Billy, my father's closest sibling, by all accounts an honest and forthright man and stellar marine. A large portrait of Billy hung on the wall in my grandparents' family room, and I grew up looking in wonder at the portrait, made from a copy of his boot camp photo, the famous dress blue photo.

Four years after the iron-on was applied to my T-shirt, my dress blue photo would be tucked into the lower left corner of Billy's portrait.

While my mother worked on my iron-on, my father paid bills or wasted time inside his study, either unwilling to take part in the historic moment occurring in the kitchen or simply disinterested in the elite future his son might grasp, the USMC iron-on considered with the same paternal irony as Boy Scout camp and trumpet lessons and Little League, money gone and time possibly wasted but what's the hurt, this is life, and life goes on and children live happily if we're lucky and raise them well.

Finally my mother peeled away the backing and steam rose from my shirt and on the shirt the glorious Eagle, Globe, and Anchor pulsed like a heart. What splendid colors, scarlet and gold! By air, land, and sea! From the halls of Montezuma! I'd first sung "The Marines' Hymn" in grade school choir and now I belted out the first verse at the top of my lungs as my mother stood back from her ironing board. I thought I saw fear in her eyes. I ripped off the shirt I'd been wearing and poured my body into the USMC shirt, and the heat from the icon warmed my chest and my chest grew and I had become one of them, the Marines! At the ripe age of fourteen I'd decided my destiny. I would war and fight and make good for those poor boys dead in Lebanon, for my poor dead uncle killed not by the enemy but poisoned milk, for all of the marines of all time killed and dead in all wars and all cheap moments of peace.

But it was not cool to want to be in the military, so I kept this desire to myself. I wore the Marines shirt only on my paper route and occasionally to school during cold weather when I knew I would never remove my sweater. I kept most of my life to myself, not willing to share what would be ridiculed and tainted by the kids smarter and hipper and better dressed, the better athletes, the better students, the kids who'd fucked already, the punk rockers and the metalheads and all of them—any of the groups to which I could never belong.

By early December the weather has cooled considerably; the high temperature hasn't hit eighty in over a month, the mornings are wet with a heavy dew, and occasionally a light rain lingers through the day.

In America the antiwar movement gains momentum. My friend Jenn sends me articles opposing the buildup in Saudi Arabia and what looks to most observers to be inevitable offensive operations. The articles generally link the Gulf conflict with U.S. energy and economic policies that rely heavily on fossil fuels and the defense of low prices for those fuels. But we marines of STA do not care about fuel, we care about living and shooting.

Heavy-equipment operators from the Combat Engineers have built a rifle range in the middle of the Triangle. With their Caterpillars they gouged the shooting berm from the belly of the desert, one thousand yards from firing berm to target, each fire avenue demarcated by the tracks of the big diesel machines.

Below the sand of the Arabian Desert is, quite simply, more sand. We've dug fighting holes, but the Caterpillars have reached much deeper. I don't know what I expected to see, perhaps bedrock, which certainly exists at some level, but the blades of the tractors have not gone far enough, and this disturbs me. Sand—we can't get away from it, and if we die and are abandoned, we'll be buried in a sand casket.

We acquire one thousand rounds of match-quality ammunition (match quality meaning that the ballistics of the projectiles are up to competition standards), the famous boat-tail round, the most precise, most severe round fired from our rifle, the round the rifle was made for, the round that was made for the rifle. The school-trained snipers wear a hog's tooth—slang for the boat-tail projectile— around their neck, and the rest of us tape our hog's tooth to our dog tags or carry one in our left breast pocket. I stow mine in my pocket, and just as old punished philosophers and characters from fiction have done with stones, I often take my hog's tooth into my mouth and suck on it. The taste is of the earth and I recognize the sweat and labor of the first rifleman, wherever he stood and fought and crawled and died on whatever battlefield, for whatever sorry cause. The warrior always fights for a sorry cause. And if he lives, he tells stories.

At the long-distance range, Crocket and I use duct tape to attach targets to the hulks of bombed and shot-up vehicles. It looks like a quarter acre of junkyard has been shipped to the Desert.

The platoon shoots for an hour, and after pulling the targets a few times and confirming that we're consistently hitting in the bull, we stop bothering with the targets and simply fire away. Just as the point guard knows the instant the ball leaves his hands whether the shot will become a basket or a brick, the sniper knows as soon as he pulls the trigger whether the shot will become a kill or a miss.

The M40A1 magazine holds five rounds. The trigger pull, at three to five pounds, varies from rifle to rifle. Some shooters might liken the trigger to a clitoris, and the well-placed shot to the female's orgasm, but in STA 2/7 we refrain from anthropomorphizing our weapons. To do so would introduce a human element into an entirely mechanical relationship. To do so might humanize our enemy, a certainly fatal mistake. Trigger pull is trigger pull. Period.

The preferred shooting position is prone. Some shooters use a tripod to steady the weapon; most use either a ruck or a sandbag filled with dirt or sand.

The spotter lies to the right of the shooter, and depending on the size of the hide, he might drape his left leg over the shooter's right. The spotter situates his scope just behind the shooter's right elbow. Some people argue that the spotter's job is more difficult than the shooter's, and before the trigger is pulled much of the workload truly belongs to the spotter, who must acquire the target, assist the sniper in acquiring the target, call the distance and wind, compute the dope, advise the sniper of the dope, and call the shot. But only one person is credited with the kill.

There is a moment when the target disappears, when the shooter sees only the clear, lovely intersection of the reticle, as if a bucket of sun has been poured into his scope, and the light means it's time to pull the trigger. For the best shooting teams this is the exact moment that the spotter begins his soft, religious chant: *Fire, fire, fire.*

Well before the shot is taken, the spotter will have drawn a field sketch, so that distance is easily estimated and the target rapidly acquired. The spotter might say to the shooter, "Officer without insignia, directing troop movement. Three o'clock from the stand of trees." Of course, in the Desert we anticipate exactly zero trees in our field sketches. We assume our points of origin will be the burnt hulks of personnel carriers and tanks and the occasional gentle rise of the desert.

I return to the disturbing nature of the terrain, the lack of variation, the dead repetition, and constantly, the ominous feeling that one is always in the open. The open, we were told as early as boot camp, is a poor place to find yourself. In the open you die, and your friends, when they try to save you, they die. But the whole goddamn desert is the open.

After the shoot we clean our weapons on the berm. Generally, the sniper sits cross-legged while cleaning the rifle, a pose not so unlike the lotus position of the Buddha under the fig tree, but of course, the sniper does not eat figs.

The bore-punch rod is made of brass, so as not to disturb the rifling of the barrel, one right-hand twist per twelve inches. It takes two men to punch the bore, one to punch down from the crown, and the other to remove the cotton pad after it has opened, flowerlike, into the chamber. There is something meditative in rifle cleaning, as with most tasks that might help save your life.

I hold the rifle and Johnny punches the bore. We're talking shit to Combs and Dickerson about how many bulls we made, invisible bulls never to be counted, ghostbulls, but that doesn't mean we can't claim them.

My team is the duty team, so while the rest of the platoon returns to base camp, we police the range, retrieve what remains of our targets, and attempt to make radio contact with Range Control to inform them that our shoot is over and the area clear. While I'm attempting, unsuccessfully, to contact Range Control, I notice four Bedouins nearby. I retrieve my binoculars and watch the men remove a piece of plywood from the soft side of a rise and begin to enter the rise. I call Johnny over, and he uses a spotter's scope to gain visual.

We often see Bedouins in the Triangle—it's their home, and we're visitors—but the behavior of these men is abnormal, and we've never seen a subsurface structure before. It might be a cache of food or other supplies, but we're concerned that the men might have observed our shoot or that they're hostile and entering a weapons bunker or long-term observation post.

Crocket and Dettmann remain on the berm with a sniper rifle, and Johnny and I approach the Bedouins on foot, he with his sidearm and me with an M16, both of us locked and loaded. I switch my trigger selector to burst. Johnny leads the way. The men are four to five hundred yards from the shooting berm.

I'm nervous and quite prepared for my first firefight. The walk is long, in the wide beige open, and with each step the heat seems to increase and the distance between us and the possible aggressors to grow larger. Their robes warp in the mirage until they look like a battalion rather than a squad. Could they be retreating, or the desert splitting open between us? I decide the men are Iraqi spies, sent across the border in the early days of the conflict and working reconnaissance ever since, blending in with the local tribesmen. I struggle to recall the phrases of Arabic I learned during the first few weeks in-country: *I am your friend, Drop your weapons, You are surrounded, I am from the United States military, Stop or I'll shoot.* Since I can't recall any of the Arabic, I plan to shout all of these phrases in English—if the men are spies, they were probably trained in Western schools and they might understand my English, though they'll also understand my fear.

Johnny carries the PRC-77 radio in his ruck, but he's unable to establish communication with the CP. He says, "If something goes down, we're on our own. If you see any weapons, shoot first. Who knows how many people are down in their hide. It might be a whole fucking platoon."

I've been on thousands of training patrols, and since being in Saudi, dozens of supposedly live patrols, but we've never actually seen potential enemy. The enemy has remained abstract, as difficult for me to comprehend as my own birth. I need to see the thing to know the thing. I'm on my way toward new knowledge. But the sensations of this first, actual patrol are no different from the sensations of the other patrols I've run in-country. A patrol is always equal parts boredom, frustration, and anticipation, and even in this small time frame, the few minutes it takes us to cover five hundred yards, the same principles of the patrol apply. I begin to daydream, to think of the place I will eat my first hamburger, Nationwide Freezer Meats in downtown Sacramento, a double french with cheese, and when Johnny stops, I nearly run into him. He glares at me, aware that I've been somewhere else.

Three of the men are squatting atop the rise and staring at us. We're within one hundred feet. I could, in two to three seconds, produce fatal injuries to all three of the men. This thought excites me, and I know that whatever is about to occur, we will win. I want to kill one or all of them, and I whisper this to Johnny, but he doesn't reply. In a draw to our right I see five camels, obviously belonging to these men. The camels are, as always, indifferent.

We stare at the men and the men stare at us, and this continues for many minutes. Johnny can't decide what to do, and he attempts to establish communication with the CP. With my right thumb I switch my fire selector from burst to fire to safe and back to burst, again and again.

Safe, fire, burst . . . burst, fire, safe.

One of the men on the berm waves to us, and Johnny waves back. This gesture is both alarming and comforting.

This man, who an observer might call their emissary, approaches us. He's young and handsome and smiling, and he again waves and we both wave, and I slowly settle my trigger selector into the safe mode. The man squats a few feet in front of us and draws in the sand, in the same way a team leader will draw in the sand with his index finger, issuing the patrol order. The man speaks a frantic hybrid of Arabic and English.

While he points at the camels, a few men exit the hide with bundles of supplies in their hands. Now eight men are visible and I begin to see that his complaint has something to do with the camels. But we still don't understand. We're huddled over his field sketch of sorts, and he slowly reaches for my rifle. I place my palm on his head and with little effort push him to the deck. I realize his move was not violent, but rather a desperate attempt to communicate. I remove my magazine and eject the round from the chamber, and the brass jacket drops into my palm.

The man is on his ass, with his arms splayed behind him, and I watch him as I perform this task, the removal of the live round, for me a movement as natural as a yawn. In his eyes I see a mixture of wonder and fear. I offer a hand to help him stand. He pauses before taking my hand. I submit my rifle to him. He takes it the way a child might, and holding it from his hip, he points the weapon toward the camels and makes firing noises. Johnny and I look at one another. Eight men, five camels. Some of their camels have been shot, and they think we're responsible.

The man inspects my rifle. I wish the colonel would run an inspection like this, delicately peering into the chamber, afraid of the weapon. I know the man wants to find gunpowder, evidence that the weapon has recently been fired, fired at his tribe's camels. I take my rifle from him and break it down shotgun style, and I remove the entire bolt assembly and hand it to him. My M16 is spotless, as always, because I clean it a few hours a day and I haven't fired the weapon since the States. All that comes off on the man's fingers is cleaning/lubricant/protectant. I reassemble my weapon. The man turns and speaks to the others gathered on the berm, and those men go back to their business of retrieving bundles from the hide.

Johnny tries to apologize to the man, but he walks away before Johnny finishes. I yell, "Hey!" The man turns around and I wave, and he waves back. Johnny and I patrol backward for a hundred or so yards, watching the men load their supplies on the camels. I retrieve my hog's tooth from my left breast pocket and pop it in my mouth.

Johnny says, "I'm glad we didn't have to shoot anyone. I wonder who played target practice with their camels?"

We drive back to the Triangle on the superhighway and I sit in the back of the Hummer with Dettmann and Crocket and tell them what occurred with the Bedouins. They think the story is funny, and they both laugh and make jokes about "camel jockeys." I'm not happy to be in the Triangle, and I'm even less happy about going to war as a hired man for another government, but I find their heart-lessness particularly disturbing. I want to defend the Bedouins against this assault from these ignoramuses.

The Bedouins are not our enemy, the Bedouins will not try to kill us whenever the Coalition decides to act. I've just experienced a human moment with the Bedouin, free of profanity and anger and hate. Because they are ignorant and young and have been well trained by the Corps, Dettmann and Crocket are afraid of the humanity of the Bedouin, unable to see through their desert garb into the human.

Before I have a chance to tell Dettmann and Crocket the reasons they are wrong, before I have an opportunity to explain the differ-ence between the Bedouin and the Iraqis, a Mercedes sedan approaches from the rear, traveling at high speed. We occasionally see large Mercedes sedans on the superhighway, a Saudi male driving with a female or a few females in the backseat, each wearing a *hijab,* the traditional Muslim head covering. These brief, high-speed glances are our only exposure to the citizens of the country we're protecting (the Bedouins are less citizens of the country than denizens of the land). We're sure the Saudis prefer this arrangement. We are the ghost protectors. As the car closes in, Crocket stands in the back of the Humvee, holds the crossbar with one hand, and puts his other hand to his mouth, flicking his tongue between two fingers. The driver of the Mercedes turns his head slowly, a little late to see Crocket, but one covered woman sits alone in the backseat of the car, and I watch her eyes follow Crocket's crude gesture. I don't know if she's registering shock or confusion or disgust, but I know I will always remember her eyes, locked on the crude young American.

The Mercedes blows past and Crocket and Dettmann yell profanities and excitedly slap each other on the back. Dettmann calls Crocket a "ballsy motherfucker," and Crocket says, "That bitch will never forget me. She wanted me."

The mail generally arrives two or three times a week. I especially enjoy receiving letters on Sundays because it makes me feel as though we're being treated with special consideration, getting mail on a day of the week that no one in the States will.

In the middle of December we begin receiving shipments of Any Marine letters. We don't know who is behind the campaign—the Red Cross, the USO?

The first few Any Marine shipments are modest, probably a few hundred letters for the battalion. STA Platoon is given six of the letters. Sergeant Dunn and Johnny decide they'll disburse one letter to each scout team and that the letter should go to the marine from each team who's received the least mail from home. In my team that's Cortes, who after a few months of deployment has only heard his name shouted four or five times during mail call. He's even tried to communicate with prisoners at the Valley State Prison for Women, Chowchilla, California, via an ad in the back of *Hustler*, with no luck.

The six Any Marines are like new kings, smiling as Dunn and Johnny hand them their envelopes. Cortes, just barely gracious, brags about how he now has a stateside hookup.

"Fuck Larry Flynt," he says.

Cortes's letter is from an eleven-year-old boy, and Crocket opens one from a grandmother of three. We laugh and Dickerson calls Cortes a pederast and Crocket a sick fucking pervert. Kuehn, happily married despite the lack of correspondence, gets a seventeen-year-old vixen from Los Angeles, a girl ready to fuck anything that moves, or so she says in her letter. She has included a snapshot and we are all momentarily saddened by her youth and what we might've considered innocence if she hadn't been so graphic and honest about her grown-up desires. Dettmann, married to his Harley, finds a nice card from a freshman attending college near his home. Her card is so sweet and wholesome she's silenced us, and I'm sure we all wish we'd received her. Goerke's envelope is postmarked Cody, Wyoming, but the letter has fallen out. Atticus's letter is actually a short note scrawled on a pink index card, supposedly from a recent university dropout: *I just quit Yale. I like to fuck a lot and drop acid. Write me soon if you like to fuck a lot and drop acid. Thanks.* Obviously, Atticus has hit the vein. The other Any Marines look defeated. We all gather around Atticus to read the soon-famous note ourselves and make sure he isn't lying. *I like to fuck a lot and drop acid* becomes one of our rallying cries, better than any *Ohh-rah* or *Semper fi.*

Atticus writes the Acid Girl, even though he's never dropped acid and by his own account he's only fucked two and a half times. She never replies. This saddens us all.

But soon every one of us carries an Any Marine letter or two in his ruck, sometimes with a portrait or a snapshot taken from the young writer's pure and heavenly and patriotic life. Most of the letters are from young women, high school seniors and college freshmen and sophomores, girls just our ages or a year or two either way.

Atticus says, "The ones that aren't legal, by the time we get out of this motherfucker, they will be. We can't get arrested for writing letters. It's part of war, it's a tradition, romancing the ladies back home."

Sometimes we respond to the girls, but no long-term correspondences, no lifelong love affairs, will be started. These are blind dalliances that accomplish a simple task on both ends—the girl in York, Nebraska, feels as if she's doing her part for the Coalition to Free Kuwait and the jarheads of STA Platoon 2/7 can come together during Any Marine call for a little fun and, as with the Acid Girl, some real excitement. And there is no such thing as too many photos of pretty girls or an excess of possibilities, no matter how remote.

I keep a photo of a girl—she's from Iowa—for a few months. I write her after her initial gesture, and I write things that make me think I sound smart and sexy and brave, ready to die for my country. She probably thinks I'm crazy. What a genre, the response to the Any Marine letter! She writes me back and includes her senior portrait, and on the back of her portrait she writes that she loves me and that she is busy praying for my safety. The next time I'm in the rear, after laminating our newly issued maps of southwestern Kuwait, I laminate her photo along with a dozen others for guys in the platoon.

Eventually so many Any Marine letters are floating around battalion that they've become a nuisance. One evening after our first hot chow in three weeks—red beans and rice that was cooked sixteen hours prior in Riyadh—First Sergeant Martinez calls an impromptu company formation. The sun is not yet down, but the temperature has begun to drop, and a light wind snaps across the desert. Because we are unshaven and have not showered in weeks, the formation is casual, and in some of the ranks men are talking in low whispers as their platoon commanders report to the first sergeant.

Martinez explains that the Marine Corps Band, expecting a quick and concise war victory and shortly afterward an increased demand for band performances, has found itself low on trumpet and cornet players, and there's an ALLMAR (All Marine Corps) call for potential band members. Battalion-level tryouts have been ordered, and Martinez hopes to fill the band with former proud members of Headquarters & Support Company, 2/7. He asks for volunteers, anyone who can claim even minor competency with a horn, and he stresses that the lucky few will be cut orders the next day—by the commandant himself, for Washington, D.C., and duty with the famous band—thus they will narrowly miss the carnage that awaits the rest of us poor, sad fuckers. Five marines volunteer, and Martinez orders them into line in front of the company. I think I know what awaits these jarheads. The men are all boots, new to the company since we arrived in Saudi; I recognize a mechanic from the motor pool and a supply clerk. They are smiling as Martinez whispers to them. They look proud, as though they're about to receive medals for heroism. Martinez must be assuring them that their honor and valor will in no way be compromised if they are picked for the band. Then he pulls a handful of plastic kazoos from his pocket, gives each candidate one, and says, "Welcome to the band! Play, you coward motherfuckers, play!" He orders them to blow "Mary Had a Little Lamb," "Silent Night," and "Come, All Ye Faithful."

When the players are finished, and the entire company is debilitated by laughter, Martinez hands each of the marines a clear garbage bag full of Any Marine letters and says, "You marines read and respond to every one of those fucking letters! Make those girls feel good! And remember, you're lucky to be in this combat infantry battalion! You're lucky to have a home!"

Martinez was being nasty and harsh but he wasn't lying about the boots being lucky to have a home. I'd always worried about losing my home and running out of everything—out of love, money, food, shelter, and transportation. As a teenager I often suffered anxious daydreams of becoming homeless, out of a job, unskilled and unloved. I pictured myself on street corners, in the rain, with a filthy dog I couldn't afford to feed. These worries occurred during the Reagan administration, when the topic of homelessness received much media attention, and certainly this fueled my fear. Reagan had been the governor of my state, his mansion was a few blocks from my home, and my parents had voted twice for his presidency, so I was intimately connected to his policies and failures, I thought. Sacramento had become a key destination for the homeless, and each Sunday at Mass, after the general collection, another collection went out specifically for homeless shelters. Obviously, these weren't the only reasons for my fear of homelessness: my family was disintegrating because of my father's disinterest and infidelity, and I projected his emotional distance many years further into my own life, when I too would become a lonely and despondent man.

I joined the Marine Corps in part to impose domestic structure upon my life, to find a home. But Marine Corps domesticity always ends. As much as you love your fellow jarheads and love field life and training and firing weapons, you will someday have to leave the Corps, at least spiritually, and find a partner and possibly have children and create a realistic domestic realm. The simple domesticity of the Marine Corps is seductive and dangerous. Some men claim to love the Corps more than they love their own mother or wife or children—this is because loving the Corps is uncomplicated. The Corps always waits up for you. The Corps forgives your drunkenness and stupidity. The Corps encourages your brutality.

By late December I'm no longer writing to Kristina. I regularly exchange letters with my friend Jenn, whom I slept with twice in high school and regularly when I returned to Sacramento on leave (once in the backseat of Kristina's car). Now Jenn is at school in Santa Barbara. I look forward to her stories of college life, parties and love affairs and literature classes, a world far removed from the Desert. Later, she will tell me that her mother urged her to write me throughout my deployment, and even when she was with a long-term boyfriend, her mother advised her not to tell me about the boyfriend because I needed hope. Her mother had written to a boy in Vietnam the same way. At first I was insulted by this revelation, but eventually I realized that it was her mother's way of telling her daughter to take care of someone, anyone, if you can, an ultimately humane if somewhat vainglorious gesture. So Jenn, among others, keeps me hoping.

I also write to a friend of Kristina's named Katherine, a woman a few years older than me whom I've met once. Katherine is pretty, and not just pretty but glamorous, and probably she writes me for some of the same reasons Jenn does. Katherine must know well enough about Kristina's infidelities, and while Kristina writes letters peppered with jealousy and deceit, Katherine writes me as a caring friend. I know I'll never sleep with Katherine, but this doesn't mean I can't attach at least some lusty excitement to responding to and receiving her kind letters. Katherine is engaged to a German air force officer and now living in Munich. She met him while working at the same hotel where Kristina works and found her boyfriend. I fantasize about traveling to Germany after the war and stealing Katherine from this Aryan.

Katherine's handwriting is beautiful, each delicately crafted letter like a fine sketch, and everyone in the platoon asks to see her envelopes before I open them. Her middle name is Mary, and she is deeply Catholic and always signs with all three of her names, and this adds to the aristocratic look of her letters. Also, her envelopes smell faintly of a rich European perfume. Troy is convinced this is a sexual overture, but I insist that the letters pick up the scent while being transported to the post office in her purse. Perhaps Troy is correct and I should pursue Katherine romantically, but I know it's easy to fool oneself with perfume and distance.

In late December I receive a note from Yumiko announcing her marriage to a man I haven't heard of before. The announcement arrives in a black lacquer box, and also inside the box she's packed a Japanese pear, wrapped in foam. I ask Troy to go for a walk with me, and as we pass through the perimeter, I share the pear with him, and the news of Yumiko's marriage. I'm not saddened as much as stunned, and Troy understands this, as he always understands me. After we each take a few bites, I throw the pear, and when it lands, sand attaches to the moist fruit, like memory to the soft parts of the brain.

In December's mail I learn of two other marriages. The first is of my longtime friend Cliff, one of my pals from grade school and the newspaper route days. He'd known the girl for a few weeks and it was possible that she was pregnant, so one afternoon they drove to Nevada and got married at the Chapel of the Pines with no one in attendance. He's sent me pictures from the backyard reception that took place the next weekend at his parents' house. He doesn't specify dates, so this might have occurred in late August or two weeks ago.

One afternoon I open a letter from my younger sister, the photo chronicler of all family events. I look at her pictures before reading the letter. I think I'm seeing scenes from a birthday party, but I can't think of anyone in the family who's had a birthday recently. My niece wears a red velvet dress and both of my sisters wear white, along with my mother. I've never met my mother's current boyfriend, Mr. George, but my younger sister has described him as "a round man who looks like a bald woman when he shaves his beard." The beardless, round man in the white tuxedo does indeed look like a woman, and he's kissing my mother in one picture and placing a diamond ring on her finger in another.

I must've sworn loudly because Troy lumbers over to my cot and asks, in his comforting Michigan nasal drone, "What the fuck is your problem?"

I hand him the pictures. "What does this look like to you?"

He shuffles from picture to picture as a homicide investigator might go over crime scene photos, and he returns once or twice to the most expository shots. He says, "Hell, Swoff, it looks to me like your mom just married some fat dude. Bitch didn't even ask your permission."

Troy is one of those rare guys who can casually call your mother a bitch and make it a term of endearment, invest the word with all that is good and wholesome and loving about the woman.

He's also quite capable at moving the conversation along, picking up and dropping other topics, some relevant, some not, and finally obscuring and even obliterating whatever might have been bothering you, like a jazzman might obscure the pain of living, though likely he'll bring up some other troublesome topic.

I say, "My mom married some guy I don't even know. She could've waited until I fucking died in the war or made it home alive, don't you think?"

Troy says, "Nothing you can do about it. We're jarheads, man, nobody gives a fuck. They want us to fight. It's our job. I like your mom. I've met her. She's a nice lady. But she can't wait for you to come home before she goes and gets married. Would you wait for her?"

"It doesn't matter if I'd wait. She's my mother and she married a stranger! She made me a stepson and I had nothing to say about it! What if I don't like the motherfucker?"

"Swoffie, you got nothing to say, man. It's not really your business. Your mom fell in love, she got married. You're a grown man, she's a grown woman. She couldn't wait."

"I think some people are waiting. Don't you think Lisa is waiting for you, or Erica? Christ, Erica joined the Suck for you. She's going to be a jarhead for you and you've never even met! Jenn and Katherine are waiting for me."

"Erica is different. She'll know the Corps, so she'll know me. Jenn and Katherine only know the bullshit you write to them. If you were in the States, they wouldn't write those letters to you. Those women have set conditions. Distance is one of them. If we were in the Palms and you called Jenn and said, 'Hey, how about I come up to Santa Barbara this weekend?' she'd say, 'Hey, how about you don't.' And let's say you happened to be in fucking Munich, Germany, and you called Katherine and said, 'Let's meet down at the Hofbräu,' she'd say, 'Let's not.' Why? Because you are a jarhead, and you don't fit in anywhere, except in their little letters."

"Then what about the Any Marine girls? Why are they writing?"

"They never have to see us. It's safe. Your little Iowa girl, she's got a boyfriend, *all* of those girls have boyfriends! They're using you. They're using all of us! We think we're using them, laminating their senior portraits and jerking off to them, but we're wrong. We're the ones being used! The Any Marine girls are sitting together in circles laughing at us because we're about to die and they'll feel better about themselves because they've written us letters!"

"Fuck you," I say. "All you've ever slept with is PI whores. What the fuck do you know about why a woman is writing letters?"

"Every whore I ever fucked I loved her first and she loved me. I know you're a jarhead. That's all I need to know."

Troy begins singing "The Marines' Hymn" and everyone in the hootch follows, except me. They've all been watching to see how I'll react, and of course I've reacted poorly, because what he's said is true. And now they will play with me.

But they only make it through a stanza and a half before Johnny enters the hootch and says, with much fake malice, "Give me a fucking break, you jarheads! You cumsuckers don't love my Corps. You shitbags disparage the memory of Chesty Puller every day with your lazy carcasses lying around on these cots like goddamn desert princesses jerking your rotten clits!"

Hearing Johnny, the mildest of characters, concoct a hard-assed drill-instructor persona is always enough to flood the hootch with laughter. I forget that Troy has just tainted my primary lifelines to the States, the civilian world, and freedom. And even though my mother has completed the crucifixion of my family, I can forget that she's now married to a man I've never met. I don't need to meet him. The men of STA Platoon are my family. Mother, father, sister, brother, we play each of these to one another, because we must. This is when I begin to understand that when you are a part of a war, life goes on for the people who aren't. They don't stop living to write you letters and keep you abreast of how they've stopped living. They marry the right or wrong people, make bad investments, get in car wrecks, die, birth children, get drunk, use drugs, have sex, become infected with diseases, and eat civilized meals.

We all join Johnny in a competing chorus of DI-ese, the language of our initial oppression. Troy mock-thrashes me, yelling, "Bends-and-thrusts. Bends-and-thrusts. My grandma is harder than you, Swofford."

Dickerson insults Atticus and questions his lineage, asking whether it includes animals. Crocket and Kuehn go back and forth, pointing fingers in each other's faces, impersonating their favorite DIs, the men they'd hated most, the men who'd taught them the most. We turn the inside of our hootch into a circus, and inside of this circus we cannot be injured, inside of our circus we cannot be touched.

But we are insane to believe this.

In early January I realize it's been weeks since anyone has bitched about the Desert. I know now that it has ceased to be simply a place and instead is a part of us, in us not only through the mouth, nose, ears, ass, and eyes, but in our souls. We've made the desert our comfortable home.

But that's about to change. We now know that the U.S. Congress supports President Bush's desire for offensive action against Saddam Hussein's military.

Sergeant Dunn reads to us from Hussein's Army Day speech, commemorating seventy years of the Iraqi army. Hussein calls Kuwait the branch that must be returned to the tree, the nineteenth governorate of Iraq. He advises the Iraqi people that the sacrifices they must make for this war are equal to the importance of the victory. Jihad, he says, is the way of all Arab people, and Iraq is the center of Arab pride.

Kuehn asks what jihad is, and Dunn says, "It means he thinks they can kick our asses with the help of Allah. We are the sinners, we are the infidels, and thus easily defeated, due to our sinning and other bad behavior."

Kuehn says, "I've been sinning since I was fourteen. They don't know that in America sinning makes you strong!"

The next day, STA Platoon is ordered to guard duty at First Marine Division Headquarters. We deploy two sniper teams to the roof of the four-story building, twenty-four hours a day. Mostly we pester the grunts who man the bunkers below. The dumb bastards stand outside their positions at night and smoke cigarettes, so we call to them on the freq, *Bang, bang, you're a dead fucking grunt.* This pisses them off, and they despise STA Platoon anyway, so we're offering them more reasons to dislike us.

We read the *Stars & Stripes* every few days and occasionally our captain acquires a copy of the *Arab Times.* The problem is, we can't believe anything either publication prints. We're stuck in the middle, and the flow of information becomes rather gooey and imprecise when we ask questions. For instance, we have no idea the air war is about to begin. Two or three deadlines have passed, Iraq is still in Kuwait, supposedly raping and killing, we're still ready to go, but where and for what, we don't know. We want to get there, we're tired of the rumors and false starts; we're exhausted from constantly training.

Our captain assures us that our current guard duty isn't a training cycle—it's highly probable that Iraq has operatives in Saudi Arabia who want nothing better than to take out a marine general and a handful of staff officers in the midst of planning the Coalition ground offensive.

But we don't believe this threat. For one thing, there isn't another building (a possible hide for enemy snipers) within two thousand yards of the command post, and the perimeter is so heavily armed, with both an infantry and a weapons company, that the sorry bastards who try to make it through would be shredded to nothing by the time a sniper gets a shot off—we'd be shooting at piles of human hamburger.

I assume that if an attack is committed, it'll be Lebanon-style, a five-ton truck loaded with enough explosives to blow the entire building to ash. We're ordered to shoot to kill any intruder, and if they're barreling toward us in an explosives-heavy vehicle, we'll try like hell to hit the driver.

*   *   *

A week into the guard-duty rotation we're fortunate enough to receive a .50-caliber sniper rifle and the training to go with it. The Marksmanship Training Unit, at Quantico, Virginia, has been working on retrofitting a civilian .50-caliber semiautomatic rifle into a combat weapon. They've been at it for a few years, and the rumors were it would be a few more before they'd roll it out. But the Desert accelerated their schedule. Twenty Barrett .50-calibers have been shipped for ALLMAR disbursal. In the middle of the desert, on a range out to two thousand yards, one hundred or so of the best shooters in the world will test a new weapons system.

The captain calls four sniper teams to the guard shack. He gives us map coordinates, tells us to bring enough chow and water for a week, and to go get our present. Me, Johnny, Troy, Dickerson, Fountain, Combs, Dunn, and Kuehn jump in a Humvee and head toward the middle of the Triangle.

We arrive at the coordinates and the area looks like a Gypsy camp. Forty or so Humvees are haphazardly parked with IR netting covering some of them, blue tarps over others, some fully exposed, and a few hosting what look like tailgate parties, as snipers from all over the Marine Corps are meeting up for some serious rifle time. We attempt to locate other snipers from our regiment, with no luck, so we park near the Battalion Recon team we trained with in November on the coast.

One of the great things about the Marine Corps is the lack of regalia that you're required to attach to your uniform. You can look at an army guy, for instance, even in the field, and read his life story on his sleeves and chest. And in the Marine Corps everyone wears the same cover, no silly berets or baseball caps. So this gaggle of marines, this clutter of snipers and recon gurus, all look the same. We're wearing desert cammies with boonie covers and nothing else. The only variation occurs with boots, and even there, little variation is visible because we all buy our boots from the same high-speed mail-order catalog.

Guys wander from unit to unit and reunions are occurring here and there as snipers share stories from the different schools they've attended: Scuba, Jump, Sniper. I'm not division-level school-trained, so in the eyes and hearts of the division-schooled snipers, I'll always be a lesser shooter, a Pig. This doesn't bother me because I know the job, Pig or not—I know I hit the same targets at the same distances, handle the compass and map with the same expertise, call in bombs and artillery just as swiftly, crawl on my belly for thousands of yards in awful terrain and weather, wait and wait and wait, and I know I'm as ready as the Hogs for combat.

My STA mates have fanned out to find friends and talk trash, but I sit in the back of our Humvee and read *The Iliad*. I rarely socialize with other units, and sometimes this causes me trouble, because people assume I'm either a sniper elitist or simply an asshole, but around other snipers and recon marines social disorder and dysfunction are expected, and I can sit in the back of our vehicle and read all day without offending anyone or inciting a fight.

A recon sergeant has started a wrestling tournament, and in the middle of the bivouac site, sand rises into a storm as snipers from all over the Corps wrestle and cheer their fellows. All around me jarheads fight and wrestle and swear and trade war stories, and I read my book.

Two jarheads who have lost their first wrestling matches are consoling and coaching one another when one of them notices me. He approaches my vehicle and says, "What the fuck are you reading?"

"*The Iliad.*"

He reaches toward me and I hand him the book and he examines the back cover. He says, "That's some heavy dope, sniper. Cool." And he returns to grappling with his partner.

For the sniper, dope is anything that helps him acquire a target.

In the middle of the afternoon the Quantico instructors call the crowd to order and commence classes on the .50-caliber. They've aligned the weapons on sheets of plywood, an impressive and deadly display. One of the instructors breaks down a weapon and explains the nomenclature and capabilities. The rifle is matte black and a few inches longer than the M40A1. It has a pistol grip, a comfortable-looking stock, and an octagonal barrel and triangular flash suppressor that resemble a whale harpoon. The weapon looks truly devastating, as though you might create casualties simply by flashing it on the battlefield. Yes, the motherfucker looks so deadly it makes me giggle and blush.

(I don't know this in January of 1991, but the Barrett .50-caliber sniper rifle will become a controversial weapon in America. After the Gulf War, the militia movement and white separatists will latch on to the Barrett as a standard for the individual's potential power against the tyrannical state. The Barrett will make junkyard relics of "bulletproof" limousines and the safety glass that surrounds public podiums. Presidential candidates will never stump the same way again when the shooter has an effective range of a mile and a half. The militia will adopt coveted scout/sniper sayings—One Shot/One Kill and Death from Afar—and print them on their T-shirts. After the bombing of the Oklahoma City Federal Building, reports will emerge that the truck-bomber, Timothy McVeigh, owned a Barrett. The Branch Davidians in Waco, Texas, will force the ATF and FBI to use military troop carriers as cover against their .50-caliber sniper capability. And in Phoenix a man will make half a million dollars a year selling untraceable "build your own fifty" kits through the mail. Representative Henry Waxman of California will become a major opponent of the idea that your neighbor might own a gun that can fire rounds through your living room and on through the living rooms of the next ten houses down your block.)

The Marksmanship Training Unit has affixed the same scope that we use on the M40A1 to the Barrett, the ten-power Unertl. This is controversial because the Barrett needs a scope manufactured to match the trajectory of the .50-caliber round. The Unertl ten had specifically been manufactured for the M40A1. The point target maximum effective range for the Barrett is advertised at two thousand yards, but the ten-power Unertl cuts that down to sixteen hundred. The Barrett has more problems than just the scope. The five-round magazines we've been issued are cheap and thin, made from subpar sheet metal by slave laborers in China, maybe sufficient for the civilian shooting in pleasant weather, wearing a fancy shooting glove and jacket, but they're not well built enough for extended use during combat. The rounds catch in the magazine, interrupting the feed, interrupting the supposedly sustained and oppressive pinpoint fire. We're forced to use a metal file to customize each magazine to each weapon, and this is a pain in the ass and absurd. The weapons must have cost over $5,000 apiece and Quantico went out and bought magazines for a nickel per, from the Communists. But when we complain, the instructors tell us to shut our holes, that we're damn lucky to receive the rifles, that they've been working their asses off since early August trying to deliver the weapon to us, and that we're making marksmanship history, integrating a .50-caliber sniper rifle into the armament. They tell us we'll really make marksmanship history when we tear the asses out of the Iraqi armored brigades from sixteen hundred yards.

But do I really care about tearing the asses out of the Iraqis? This is what I ask myself as I fire my one hundred rounds for the afternoon. From sixteen hundred yards away I'm achieving tight groups and punching armor-piercing projectiles through hardened steel. This is marksmanship magic. But also, this is death—the war moving closer, encroaching upon me. How long before I'm *really* pulling the trigger? Who is that man quartered in my crosshairs? Who will sight in on me?

After the shoot, the instructors treat us to a hot meal. Some of us haven't eaten hot chow in weeks or even months. We're being pampered for some reason, as pampered as one might get in the Triangle. Not only have they trucked in hot chow, but there's a whole Humvee full of pogey bait, and it's free.

The head instructor says, "Take what you want, it's on the commandant. He's excited about this weapon."

They pull out cases of iced Pepsi, and two of the instructors build a bonfire, because the sun has gone down and it's January and even in the desert it gets cold at night in January.

We break into four groups and we're supposed to sit around the comfy fire and have a little talk-talk about the Barretts, but the session quickly widens to include anything on anyone's mind that's worth some wrath.

One of the recon marines I know becomes especially animated, jumping to his feet, throwing his boonie cover at the instructors for our group, and yelling, "I want that goddamn four hundred yards. If I fucking die because you make me crawl four hundred lousy fucking yards closer to a goddamn raghead armored brigade, well, fuck; well, fuck me, I'm not crawling four hundred yards closer, you are going to shit me a scope that hits at two grand."

Kuehn says, "The motherfucker weighs enough. Plus the ammunition. We've been so happy pissing all over ourselves we haven't talked about deployment. Are we going to carry a forty and a fifty in each sniper team, plus an M203, an M16, a pistol, and a freaking radio? Jesus, two men with enough firepower to take out a rifle company, but they won't be able to fucking walk because the shit's so heavy. We'll be dead in the sand."

Dickerson says, "I'm turning my M16 in at the armory. And my pistol. And the radios don't work anyway. When's the last time anyone had a Prick work for more than a day without having to take it to the comm shop? The army is using satellite systems and we're carrying fifteen pounds of dead radio. I'm gonna use smoke signals."

"We can do like the Saudis and hire some Flips to do the hard work," a recon sergeant says. "We trained some fucking Saudis last week, we worked all day digging a defensive position, while the fuckers watched, then we told them to do the same overnight. Come back in the morning, and the bastards had driven to town and hired ten Flips and a couple Koreans to dig their fucking holes! Can you believe that shit? They said, 'We don't dig holes.' I told them to fuck off and we left 'em there. All I got to say is expect an opening bigger than the parting of the Red motherfucking Sea when the war starts. Every A-rab in-country is gonna step aside for the U.S. of fucking A. to go get chewed up. That's us, you dumb bastards."

The instructor breaks in. "Hey, gents, can we talk about the rifles? It's not news that this war is gonna be all-American. I'm here

ANTHONY SWOFFORD

to teach you how to kill people and disable vehicles with your new toy. By the way, you all know you can't hit a human target with a fifty-caliber weapon, right? It's in the Geneva Convention. So you hit the gas tank on their vehicle, and they get blown the hell up, but you can't target some lonely guard or a couple of towlies in an OP calling in bombs. You'll have to get closer with the forty or call in your own bombs."

"We can't shoot people with this thing? Fuck the Geneva Convention," a sniper from the Fifth Marines says.

Dickerson says, "You fuck the Geneva Convention and I'll see you in Leavenworth. That's like shooting a nun or a doctor. Where'd we find this retard?"

The recon sergeant says, "The Fifth Marines. They collected every jackass in the Corps and shipped them all to the Fifth Regiment. All the inbreeds and degenerates. They came from the same mama somewhere in the woods of North Carolina. A big old green, wart-covered jarhead-mama. She shits MREs and pisses diesel fuel!"

The instructor interrupts again. "What I want to talk about is the Barrett! How did you feel behind the weapon?"

"It's an amazing weapon," I say. "The recoil is nothing. It feels like an air rifle, with that ten-foot spring in it. I don't like the scope. I love that scope on my forty, I just don't like it on this weapon. It doesn't feel right. And I'd like my four hundred yards back, just like Lips over there."

"Yeah. If the commandant loves me so damn much, where's my four hundred?" the recon marine asks.

"I don't care about the four hundred. I don't think we'll need it in this war. Hell, I don't know if *we'll* be needed. The war's going to be moving too fast. Sixteen hundred yards is nothing. Sixteen hundred yards was two weeks of fighting in Vietnam and a whole goddamn year in World War One. It'll last about five minutes out here, if you ask me."

This is Johnny, a guy who everyone listens to. Strangers watch Johnny for about two minutes and they know his dope is dialed tight.

He doesn't look at anyone when he speaks, he half looks at the sky and half turns his eyes back on himself. When he's done talking, he looks down at his hands, and the entire conversation stops, because he's brought up what everyone else was talking around—the possibility of our obsolescence. The Barrett has been introduced to bring the sniper up to desert speed, but Johnny has stopped us.

The instructor says, "Listen, snipers. You're always needed. You all know this. I won't lie, the war is going to be high fucking speed, but that doesn't mean the colonels don't need snipers. You snipers have a good night. I've got you for four more days and about forty thousand rounds. And I'm trucking in hot chow every night. So let's tear it up, all right, snipers? Remember, you are the most effective psychological weapon on the battlefield."

I say, "The most effective psychological weapon on the battlefield is the nuclear bomb. And then gas, and the bastards have gas and we don't. Or we won't use it. Tell us, Quantico, are you taking these goddamn pills three times a day?" I pull the foil-wrapped pills out of my cargo pocket. "Fuck no, you aren't. In six days you'll be on Virginia Beach drinking rum runners and fucking your wife. They haven't even told us what's in these pills. They tried it on rats, and they say it might be an antidote to nerve gas! Fuck yes, I'll take the pills. But in a year my asshole will turn inside out and start talking to me!"

Johnny pulls me aside as though I'm a drunk relative at the family reunion. "Hey, Swoffie, cool down. We can't control anything but our crosshairs."

Over the next four days we fire hundreds of rounds through the Barrett. Due to some strange interchange between the scope, Johnny's thick eyeglasses, and his weird eyesight, Johnny hits consistently at eighteen hundred yards, farther than anyone else on the firing line. Because of this, and other reasons one can never know, STA 2/7's Barrett is assigned to me and Johnny, which means, among other things, we now carry more weight on our backs. But we also own the best gun in the desert.

We arrive back at First Marine Division Headquarters, where the other sniper teams have spent the week bored to death on the roof. The only excitement occurred when a boot lieutenant accidentally discharged his pistol inside the building. No one was injured, but the sergeant of the guard went "about ape shit," as Dettmann put it, trying to find the culprit. Accidental discharges are always a concern when two-thirds of the Marine Corps have live ammunition hanging from their bodies.

There are also the accidental *on purpose* discharges, when the marine decides it's about time he fires his rifle or blows something to hell because there he sits with all this firepower and who knows when he'll be allowed to use it. The AOPDs usually occur when two marines have been sitting together on an observation post for days or weeks, looking for what they're not sure, and they've talked themselves nearly to death, they know more about each other's sex life than they ever wanted to know, they know every childhood victory and failure, every love lost and love gained and love just barely missed, the dreams and sick fantasies that fuel each other, and finally, more than anything, they know that when they get out of the Marine Corps, they never want to see another jarhead for as long as they live because jarheads are sick and fucked-up, and if jarheads are sick and fucked-up, that means they are too.

And after the long silence that follows this troubling recognition, one of the jarheads says, "Let's shoot something or blow some shit up. Isn't there a Claymore around here somewhere?"

This must have been how it occurred with Fowler. Though he might've been alone. No one really knew. Often, the stories jarheads tell are impossible to confirm.

On OP one night Fowler says to me, "You should see what the forty does to the head of a fucking camel!"

I ask, "What does it do?"

"It turns it inside out into about three fucking knots. The goddamn slow things are an easy target too. Headshots like a motherfucker."

I don't believe or trust or like Fowler, but I assume his story is true because of my recent interaction with the Bedouins, and my knowledge of his act is potentially harmful to my rank, my paycheck, and my freedom, so I ask him no further questions. This is one way stories become clouded and imprecise, because often the storyteller is a jarhead no one cares much for—a loudmouth or a shitbag or the guy who has seen it all and is here to tell you about it, and once he begins speaking, other jarheads do anything in their power to shut him up, or they walk away, because he's either lying or he's telling the truth after committing a heinous act.

Since we're in an OP, and I'm unable to leave, I change the subject to the only thing Fowler and I share, unfaithful girlfriends. We spend the next eight hours talking about his girl and how she ruined his heart.

But with a storyteller like Fowler, if one asshole jarhead won't listen, he'll go to the next because at the root of all of his storytelling and the acts he either commits or fabricates in order to have a story to tell, at the sick root is a desire to be held in awe by others, so that he can feel better about himself. Over the next few days the whispers around the platoon and the division are that Fowler has shot at least one camel, maybe three, with his forty, and *what a crazy motherfucker.*

Fowler is bad for morale, and the camel rumors haven't helped his standing with our leaders. Because he considers himself a more skilled shooter than anyone else and he spends a lot of time telling all other members of the platoon how stupid and incompetent they are, he couldn't have noticed the tide turning against him, and he must be genuinely surprised when Staff Sergeant Siek and Captain Thola approach him and tell him they think it best for STA Platoon and best for the mission and the safety of the battalion if they find another job for him. In fact, they've already found another job for him, as Headquarters & Support Company police sergeant, the man in charge of handing out five-gallon water jugs and rolls of shit paper.

Years later, at a house party in Sacramento, on the bluffs of the American River, a man I knew approached me as I chatted with a pretty girl from the local state college, a communications major, bound for big things in the news business, or so she said. He asked if I knew Tom Fowler, if wasn't I the guy who had served in the Marines with him, and if so, I should come inside and have a listen.

I left the news girl and followed the man inside to find Fowler, Headquarters & Support Company police sergeant, master of shit paper, telling a crowd of fifteen or twenty people, mostly women, about the time in the Gulf War when he'd fought hand to hand with four raghead bastards, how he'd run out of ammunition after killing a few of their comrades in a fucking fierce firefight and was now using his bayonet, he screamed, his fucking bayonet, like Dan Fucking Daly at the Boxer Rebellion killing the fucking Chinks by hand, and that's what he did, stabbed each of the Iraqis in the heart with his bayonet, thus saving a crowd of Kuwaiti women and girls, next up to be raped by the aggressors.

After the war, and after I'd attended Army Airborne School, Fowler wouldn't talk to me except to tell me to fuck off. He'd leave any room I walked into; once he left a full beer at a bar. Even though he'd handed out shit paper during the war, he thought he rated jump school, or at least he was certain that I shouldn't have received the battalion's only billet. I couldn't have cared less. Airborne was an easy school, the simplest thing I'd ever accomplished in the military, and a good bit of fun, jumping out of an airplane five times, five-jump chump, and I wore the handsome jump wings on my uniform and good-naturedly joked with my platoon mates by calling them Legs, but otherwise Airborne School didn't matter to me. Though I did enjoy that it burned Fowler's ass. It must have been because we were from the same town that my jump wings so disturbed him, and his nightmare was that I'd show up at the party where he was crying his heart out, but I'd have more shit on my chest and know what he really didn't do.

The women in the small crowd cried and the men looked proud to be Fowler's friend, or his new friend, and as Fowler wept and hugged one of the women, he saw me, and he froze. But I said nothing. I walked outside and found my friend in communications. A few hours later when I left the party with her, I saw Fowler lying on the couch, his head in a woman's lap, she patting his small, bald head and helping soothe his pain as he wept from the horrors that haunted his waking and sleeping hours.

Unfortunately, I encountered Fowler a few more times, at bars and at parties, replaying the same story, so that I knew he believed himself, just as when with our platoon he'd believed he was the best shooter, the most competent camouflage artist, the master mantracker, the chief of chiefs.

The last time I saw Fowler I was out late at a bar frequented by off-duty strippers. I wasn't necessarily there for the strippers, but for the cheap drinks and the proximity of the bar to my friend Cliff's house. Cliff had heard me speak of Fowler and had even met him once, and a few drinks into our night, he pointed toward the dance floor, toward the biggest fool on the dance floor, and said, "Jesus Christ, isn't that that Fowler guy?" And of course it was Fowler, dancing with a rather degenerate-looking stripper, probably not off-duty but years out-of-service, strung out, she looked, with teeth ground down to the gums and her broken arm in a cast. The sight of the short, bald, and extremely drunk Fowler dancing with the burnt-out stripper nearly toppled me out of my chair. I had witnessed many comical and sick moments in my life, but this beat most of them. I nodded and smiled at Cliff, the sign that we should finish our drinks and exit the bar, but we weren't fast enough, and within seconds, Fowler stood beside me, smiling.

He yelled in my ear, "If it isn't fucking Swofford! Here to beg some free tittie?"

"We're leaving."

"Come on, Swoff, just like the old PI days, we'll get all fucked up and screw some whores! I know you still got the hunger, you're a fucking jarhead until the day you die!"

"This isn't the PI. Get the fuck over whatever is bothering you. So you handed out shit paper during the war? Nobody gives a fuck about that war."

"They have to! I'll make sure of it! They fucking have to, Swoff. It was our goddamn war! The only one you'll ever have."

"I don't want any more. Fuck the Suck."

"I'm back in! I joined Reserve Recon. I finally went to jump school! You don't have shit on me anymore!"

He'd always spoken loudly, as though to help convince you that what he was saying wasn't a lie; he needed to turn up his volume so you might not hear the lie but only the noise surrounding the lie. But I believed that he'd reenlisted and gone to jump school. I could see the pure joy in his eyes—he'd finally gotten one over on old Swofford. *Fuck you, Swofford,* his eyes said.

I recalled that after his reassignment to police sergeant certain people had taken to calling him Huggies, as in the diaper.

I said, "That's great, Huggies. I'm glad to hear it. I'm sure jump school is still a piece of fucking cake."

"I think it's a little harder than when you went through. There's more running and shit. They've toughened it up. They even dropped a couple of jarheads from my class!"

"I bet they did. Maybe it's so tough now they'll go back and take it off my DD-214."

"That'd be fucked up. But I'm glad I got my wings!"

"Shit, Huggies, all you had to do was ask. I'd have given you a spare set. You could've carried them around and showed them to people without reenlisting. Hell, you could've pinned them on your civilian clothes like a cracked-up Vietnam vet."

"You're still a funny guy, Swoff. But I got bigger news than jump school. You're gonna shit, man. You are going to shit. Guess where I'm going tomorrow?"

"Where are you going, Mr. Police Sergeant, Mr. May I Wipe Your Ass?"

I was enjoying talking some trash. It had been years since I'd broken it down like that, speaking jarheadese, pure profane smack.

"I'm going to gay fucking Paris to join the French Fucking Foreign Legion! You'll never see me again! You'll hear that the Legion has done some crazy shit, some crazy fucked-up shit, and you'll know I was in on it, with a new name like Pierre, but you'll know it's good old fucked-in-the-head Tommy Fowler, still tearing shit up!"

He smiled as wide a smile as I'd ever seen and his drunken-red cheeks beamed like stage lights. I was a bit surprised, shocked even, over the Foreign Legion news. But again I believed him, because his eyes were still saying, *Fuck you, Swofford, fuck every jarhead who never believed I was bad enough and mean enough, fuck every jarhead I handed shit paper and water to, fuck you all, I'm big, bad French Foreign Legion Tommy Fowler!*

He told me he could get me on the plane with him, I could purchase a ticket overnight for a grand, all I needed was my DD-214 to prove my background, and in ninety-six hours we'd be in North Africa, together again, Swoffie and Fowler knee-deep in the shit.

"Or maybe you don't have the balls," he said.

I told him he was correct, my balls had been used dry. I wished him well. I even bought the bastard a drink, and I bought a drink for his stripper with the broken arm. And I sat there for a few minutes with my friend and we watched Tommy Fowler dance himself closer to oblivion or North Africa.

I don't know if Huggies joined the French Foreign Legion, but

I lived in Sacramento for a few more years, and I didn't run into him again, so he may well now be a Pierre or Jean-Luc, living in the desert, getting even for all of those rolls of shit paper, attempting to reshape his past, to make sense out of nothing, in his peculiar and perpetually fucked-up fashion.

All over headquarters, marines are excited to hear that a .50-caliber sniper rifle has been installed on the roof. Jarheads dial our guard frequency all day, asking questions—How far does that bitch shoot? How many rounds in the magazine? Bolt-action or semiauto? How the hell can I get me one?

One night on the headquarters roof, Johnny notices that we can look straight into the general's office, and if we use a pair of binoculars, we can see every symbol on his wall map, every symbol that reflects troop strength and movement, both enemy and friendly, and so, with a little bit of sniper ingenuity, we construct our own model of what the hell will occur at the border.

After three nights of constant map observation, and transferring all we've seen on the general's wall onto our own maps of northern Saudi Arabia and southern Kuwait, we're quite sure that we'll soon be some dead jarheads. Two-thirds of the Marine Corps is in-country, the First Marine Division, our division, and the Second Marine Division, plus attachments. The map locates the First directly south of the Burqan oil fields in southern Kuwait, about fifty miles inland, with the Second directly to our west. Coalition Arab forces are to our rear in "support positions." A Marine Expeditionary Unit with amphibious and air assault capability floats off the Kuwaiti shore. Farther west of the Second Marine Division, army airborne and mechanized armor units are positioned for attack into Iraq. Across the border, after the two minefield/obstacle belts, the Iraqi forces look formidable if not intimidating. Johnny does the math, and he has us outmanned at the infantry level by three men to one. Directly north of the First Marine Division assault route we count fifteen artillery batteries, to our three. An Iraqi armored brigade is spread west to east across the middle of Kuwait, and an armored division holds defensive positions directly south of the Burqan oil fields. There they are, the enemy, our first sighting.

We haven't talked about body bags for a few months, but we start again. Word is they have about one hundred thousand of the damn things waiting in Riyadh. We wonder if they don't come in sizes, because a small jarhead about Goerke's size, you could fit two and a half of him in a bag that would barely fit a Combs, big Oklahoma bastard as thick all over as a tree.

We decide that the size of the bag doesn't matter, only that you're dead and on your way out, shoved in the cargo hold of a plane, stinking the place up with your death and the death of those gathered around you, maybe jarheads you knew, maybe a few of the jarheads you're joking with right now, about body bags and dying.

It's been a few months since the command ordered an official dog-tag check, so we perform one of our own—you need at least one around your neck and one strung in the lace of your left boot.

Without looking, I know that my tags misrepresent me as a Roman Catholic. I'd prefer to be known as a nonbeliever, but Johnny says, "I don't care if you don't believe in God and some padre tries to give you the last rites. Anyway, when we get hit, there won't be a priest within miles. Just make certain your blood type is correct. And wouldn't you rather get some useless last-breath religion than the wrong goddamn blood?"

He has a point. And I can't not believe in blood.

My parents were converts to Catholicism, my mother from Methodism, while my father was in Vietnam, and my father, after a troubling Southern Baptist upbringing, converted when he returned from his tough tour through war. I was born a few weeks after my father's baptism, and the same priest baptized us both.

I enjoyed being an altar boy for a few of my teenage years. I solemnly performed my duties, and I considered our leader, Father Bill, a mentor and friend. My high moments of Catholic belief occurred during the fifteen minutes before Mass started each Sunday, when I'd be alone in the sacristy with the priest and my fellow altar boys as we donned our vestments and prepared the wine and host.

When I joined the Corps, I called myself a Catholic.

At boot camp I was chosen Catholic lay reader. When all of the Catholic recruits had been herded into one corner of the squad bay, I was within arm's reach of Drill Instructor Seats, who grabbed me by my collar and said, "You, fuckface, you're the goddamn Catholic lay reader. Whenever a Catholic recruit wants to pray, you lead the fucking prayer. If a Catholic recruit wants a goddamn Bible, you shit him a Bible, pronto. You lead the Catholic prayer every night. This is the catch. There really isn't a Catholic prayer every night, there isn't any prayer every night, except the one your drill instructors tell about praying that you shitbag recruits become mean, green killing motherfuckers. On Sundays, you march this shit bucket of Catholics over to the church. This is another catch. There isn't a church, but there's a big goddamn theater, and from ten hundred to eleven hundred the Catholics own the theater. That's when you march over there. You do your damn praying and singing. And then you march back. If it's taps, and the officer of the day walks on deck, and one of your drill instructors says, 'Pray, recruits,' you better start praying, pray like a motherfucker, like you do it every night, like it's as natural as sucking on your mommy's nipple. And any other time your drill instructors decide it's time for the Catholics to pray, you better shit me a prayer, do you understand, fuckface?"

This sounded like a lot of pressure, and I considered asking Seats what exactly it meant to *pray like a motherfucker* and if someone more devout than me might be better for the job, but after my altercation with Burke, I was smart enough not to ask.

171

My fellow Catholics seemed disappointed in their lay reader. Often, on Sundays, I'd forget about Mass, busy as I was cleaning my rifle or spit-shining my boots, and one of the Catholics would find me sitting in front of my rack at 0955 and say, "Recruit Swofford, we need to get to church." And I'd run us Catholics in double time the mile to the theater. On the rare occasion that the DIs ordered prayer in the squad bay, I'd muster the Catholics, and they'd all look to me for guidance, because they were required to, and I'd suggest, like every other time, "How about a couple Hail Marys and an Our Father?" And we'd mumble our two simple prayers, led by me, while at the other end of the squad bay the Protestant lay reader was busy sweating and throwing down some serious fire and brimstone.

Because of my lay reader assignment, the base chaplain contacted the monsignor from my church of record, and I received a kind letter from him. He remembered me as a young boy, and then as an altar boy, and he wished me well in my current incarnation as a marine. I remember being happy to hear from the monsignor, a man whose homilies I'd found complex and inspiring, but his letter didn't buttress my crumbling faith.

Already, I recognized the incompatibility of religion and the military. The opposite of this assertion seems true when one considers the high number of fiercely religious military people, but they are missing something. They're forgetting the mission of the military: to extinguish the lives and livelihood of other humans.

What do they think all of those bombs are for?

I tap the dog tag laced into my left boot, and I reach into my blouse and retrieve the multiple tags—they are icons, really—hanging from my neck. I tell Johnny that even if they are incorrect about my lost religion, I have the proper number of tags, plus some.

Before going to war, the marine is afforded ample opportunity to order additional dog tags. You are only supposed to order more when you've actually lost a dog tag or a set (two tags to a set), or you need to change some of the information, and the only information that can possibly change is your religion of record. You either have a religion of record, or they stamp NO PREFERENCE on your tag, but this still makes it sound as though you want something, in fact it makes you sound like a religion whore, as though you'll take it in any hole, from any pulpit. They make it hard for a nonbeliever.

Shortly after joining the Seventh Marines, I ordered new dog tags, and I requested that NO RELIGION be pressed into the metal, but when I received the tags, prior to deploying to Okinawa, I realized I was still a Roman Catholic, according to my tags. I ordered a corrective pair, and they came back the same way, and over the years I ordered numerous NO RELIGION pairs, and I requested, finally, NO PREFERENCE, but still the tags came back ROMAN CATHOLIC. My mother insisted these typos were signs from God, but I knew better. Eventually I realized that I enjoyed ordering new sets of dog tags, and that it didn't matter to me what they listed on the religion line, I didn't care: I enjoyed receiving the shiny new set of dog tags, removing the tags from the tiny Ziploc bag, and I liked the noise the new tags made when clanked together.

New dog tags afford the marine the opportunity to replace or reassign an old set. For example: reassign a set to your mother and your little brother and your girlfriend and maybe even that casual sex partner from the town outside base (how many sets with different SSNs does she own?). Now decide exactly how you will make the new set tactical, because as much as the clank of the new tags sounds clean and crisp and alive, such noise might be deadly. And you're ordered to separate the tags; per regulation, one should hang around your chest and one through the lace of your left boot. But the jarhead does things to his dog tags that aren't regulation, such as spray-paint them, usually olive drab but sometimes shit brown, or he'll stack five or six tags on top of one another and wrap camouflage duct tape around them. He'll also tape odd heirlooms to the dog tags, such as strands of his girlfriend's pubic hair or the projectile from his favorite rifle. If you ask him, he'll unpeel the mess of dog tags and tell you exactly where he was—on what ship, in what port, stationed on what shithole base—when he received each tag, because though to the untrained eye each dog tag looks exactly the same, the jarhead knows the difference between the dog tag press at Camp Pendleton and the one on the amphibious assault ship USS *Peleliu* and the one at Subic Bay and the one at Cherry Point Air Station, North Carolina.

So the joy of dog tags is ordering new sets and deciding exactly how to wear them and who will be fortunate enough to receive an old set if you already have many tags hanging around your chest and hidden in enough lucky places.

The comfort of dog tags is surrounding yourself with and disbursing so many pairs that there is no way you could possibly die, because your goddamn dog tags are everywhere: in your boot; five pairs hanging from your neck; in your mom's jewelry box; in your girlfriend's panties drawer; buried in your backyard, under your childhood fort; discarded at sea; nailed to the ceiling of your favorite bar in the PI; hidden in that special whore's mattress; hanging around the neck of the mama-san seamstress on Okinawa, the one who sewed your chevrons perfectly every time. There's no way a jarhead with that many dog tags—his name and SSN and blood type and religious preference stamped into so many pieces of metal, spread so far and wide—will die.

This is the only true religion.

The evening of the sixteenth of January we're redeployed north of the Triangle with the rest of the battalion. We've never been so far north, and because of this we assume the war will soon begin. We want the war to start or we want the war to never start. We know nothing—we look at our maps covered with troop strength and movement symbols and minefield and obstacle locations, and we still know nothing.

I'm happy back in the field. It will rain on and off for a month, usually in the afternoon, sopping downpours that last a few hours before the sun breaks through—I'll later see this recorded as the worst winter in fourteen years for the Arabian Desert.

Some mornings, I find my way to the nearest rise and stand and watch the soft haze burn away, and if I've found a quiet moment with no ground traffic from mechanized units, I might easily convince myself that where I stand is *nowhere,* that I'm an exile, stuck between worlds, between many worlds, a prisoner held captive by sand and haze and time. By politics and rhetoric too.

I'm a soldier, in a "conflict." A "conflict" is much easier for the American public to swallow than a war. *War* still has that messy Vietnam feeling—the Vietnam War was not an official war either, but a perpetually escalating conflict with many poor, dead, sad fuckers.

Conflicts—or even better yet, a series of operations—sound smaller and less complex and costly than wars.

A half million troops are deployed to Saudi Arabia, more than enough to start the fight—more than enough frontline bodies to accept mortal injury and still have numerous poor, sad fuckers in reserve. Call it whatever you'd like: the troops are sturdy, their training has been extensive and intense.

The war begins. Within hours of the first U.S. bombs dropping on Iraqi forces in Kuwait and Iraq, on the seventeenth of January, the Iraqi air force threat is demolished. Two days later, the Coalition has flown over four thousand missions with the loss of only ten aircraft. The Iraqis are not so lucky. After the loss of many aircraft, and the transport of over one hundred Iraqi planes to safe airfields in Iran, the only semi-long-range air-delivery capability the Iraqis command is the Scud.

The potential Scud interceptor, the Patriot missile, is a darling of the American press. Across the country, at gas stations and dime stores, in front of sports stadiums and at church bazaars, citizens spend good, clean American dollars on T-shirts printed with the slogans PATRIOT MISSILE: SCUD BUSTER!! and I'D GO TEN THOUSAND MILES TO SMOKE A CAMEL!!

The Scuds are Soviet-built missiles originally intended for the delivery of antipersonnel bomblets, chemical weapons, and small nuclear devices. In the late 1980s, for their war with Iran, the Iraqis modified the Soviet Scuds, increasing their maximum effective range and renaming the missile the al-Hussein. But the increased range decreased the accuracy of the missiles. It's believed that the Iraqis have thirty-six mobile Scud launchers, but due to mobility and camouflage, it is anybody's guess how many launchers are currently combat capable.

On January 18, Iraq fires Scuds at Tel Aviv, Haifa, and Ram Allah, and by the end of the day Israel has been attacked with the Scud eight times, causing dozens of injuries and a few deaths by asphyxiation due to incorrectly donned gas masks. Initial reports that the Scuds contained chemical weapons are false. This same morning, the Patriot missile battery at the combat air base in Dhahran, Saudi Arabia, destroys an incoming Scud.

The Patriot is fired in the vicinity of an incoming missile, and the Patriot's warhead explodes, with the intention that the shrapnel will either detonate the enemy warhead or puncture the fuel tank, causing the missile to explode or fall short of its target. You're safe, as long as you're not in the short zone.

To keep Israel from destroying the Coalition by attacking Iraq—Saddam's intention in firing Scuds at Israel—the United States sends Patriot missile batteries to Israel, and the Patriots will reduce the Scud damage to Israeli cities.

But I am not in Israeli cities, I am on the front lines.

It's easier to dig a fighting hole in wet sand because dry sand tends to ship back into your hole, and when dry and falling into your hole, the sand is reminiscent of a timekeeping device from the board games of your youth, and as the dry sand falls into your hole, you aren't sure what you're pissed off about: the reminder that time is passing quickly and your death might soon arrive like morning, or the nuisance of the sweet memory from childhood of the family huddled around the game table dealing cards and laughing, or that the shipped sand means you must move that sand again, as though through this thankless action you might know each particle personally, as though because you now actually live inside it, you must care about this *most unstable material or medium that will make futile all effort or endeavor.*

And someone is always nearby while you complain about having to dig another fighting hole; usually a sergeant is nearby to remind you that *fighting holes save lives and if you were in the fucking army, they'd call it a foxhole, and the fox is a fiendish devil but not a fighter, and you are a fighter, so you must live now in this fighting hole you will make out of the earth with your hands God gave you.*

Now more dry sand ships into your hole and you wonder if any of this is worth it and how it all began.

And you remember that novel by Kobo Abe, the salaryman out chasing his passion, insects, only to be nabbed by the villagers like an insect himself and sent to the task of fending off burial by sand. You recall that as a teenager in Japan your brother read the novel in the Japanese but you never did, because in Japan you were too young for the novel, but your brother, at night before you slept near each other on your futons, he would tell you the story of *The Woman in the Dunes*. Now, you wish there were a woman in the dunes nearby who'd tend to your sand wounds, save you from the villagers, convince you that all effort at escape is futile. But of course you are in the wrong country and this is a war, not a novel. You remind yourself not to forget about the war.

You continue digging. The sound is of an E-tool entering wet sand.

We dig our fighting holes in the wet sand that surrounds our hootch. Our defensive posture is such that any Scud attack other than a direct hit will result in minimal damage but lots of loud explosions. We're equipped to forcefully repel a ground attack by enemy infantry, and with the help of air and artillery we will diminish the capabilities of a mechanized unit while suffering a significant number of casualties.

No one will confuse the outline of our defensive position with the ancient tradition of scarring the earth for the benefit of the gods. But we work hard to save ourselves. We spend the entire day of the seventeenth of January digging the fighting holes. We hear planes and helicopters fly overhead, and because we've all been in the Corps long enough, even the boots, not to care about a flyover and what it might mean—even though now it means we are at war, finally at war—we continue to bitch and dig while ignoring the aircraft, or if not ignoring, certainly not looking at the aircraft, because only a boot jarhead stops digging his fighting hole to watch an aircraft split the sky. We take all day to dig the fighting holes either because we are tired and we know that when we're finished someone will create another task, because now we are at war and there will be no end to tasks relevant to combat, or because we still don't believe in the existence of a credible threat to our security, our remaining breathing hours.

In fact, we go to sleep tonight, the first night of the war, without a firewatch. We crawl into our sleeping bags on top of our cots, the inside of the hootch warmer than the outside desert evening and drier certainly than the ground and a poncho.

Perhaps Staff Sergeant Siek hasn't assigned a firewatch because he knows no one will sleep.

After a few hours, Doc John asks, "Is anyone else awake?"

And we all sit up and Dickerson lights the lantern hanging from the crossbeam.

Kuehn and I leave to take a piss. During the day you piss in a general area, the area where everyone pisses, but at night, especially on a dark night, you simply walk out from your position as far as you'd like, and you count your steps, and then you piss, and then you execute an about-face and return the same number of steps. Kuehn and I piss and look at the stars. He pulls a bottle of whiskey from his cargo pocket and says, "Hit it, Swoff, we're at goddamn war."

I take a long drink, whiskey being one of my least favorite liquors, but still it tastes good, and I pass the bottle to Kuehn, and he drinks it down much farther, but I take another try, and my belly warms and I'm happy to be pissing, and drinking from a bottle of illegal booze in the middle of the desert, with Kuehn, my crazy friend from Texas.

He says, "I didn't think it would happen. All those deadlines, all that talk. It's a real motherfucking war. Bombs and shit. Chemical weapons."

I say, "I didn't think it would happen, either. We've been here too long. It's our home, so how can it all of the sudden be a war zone?"

"Bastards were just waiting for us to acclimatize, for the cool weather to get here. They think they're doing us a favor by waiting this long."

"Welcome to the motherfucker."

"Welcome to the motherfucker."

We finish the bottle and return to the hootch. Troy, Dickerson, Combs, and Dettmann are playing poker. Goerke is in the corner, using Troy's tape recorder to make a good-bye tape for his mother. Sergeant Dunn, Staff Sergeant Siek, Johnny, and Fountain are playing a board game, Axis & Allies. Martinez flips through a smut magazine. Cortes bought cigars from the Egyptians last time we were in the rear-rear and he's pacing in circles outside the hootch, smoking. He announces that he's not going to stop pacing until he smokes his entire box of cheap cigars. He thought he'd save them until the war was over, but, he says, "Fuck it, I'm smoking." Occasionally I hear him trip over a fighting hole or his own feet, and he curses, and Dickerson yells that if Cortes is out there filling up all of our fighting holes with sand, he'll be the one digging them out. Vann is outside the hootch as well, crouched in a fighting hole, using a flashlight, writing a letter to his wife and son, Little Vann. Soon, his wife will have another child. Sandor Vegh has a wife and a son at home in Ohio, and he's on his cot writing a letter, a letter that must begin, *Honey, the war started today, but you already know this, you probably knew before I did.* I assume Vegh was raised poor, because he will not allow potatoes in his home, and he occasionally makes vague threats out loud, such as, "If I find out she's serving potatoes while I'm gone at war, I'm going to be pissed." He says so again tonight. Vegh often thumbs through pictures of his family. He's a first-generation Hungarian-American, and I wonder if his parents brought their family to the United States to send a son to war for their new country. I wonder if his parents are proud or desperate, and how many generations it takes to be fully vested in a country, vested enough to lose sons at war, certainly more than one generation, I think. What if next year you decide to return home; what has your son died for, a half country, shadow country? Troy asks Doc John for sleeping pills and Doc says he's out, and Troy asks what kind of doc is it that doesn't have sleeping pills on the first night of the motherfucking war? Doc says he'll raid the battalion med locker tomorrow. *Tomorrow, tomorrow, I'll love you, tomorrow,* Troy sings. Meyers is frantically cleaning his already clean

M16, and he loses his firing pin in the sand, and three or four of us spend half an hour sifting through the sand beneath his cot before Troy finds the firing pin, and he offers to sell it to Meyers for $5,000. And so the night continues, the first night of the war, no one sleeping, Cortes smoking, Troy singing, Vegh worried his wife might be serving potatoes in Ohio, a World War II board game being played in the corner, Goerke passing the tape recorder to Atticus, who passes it to Troy, and around to others in the hootch, but I decline the offer. A "good-bye, I love you" tape is disturbingly fatalistic this early in the war. And to whom would I say these last words? I will wait for the bombs to land closer.

The next morning at a hastily arranged battalion formation the colonel announces that we are now involved in an offensive operation named Desert Storm. He tells us that we are both the tip and the eye of the storm. I think he's blending metaphors, and that most of us don't know what a metaphor is, and that he's confusing the troops. The colonel insists that chemical-laden Scuds are still a serious threat to our safety and that an Iraqi ground offensive is possible, so we need to fortify our defensive positions, and he adds, "Please do not consider this a bunch of bullshit." After the formation we thousand or so marines of 2/7 walk slowly to our fighting holes, kicking up a sandstorm, as though by walking so sloppily with such disregard for tactical movement we might obscure the words of the BC, that by kicking the sand and saying to ourselves or others *Motherfucker,* we might bring peace to the region, assuring our safety and the cessation of hostilities.

Staff Sergeant Siek decides that a trench between each of our fighting holes is necessary to further solidify his command and control. The trenches need only be deep enough for a body to crawl from hole to hole. We are lazy from the prior night's lack of sleep, and even if we'd been well rested, none of us have ever been motivated by the task of digging holes and trenches, but we dig the trenches and bitch and the sand ships into our holes and we are reminded again of time passing and the board games of our youth and the dark futility of the entire venture.

* * *

The next afternoon we are given further instruction in NBC (nuclear, biological, and chemical) defense. We listen to an officer from division NBC tell us again that the PB, pyridostigmine bromide, pills aren't harmful, that in fact they will help us, like all of the other things the Marine Corps insists we ingest. The officer disburses atropine and oxime injectors and PB pill packs. The PB is intended to enhance the effects of the atropine and oxime postexposure antidote that we'll (with any luck) self-administer to reduce the likelihood of dying from the nerve agent we've been attacked with, such as soman, an agent that produces what the NBC officer calls "immediate casualties." Kuehn wonders aloud why we've already taken one cycle of PB and are just now being issued the atropine and oxime injectors, but Siek tells him, "Shut the fuck up, Kuehn," as often happens when Kuehn asks hard questions we'd like answered.

Everything the division NBC officer tells us we know already because we've been training for the effects of nuclear, biological, and chemical attacks since roughly the eighth week of boot camp, a long time in the past for most of us.

If rather than offering a detailed and gory refresher course on nerve agents and their effects, the officer had simply said, "Hey, I know you jarheads know all this NBC crap because you've been training it since boot camp, and I'm not here to tell you what you already know, I just want to give you a heads-up and make sure you understand that such an attack is not imminent but possible," and if concerning the PB pills, our staff sergeant had said something other than, "We will have three formations per day and at each formation you will take one of these goddamn pills. Don't fucking ask me what it is. I'm taking it too. Do you want to fucking live or do you want to fucking die?"—we might not be walking toward our fighting holes with our bodies and minds full not only of NBC defense knowledge and pyridostigmine bromide but also of fear and terror.

We swallow these PB pills not because we need to, but because the intelligence is incorrect—the people at the Pentagon received bad dope concerning the number of Iraqi chemical warheads in

Kuwait, and they didn't know about the bad dope but they knew that when soldiers and marines, good old rough American boys, started dropping dead on the battlefield from nerve gas (the dropped-dead fighter the only flawless indicator of a chemical attack), the public perception of the war being a good war and worth fighting would change. I'm sure these Pentagon guys suffered nightmares, not because they were ingesting PB pills or because they lived and breathed and shat with a gas mask fastened to their body, but from watching the movie *All Quiet on the Western Front* during their lunch breaks. With chemically dead fighters on their hands, the political soldiers at the Pentagon would look bad for not doing all they could to protect the fighting soldiers and marines, and the public relations war that the Pentagon had been winning would sway toward the side of peace and diplomacy because after Vietnam no one wants to see great numbers of the boys coming home dead, no matter the proposed importance of the battle, be it a fight against Communism or for the stability of 40 percent of the world's oil fields. So the political soldiers had to find something that would promote the public sham of a Pentagon dedicated to the safety and welfare of its troops: enter PB pills. None of this has anything to do with the individual lives that might be lost to nerve gas—the immediate casualties—and everything to do with the public relations battle, the real battle occurring in America.

We enter our fighting holes and our fear and terror are with us. The division NBC officer has fucked us, jinxed us, diddled us in the ass. If listening to our banter, you will not hear pleasure coming from our holes, you will hear despair. We have no confidence in our protective gear. How will we be saved?

(Later, I will read that the pyridostigmine bromide has been approved under the condition of full disclosure, that is, the troops must be informed fully of the potential effects of the PB, both positive and negative, and then the individual service member will choose whether he or she wants to take the pills. This, of course, is not the way it works in the military. The history books tell me we were supposed to take the PB pills three times a day for a week. I recall ingesting many more pills than twenty-one, for longer than a week. It makes sense that we would want more of the pills, even though we had no idea of the possible side effects. Why not take more of something that you've been told might save your life? If twenty-one pills are good, forty-two must be better and sixty-three will turn me golden.)

Now we stand in our normal platoon formation, two ranks of twelve men, two scout teams per rank, and Staff Sergeant Siek issues the orders:

"Remove one pill from your PB pack."

"Place the pill on your tongue."

"Stick your tongue out so I can see the pill."

"Take your canteen from your war belt and swallow water and the pill."

"Show me your tongue."

"Now, don't you feel better?"

Kuehn is the only one of us who spits his pills out and buries them in the desert. Kuehn isn't smart enough to rebel against ingesting an experimental drug into his body, but he's angry enough to rebel against anything the Marine Corps orders him to do that doesn't produce immediate and positive results.

Me, I'm afraid. I rarely if ever disobey orders. I believe that the Iraqi army has tens of thousands of artillery rounds filled with chemical weapons. In my dark fantasies, the chemicals are gassy and green or yellow and floating around the warhead, the warhead on its way to me, my personal warhead, whistling its way to the earth, into my little hole. I too think of *All Quiet on the Western Front*. I can't remember if chemicals were used in the book or the movie, but I know that during the early years of the Great War nerve gas killed tens of thousands, and I don't want to die that old terrible way, not the way of books or movies, but the way of war.

I also know that in 1987 and 1988 Saddam Hussein attacked Iraqi Kurds with chemical weapons, and that thousands died and suffered, and that, already, deformed children are being born to victims of the attacks, children with seven or eight toes per foot, without anal openings, blind babies, stillborn babies, babies so retarded they'll be dead within years or killed sooner out of mercy and despair.

I take the pills.

We pass the weeks of the air campaign living between our hootch and those joyless fighting holes, each day removing sand that has entered because of fierce winds or walking too near the edge. We run patrols that are advertised as live, but we see nothing live other than each other. Most nights a Scud alert goes off. The alerts, soon viewed with great doubt, are made with an air siren emitted from a can, such as you might buy at the hardware store to add to your home-safety kit, the type the coach uses at track practice when running his kids through the hurdles. The man responsible for tooting the Scud alert is usually a lance corporal from the comm shack. While listening to the theater-wide freqs, he will receive the alert from someone else, some other Paul Revere farther up or down the line, and he'll run out from his comm shack and toot his horn, usually at 0300 or 0400, and everyone who's awakened will yell, "Scud alert! Scud alert!" And we'll don our gas masks and helmets and flak jackets, grab our weapons, and stumble to our holes before settling in the sand, waiting for someone, usually the same lance corporal, to call *All clear* because the Scud has either landed in Jerusalem or burnt up in the sky before penetrating American or Coalition positions.

Once the air campaign begins, I never sleep through the night. Three hours is the longest stretch of uninterrupted sleep I experience, and this occurs during a bogus patrol when Johnny says, "Let's get some sleep," and we take off our helmets and flaks and sleep in wet sand. If a Scud alert doesn't interrupt our sleep, someone screaming from a nightmare or wide-awake anger and fear will awaken the entire hootch. Doc John Duncan passes out sleeping pills to those who want them, but I'm afraid of sleeping through a valid alert, and anyway, the guys who take the pills wake up just like those who don't. The synthetic chemical for drowsiness is not as strong as the naturally occurring chemical called fear. After an alert, a game of poker might start, or if not, at least a game of sitting awake and talking shit, either about women back home, real or imagined, or the hunting in the bayou versus the hunting near Hannibal, or southern versus northern California beach breaks.

One night after an alert, Welty announces that he's going to sit cross-legged on his cot and throw a soda can into the air above his head and catch it behind his back, and that he will continue this act, without dropping the can, until morning. The hootch divides into two groups, those for and those against Welty, and bets are made.

I'm not sure what has compelled Welty to play such a silly game, but I know that we're watching him because we need the assurance, or at least the hint, that such simple pleasures, such mindless pleasures as playing catch with yourself, with a soda can, are still possible and even important. This is of course a throwback to boyhood, when we could've kicked a can for miles through a city or down a country road, when the most important question was, Where will I find my next can? Now we must ask ourselves, When will their bombs find me?

We stay up all night watching Welty toss his can, rooting for him or jeering him, all of us entranced by the mystery of his endeavor, happily entranced because he's enabled us to forget words such as *Scud* and *gas* and *artillery*. Welty never drops the can. I lose $5.

Another night, after we return to the hootch from a Scud alert, Dettmann starts weeping and won't stop. We tell him to stop, but he won't or can't. Combs, near the breaking point himself, takes Ellie Bows outside and thrashes him for a good hour, but throughout the exhausting cycle of bends-and-thrusts and push-ups and bear crawls, Ellie Bows continues to cry.

Goerke, a bit of a humanist, joins Ellie Bows outside and insists that Combs thrash him as well, because even though Goerke isn't crying, he wants to cry, and isn't it the same thing? he asks.

During the thrashing, I'm reclined in my cot, wide awake, hands locked behind my head, eyes fixed on the crossbeam of the hootch.

Two months prior I could've killed Dettmann, and now I'm glad I didn't. I think of everything and nothing, living and dying, and I know that the answers to all of the questions I'm afraid to ask are located to the north, along the Iraqi minefield and obstacle belts, in the enemy bunkers where Iraqi soldiers are at this moment being bombed by our planes.

On the eighteenth of February we move to the Berm: the man-made obstacle made of sand, *a most unstable material or medium that will make futile all effort or endeavor,* that follows roughly the Kuwait–Saudi Arabia border. Shortly after arriving at the bivouac site, we receive incoming artillery rounds. The first few rounds land within fifteen feet of the fighting hole Johnny Rotten and I are digging. Johnny is the first to yell *Incoming,* and we crouch in our half-dug hole.

The rounds explode beautifully, and the desert opens like a flower, a flower of sand. As the rounds impact, they make a sound of exhalation, as though air is being forced out of the earth. Sand from the explosion rains into our hole. Because we'd been deep in the labor of digging our fighting hole, and the chance of an enemy attack seemed remote and even impossible, our flak jackets, helmets, weapons, and gas masks are stacked in an orderly fashion a few feet behind our position. More rounds land nearby, and someone yells *Gas! Gas! Gas!*—this being what you're supposed to yell when you have good reason to believe a chemical or biological attack is in progress. Now Johnny yells *Fuck,* what you're supposed to yell when rounds are incoming and someone yells *Gas! Gas! Gas!* and your gas mask is a few feet behind you, out of reach. I too yell

Fuck. Then I crawl on my belly to our gear, and as delicately as possible, I throw it all to Johnny and I crawl backward to the safety of our half-hole, and we don and clear our gas masks. More rounds impact, and these explosions too look quite beautiful and make it sound as though the earth is being beaten, as though air is being forced out of the earth's lungs, and I begin to weep inside my gas mask, not because of fear, though certainly I'm afraid of one of those rounds landing closer or even on top of me, but because I'm finally in combat, my Combat Action has commenced.

I've pissed my pants, but only a bit, a small, dark marker the shape of a third world country on my trousers. My heart rate climbs. My breathing, as happens when you have a gas mask on, becomes labored. Hearing is of course muddled by the gas mask, and communication thus impaired. Johnny and I look at one another and around our defensive position, the entire STA Platoon half-dug in around the battalion CP. More shells explode near us.

If the Iraqis have competent forward observers, they will adjust their fire one hundred feet north and land rounds directly on the commanding officer and executive officer of the Second Battalion, Seventh Marines. But this is unlikely.

Either because the CP has a chemical detector, or someone simply feels that no chemicals have been delivered via the incoming artillery, the all clear is called, and we remove our gas masks. The artillery assault ends.

Because part of STA's mission is to function as the eyes and ears of the battalion commander, we commence with such work and begin to look for an enemy observation post and the bastards who called in the rounds toward our command post. We're equipped with the best optical devices in the battalion. We scour the biblical range two thousand yards to our east, our bellies flat to the warm sand. Johnny, with his grossly impaired and oddly precise eyesight, is first to notice the enemy position. With his direction I gain visual, and while I can't see the individuals inside of the OP, I definitely make out the physical structure, dug into the side of the range like a wound into the ribs of a martyr. Those poor fuckers, I think, *those sons of bitches.* Johnny dials the air freqs, and Fountain and I work the coordinates. We accomplish our map work like the experts we are, while all around us marines yell that they're okay, that they haven't been hit, and *let's drop some shit on those raghead motherfuckers.* Johnny asks and I tell him that I think the best bomb cocktail would be a combination of smoke, for obscuration and marking, and antibunker, for killing the bastards. He places the handset in my hand and says, "Fuck 'em up, Swoff."

A captain from S-3 appears and pulls rank, insisting that he direct the fire mission, not me, not STA, even though Johnny has done the work of locating the enemy position and Fountain and I have acquired the coordinates. The captain has even carried his field chair over from the CP. He explains that he has bad knees from college football and that if he lies prone in the sand, it will take about three STA marines to peel him from the deck.

Johnny takes the handset from me and gives it to the captain, and we crawl backward a few feet and listen to the captain call in the planes, and a minute later the devastation starts. I watch through my spotter's scope. I've seen thousands of bombs land on targets— buildings constructed for the purpose of being bombed turning to dust and the hulks of decommissioned vehicles becoming beautifully twisted tons of steel as shocking as a Giacometti—but I've never witnessed the extermination of human life. The explosions look, through my scope, about the same size as the artillery explosions that had minutes before occurred directly in front of me. The bombs make a soft thud of a noise, like an E-tool striking a skull, that reverberates through the shallow valley. In the dust cloud floating slowly down the ridge I imagine that I can see the last breaths of these men now dead.

Another jet bombs the enemy position and we return to digging our holes. We have just experienced a formal exchange of fire. The reports will be forwarded to regimental and division S-1—we've earned our Combat Action Ribbons. But we don't discuss this. We remain quiet about the incoming rounds and the quick devastation of the enemy position. It seems as though we would talk about it, but we don't, and I suppose that during war men rarely talk about warring—they talk about war before the war, when they are full of bravado and their balls and cock swing like a clock pendulum, ticking away at time and cowardliness. And afterward they talk, because they must, to remain sane. Each man has his own story of where the rounds landed and who was hit and not and why. Some men talk endlessly until they are no longer believed or even loved. You will find these men alone, drinking in bars meant to celebrate their prior service, their labor for their country.

I continue digging our fighting hole while Johnny receives a patrol order from Captain Thola. I dig fast and I dig deep, smoothing the walls with my palms when I'm done. I use tripod poles to align our fields of fire. With my hands I dig small shelves where we might prop a photo or a charm, though I know neither of us believes in charms nor do we have photos suitable for such brazen display. I no longer doubt the existence of our enemy, but I feel good and safe and American.

I feel this way for only a short time, until Johnny returns from the patrol order briefing. Johnny rarely cusses, only when his gas mask is out of reach or the odds he's been handed are horrible. He jumps in the hole and says, "We're fucked. Will you run over to the comm shack and get two Prick batteries?"

After we had neutralized the enemy observation post, the comm shack had assembled itself on the highest point in the neighborhood, a good position for communication but not very tactical, as far as I can tell, but no one has asked me. The comm shack is about a four-hundred-yard walk or run, in the plain wide, beige open. It is the longest four hundred yards on earth. The artillery stopped over an hour ago, but that means nothing. Johnny tells me to run tactically and to wear all of my war gear and good luck and, yeah, it is damn far but we need the batteries for the sure-fucked mission we're supposed to run in two hours.

I run toward the comm shack. A world-class sprinter can run four hundred yards in about forty-five seconds, but wearing boots and equipment and running on sand, it's going to take me a lot longer than that. The exhaling sound the enemy artillery rounds made upon detonating in the sand rushes through my ears. An explosion of sound surrounds me, the sound of my breathing, the sound of my gear—ass pack, canteens, first-aid kit, six magazines with thirty rounds each—bouncing around my midsection, my footfalls in the sand, the exploding sand, my breathing, my gas mask flapping against my right hip, the comm shack closer now, I'm still running and breathing and the deadly sounds continue and I'm afraid of dying. I think, You are afraid of dying, I say aloud, "Do not die now," I think, Don't die while running after batteries for your cheap and usually inoperative communications equipment.

I make it to the comm shack and spend a few seconds catching my breath in the entry to the hootch.

A lance corporal hands me the batteries and says, "That's a long fucking run, huh?"

I reply that, yes, it is a long fucking run and now I must go back the other way.

I take my batteries and run toward my hole, where I settle safely as Johnny uses a red grease pencil to draw our patrol route on a map.

He says, "That wasn't so bad. What I've got here is much worse."

Johnny and I are to be inserted by the rest of the scout team, four members, into a hide position where we will spend forty-eight hours observing the enemy minefield and enemy troop movements across the minefield. The minefield consists of two long obstacle belts that are reportedly filled with many thousands of antipersonnel and antitank mines. To fight the Iraqis we'll first need to reach them by moving men and equipment across the border, through the obstacle belts.

There are problems. Psy-ops personnel have been dropping bombs for about a week, "soft" bombs that disperse propaganda rather than exploding ball-bearing clusters. The soft bombs deliver pamphlets encouraging the Iraqis to surrender. Some pamphlets depict a teary-eyed Iraqi soldier imagining himself dead in a desert pool of blood; others use a diptych illustrating the difference between the weary and hungry and soon-to-be-dead Iraqi soldier, alone on the battlefield, and the happy and safe and alive Iraqi soldier enjoying a picnic with his family shortly after surrendering to the Coalition. On the reverse of these flyers the flags of the Coalition countries are aligned in a fierce New World Order formation that bespeaks diplomacy and peace, but most of all, overwhelming firepower.

Because of the psy-ops work and the hope that Iraqi soldiers will soon begin surrendering, the battalion refuses to supply fire support for our mission. No air, no arty, no mortars, not even a goddamn .50-caliber machine gun sitting on a ridge, two grand back. The command has decided we are well enough armed against a squad-strength force, a squad being what intelligence tells them we might encounter, and they don't want us calling in two tons of bombs or an arty battalion for a platoon or larger of surrendering Iraqis.

There are six of us, and together we carry five M16s, three M203 rifle/grenade launchers, two 9mm pistols, one M40A1 sniper rifle, and one .50-caliber sniper rifle, plus a few dozen frag grenades and smoke, and our platoon corpsman is attached, Doc John, who carries a 9mm he isn't supposed to use. We're being possum-fucked—not only has the command denied support, but their denial of the support is a vote of no confidence in our ability to properly and lawfully engage the enemy. Twice fucked. We're *bait,* and for the first time since joining the Marine Corps and for the first time since my arrival in-country, I feel completely dispensable. Countless other times I have felt worthless and unimportant, but never completely dispensable. If we get carved to oblivion out there, it doesn't matter, as long as we don't massacre surrendering Iraqis, and the current mission is to convince the Iraqis to surrender. Somewhere, at regiment or division, or even higher, a major and a light colonel are busy crunching the numbers, and a six-man scout team or a two-man sniper team from a marine infantry battalion have been deemed worth losing.

We exit the battalion perimeter through Golf Company, Third Platoon, lines, my old platoon, but I know no one. The grunts are polite; they've heard that the CP perimeter took rounds earlier and also that we are being sent out with no support. One of their sergeants tells us that if we get caught in a firefight, dial him up and if he's able, he'll send a squad for us. The sergeant's generous offer is not smart but noble and even admirable, and, if only for a moment, he makes us feel better, or at least loved, loved in the way men love one another when they enter combat—loved as brothers love brothers and fathers love sons and sons love fathers—because they are men and they might soon die in one another's arms.

What we are about to accomplish, our first combat patrol, will void every training cycle we've participated in, every round we've fired at a paper or twisted-metal target, every grenade thrown at iron dummies. When you take the initial steps of your first combat patrol, you are again newborn—no, you are unborn—and every boot step you take is one step closer to or further from the region of the living, and the worst part is you never know which way you're walking until you're there.

Martinez takes point, Kuehn falls in behind him, Johnny mans the compass and map behind Kuehn, Dettmann with the worthless heavy radio on his back follows Johnny, Meyers and Doc John are in line between Dettmann and me. I like taking the rear, looking behind me every ten or so steps, visually controlling the entire field of battle. I don't count steps, though. The good rear man never counts steps but rather turns around when he feels he should, when the time that has lapsed since his last look is time enough for some small storm to have formed on his heels—then he turns, two, three backward steps now though his overall motion is still forward, with the movement of the unit, now a swift turn on the right foot and forward facing again, and checking both flanks, nodding toward Johnny that all is clear. The patrol must maintain 360-degree control—357 degrees leaves three slivers of time and space open, and this is where the enemy enters and now you are dead.

Hand signals are the preferred mode of communication during patrol. The team leader uses hand signals to slow or increase the speed of the patrol, to call team attention to a particular area in the patrol zone, to call certain members forward for conference, to initiate a firefight and to cease fire, among other actions. A hand signal is as authoritative as a verbal order. Sometimes, because of battlefield stressors such as exploding enemy ordnance, marines forget what the hand signals mean, and the situation becomes loud and confusing and marines begin yelling rather than using their hands.

The hide Johnny and I are supposed to man for forty-eight hours has to be built because there is no natural cover where we're going. We'll dig ourselves into the soft slope of a gentle rise. From the map, our intended position looks to offer a premium view of an area of the obstacle belt and minefield. We figure it will take five hours to dig and camouflage the hide and redistribute the sand. We've brought along an extra ruck, and we'll take turns digging and shoveling the sand into the ruck and carrying the sand-filled ruck two hundred yards behind our position and dumping the sand so that it looks natural, not as if it has just been extracted from the side of a nearby rise so that two marines can hide in the earth and with any luck watch Iraqis cross the minefield and obstacle belt.

We'll blame Dettmann, poor Ellie Bows, for what happens next. He stays on the radio too long, we'll later decide, longer than three seconds, so that the enemy triangulates us—radio geometry whereby the enemy uses two known, fixed positions to locate the position of your signal. We'll never know for sure. Possibly, we were moving too quickly, excited in the midst of our first combat patrol, not paying attention to our pace, so that the sounds from our gear, the natural movement, the tension between body and uniform and flak jacket and war belt and rucksack, times seven, became a chorus, and we were not patrolling tactically as we might each have thought, but rather as a seven-member chorus of idiots announcing their position. Maybe, when Johnny stopped the patrol and called Dettmann forward and spoke to Dettmann after exhaling, telling Dettmann to call in Check Point Two, Johnny hadn't exhaled fully, so that his whisper exited his body as a scream. Or maybe we were so goddamn quiet, so fucking perfectly tactical, the night so silent around us, that the enemy assumed a patrol must be in the area.

Somehow they know we are here, and that's why they're shooting rockets at us, MLRs, multiple-launch rockets, many rockets launching, landing, near us, exploding like fierce blazing fists, so that the command and control Johnny might want in such a situation are now overruled by our collective fear and terror, and the now of these moments is a blur, a hall mirror shattering, a shiver of bodies. I see all of our broken faces, caught in this eternal moment, and no one can find the way out. Kuehn now yelling, *Fuck this goddamn shit—oh, fuck God, I love my wife,* and Doc John laughing, saying, *Jesus Christ, are those rockets?* and Dettmann screaming, *I didn't do it,* and me yelling, *Rockets, rockets,* and forgetting, absolutely forgetting, everything I've been taught about evasive action for rockets and only knowing the word *rockets.* I stand in place and piss my pants, this time not just a trickle but piss all over and running into my boots, clear piss I know because of hydration, no underwear and piss everywhere, thighs both, knees both, ankles both, bottom of my soft wet feet both, clear piss and no underwear because otherwise chafed rotten crotch and balls from humping because Vaseline only works to mile ten and all wars and battles occur farther than ten miles from all safe points, and bloodrottenballs if you don't remove your underwear at mile ten, and rockets landing red glare and more rockets, hitting everywhere around us, but they haven't hit us, so far they have only caused great amounts of terror and forgetting.

No one is hit. We stare at the smoky depressions left in the earth and no one has been hit. The sand, where the rockets have impacted—smoke-shrapnel burnt into the desert—looks like an abstract charcoal portrait, broad strokes beginning and ending nowhere.

Then we hear the voices of the Iraqi soldiers, and the idling diesel engines of their vehicles. Johnny and I low-crawl to the top of the rise while the rest of the team prepares to cover our right flank. This is not communicated verbally or with hand signals but simply through knowing. I'm crawling slowly, my belly as close to the earth as I can force it, sand filling my trousers. We still hear their voices, their deep throaty drawl, and the engine idling and I think, What are they waiting for, do they even know we're here? Based on what I recall from Soviet armor, I know there might be up to eleven of them, and I know they will be armed with AK-47s and RPGs, rocket-propelled grenades, and possibly a light machine gun. I imagine we are better trained, but it is of course possible that these men have fought before, against the Iranians or Iraqi Kurds or as part of the initial invasion of Kuwait, though I'm quite sure little fighting occurred in early August.

We crawl. I've always admired Johnny, and watching him lead us, lead me, up this rise and into a firefight, I admire him even more, I love him for his expertise and his care and his professionalism and his fear. And then we hear the engine of their troop carrier move from idle to acceleration, and the slow, deep throaty drawl of the men's voices is gone, and we know that we've been just missed again. Johnny stops crawling and buries his head in his arms, and I roll over and look at the sky, the smoky dark sky without the stars I normally see, and the rest of the team walks upright toward us and gathers in a circle and sits and no one speaks, for many minutes no one speaks, for hours maybe, or seconds, no one speaks, until Doc John asks if we are all right and Kuehn says, "Yes, Doc, we're all right, look at us, but we could've not been, we could've not been, and that's all that matters."

The rest of the team returns to battalion and Johnny and I patrol the final klick alone, and Johnny uses the GPS to confirm we are where we need to be, and we start to dig. Dig, motherfucker, dig your grave, I think, dig with these hands. It does take five hours to dig the hide and distribute the sand elsewhere. We cover the opening of our hide with IR netting and settle in. I draw a sketch of the area, an absurd sketch because in addition to my being a poor artist, the only thing in front of us is desert. After the mission I will turn the sketch in to battalion, and rather than sketch the rises and draws and soft slopes, I want to write in bold print, THERE IS A FUCKING DESERT HERE AND NOTHING ELSE. Johnny asks me please not to, even as a joke.

We both remain awake at night, and during the day we assume four-hour shifts. We wait and watch and we see nothing of importance for two days. Occasionally an enemy troop carrier will approach the minefield, but they do not cross through the safe avenues that we know exist, and it's of course too dangerous to guess. We hear Coalition bombs landing nearby or far away, watch psy-ops pamphlets blowing across the minefield, listen to more bombs, but the Iraqis never cross their obstacles.

Shoved into this hole in the middle of the middle of nowhere, I consider the fire we've taken. The ground war has not officially begun, but we've been fired at, within close range, twice. I will never know why those men didn't attack us over the rise. Perhaps we shared an aura of mutual assured existence, allowing us to slowly approach one another and prepare to engage, but finally when the numbers were crunched, the numbers were bad for both sides, and the engagement thus sensibly aborted. If wars were fought only by the men on the ground, the men facing one another in real battle, most wars would end quickly and sensibly. Men are smart and men are animals, in that they don't want to die so simply for so little.

Because we've reported nothing with intelligence value, we're pulled out of our hide. This order arrives in the middle of the afternoon on our second day. Johnny communicates that we'd prefer to move under the cover of darkness, but we're nonetheless ordered to return immediately, so that we patrol, or rather walk, toward battalion lines in the middle of the afternoon, as though no ground war is about to begin, as though we're amateur naturalists out on a stroll.

At battalion we learn that the final-final deadlines for complete withdrawal from Kuwait are being issued to Saddam Hussein, and that the real battle, the mother of the mothers, is about to begin, within hours or the day. The battalion moves directly on top of the Berm, we actually dig our positions into the Berm. Psy-ops helicopters fly overhead all day, playing tapes of Led Zeppelin and the Rolling Stones, and I'm not sure that we aren't as unnerved by the music as our enemies might be. Iraqi troops have lit fire to hundreds of oil wells in southern Kuwait, and we're told that they're also spilling crude onto the desert floor. The oil fires burn in the distance, the sky a smoke-filled landscape, a new dimension really, thick and billowing. A burning, fiery oil hell awaits us.

In the late afternoon the wind shifts and oil from the fires begins to fall in small droplets on our gear and our bodies. Crouching into the Berm, with my poncho draped over my body, I write a few letters. In a recent letter my brother informed me he has requested transfer from Germany to the Storm, and when his transfer arrives, I should be able to go home because of DOD rules that allow families to deploy only one progenitor of the family line to a war zone. I write my brother, telling him he is late. I also tell him that I think he's shamelessly lying, that his hero pose sounds good on paper and probably over the phone to our mother and sisters, but what the fuck is he talking about, he's living in Munich, on the economy, driving a BMW and drinking good German beer and God knows what else and he has a wife and a daughter and don't they plan for more and if he's smart, he should be happy with the out. I love my brother dearly, but he has always been rather impressed with himself, and because of the events of the last few days, the incoming rounds, and the events that await me, more incoming rounds, I turn against my brother, and I insult the U.S. Army and any pigfuck who would join such a shitpoor organization, and I tell him what I've thought of being his little brother for so many years and, as far as I can tell, the rest of my life. I tell him that it's an okay gig, really, that I love and like and respect him, but when he pulls bullshit like telling me he's going to come to my rescue and fight for me, take my place in the ranks, I can't help but be angry and recall that in the family he has a reputation for largesse and falsity. I tell him I know the truth, that he's goddamn happy over there in Germany, drinking the beer and what have you, and that he's really goddamn stupid or even crazy if he thinks he'll prefer combat action to drinking good German beer, fucking his wife, playing patty-cake with his daughter, and going about the normal wasteful business of the garrison military.

But then, my brother has always fabricated facets of his life. I first realized this when I was eleven, and he told me he was a star on the local college football team. He had been a minor football star in high school, but not star enough to be a star at college, even at a small state college with a generally unimpressive football program. He told me of his star status and at first I believed him, and possibly other members of the family believed him as well. But when my father and I went to the games, Jeff sat on the sidelines and only played after the outcome had been decided. I was embarrassed for my brother. Even though my father and I had been in the stands on Friday evening, my brother would still tell us that he was a football star—he'd recount his latest impressive performance while the family shared Sunday brunch after Mass. My brother's behavior confused me, but I never talked to anyone about it.

This was about the time that I began to lie as well, to construct my fantasy world. I lied about my brother to my friends, telling them he was a local football star even though I knew the truth. I suppose I thought that continuing my brother's lie would bring me closer to him or that my lie would obliterate his. Once, a few years later, I even lied about him to him, insisting that on the wall in the weight room of our high school his name was stenciled next to a record for the bench press. He knew I was lying, and that at that moment I could bench-press more than he ever had and still it wasn't enough for a high school weight room record, but because he wanted to believe my lie, he didn't challenge me. He lied with his silence. By this time he'd joined the army after dropping out of college, and the army allowed him an entirely new world to mold around his own personality.

Growing up on air force bases, my brother had hated the military, and in moments of whispered sibling conference, he'd disparage the gypsy lifestyle forced on us by our father's career. Perhaps because my brother was the firstborn son of the firstborn son of a firstborn son, he fell automatically to the role of spoiler, agitator, and rebel, as my father had before him. My father left his family and the South with nothing to prove, but my brother needed to shout his worth, his excellence, to those he'd left behind.

In the letter, I tell Jeff how I'd followed his example as a teenager and told countless lies about myself and my accomplishments—but shortly after joining the Marine Corps, I'd stopped lying because I realized that both lying and religion wouldn't matter when the bombs arrived.

I ask him to please stop lying about trying to take my place in the war. I tell him that his lie is embarrassing and offensive, and that if he does somehow become stationed in the Desert, I won't leave.

My brother never responded to my letter, and anyway, I assume that by the time he received the letter in Munich, probably by the time the letter left Saudi Arabia, the war had ended.

We cannot plan how we will die—unless we decide to kill ourselves—but Jeff might as well have come over to the Desert and got his ass shot to death, died a hero, because as it was, he simply prolonged the lie of his living years, and shortly after separating from the army, under questionable terms, he died slowly, over a year, from a cancer. So now the advancement of my Swofford line, the Georgia Swoffords, the Douglasville Swoffords, the John Columbus Swoffords, the John Howard Swoffords, is my responsibility, resting firmly in my shorts. The pressure is immense, and I blame my brother for dying and filling my balls with so much false history and hope for the future.

I believed I'd enlisted in the Marine Corps in order to claim my place in the military history of my family, the history that included my father's service in Vietnam, his brother dying in the peacetime Marine Corps, and my grandfather serving in the army air force from December 10, 1941, through the end of World War II.

This initial impulse had nothing to do with a desire for combat, for killing, or for a heroic death, but rather was based on my intense need for acceptance into the family clan of manhood. By joining the Marine Corps and excelling within the severely disciplined enlisted ranks, I would prove both my manhood and the masculinity of the line. Also, by enlisting as an infantry grunt I was outdoing my brother, who'd spent his first few years in the army learning a practical vocation, teeth cleaning. Even before I hit puberty, Jeff and I had been in competition for the dominant male role just junior to our father's.

In the midst of my parents' divorce, my brother wrote a letter to my mother's lawyer, outlining the years of cruelty and abuse the family had suffered under my father's ironfisted rule. Largely, the letter consisted of fantasy, and my brother depicted himself as the hero of the family tragedy, wanting to run away as early as age eight but sticking around to protect his mother and siblings.

I read this letter a few months before shipping to boot camp, and I wept from the first sentence through the next five pages, and when I finished, I told my mother—a confused and angry and betrayed woman—that she couldn't use this fabricated document.

After my brother's death, among his effects I discovered my father's reply to this letter. It was full of profanity and threats of violence. My father swore that he would avenge my brother's lies and false accusations.

My father and brother didn't speak for five years after my brother wrote the letter in support of my mother. Finally, the summer my father drove to Georgia to visit his ill father and my brother was attending an army school in southern Arizona, no longer cleaning teeth but studying military intelligence, they met in a Mexican border town. I do not know what was said between the two men, if my brother apologized for the egregious lies in his letter, if my father apologized for his admittedly strict but not abusive family rule, but I do know that the first night of their rendezvous, they drank together excessively and walked arm in arm through the Mexican town, looking for my father's hotel, not finding it, and finally sleeping next to one another on the dead grass in a filthy park, and I know that after this visit the two men shared a friendship until the son died.

The first time I tried to join the Marines, at the age of seventeen, I needed my parents' consent. I'd arranged for a recruiter to meet my parents at the house, and the recruiter had the contract ready for them. I assumed that after a few minutes of consultation my parents would sign.

For many years my father had planned for me to go to college and become an architect and design grand houses for him to build, but the construction company he'd started after retiring from the air force never achieved the success he'd sought, and most of his jobs were simple bedroom-and-bathroom additions that he could draw the plans for, on graph paper or even a cocktail napkin. Along with any desire to sustain his marriage, my father had lost interest in building his company and furthering my architectural education.

My mother did not want to see another son join the military, but she'd never said no to her sons and even recalled fondly applying the USMC iron-on to my T-shirt many years prior, and she asked me if the shirt was still around or if it had died a slow death in the cleaning-rag barrel. I was too embarrassed to admit that I'd pinned the T-shirt, too small now for me to wear, inside my closet.

I can't recall the recruiter's name, but he was a short and sinewy staff sergeant of Asian descent, perhaps Korean or even Vietnamese. I liked the staff sergeant. He ran 10Ks with me along the American River and afterward treated me to dinner. There he gleefully talked to me about buying sex in the Philippines and Italy and Sweden and Panama—information my mother would never see in the brochures. The recruiter guaranteed me I could book a threesome for forty American dollars in Olongapo, PI. I'd just turned seventeen. I'd had sex three times and been the recipient of five blow jobs and fourteen hand jobs. I was sold.

I wanted to be a grunt, a rifleman, I didn't even need to hear what other options existed, and the recruiter supported this choice. "You'll be a fine killer," he'd say to me after our meals.

My mother made fresh coffee and arranged a cookie plate for the recruiter's visit and sent my younger sister down the street to play with a friend.

The recruiter arrived and my father welcomed him and walked him outside for a tour of the backyard, to show off the new built-in pool and recently landscaped lawn, and to introduce him to our dogs. The recruiter was wearing his modified dress blues with ribbons and badges, and our two dogs were disciplined enough not to jump on the recruiter and ruin the sharp, clean lines of his uniform. Our dogs understood uniforms.

Inside, my father offered the recruiter his own chair, and my father sat next to me on the couch while my mother sat in her chair and faced the recruiter.

The conversation flowed amicably: the recruiter offered my parents compliments on the interior of the house, the art and furniture from twenty years of traveling and living abroad. He asked my father about the places he'd been in the air force, and my father made a joke about the feeble air force and said something about all of the crazy jarheads he'd known in Vietnam, and before that his poor, sweet marine brother who'd died, and how he'd always believed the Corps was the backbone of the U.S. military. The recruiter accepted the compliment and said something positive yet tempered about the air force. Then the conversation moved to me. The recruiter congratulated my parents on what a fine young man they'd raised, a bright young man with a promising future, physically fit and a great specimen prepared to be molded into a hard piece of USMC steel, the recruiter said with a smile. And this is when my father said, "Staff Sergeant," and placed his hands together as if for prayer, and bit on the tips of his index fingers, and then said, "Staff Sergeant, I'll sign your contract if you guarantee me you won't get my son killed. Then I'll sign your contract. Otherwise, you should leave my house." And the polite staff sergeant began to speak and reach for one of his slick brochures, the brochures I knew by heart but that my parents hadn't even seen yet, but my father said, "Tell me my son will not die in your holy fucking Marine Corps." And this was the first time I heard my father curse, and the only time until I returned from war.

The recruiter said, "I'm sorry, sir. I cannot tell you that. I can tell you Tony will be a great marine, that he'll be a part of the finest fighting force on earth and he'll fight proudly all enemies of the United States, just as you did once. He will be a great killer."

I walked the staff sergeant to his car. He said, "Hey, we'll get you next time. Your dad wants something that's impossible. Keep up with the physical training. When you're seventeen and a half, you can join on your own."

I returned to my bedroom and looked over the well-thumbed recruiting brochures that showed jarheads running in tight formation, their voices warped into war cries; jarheads gathered with friends, on liberty, sharing photos from their various exotic duty stations; jarheads firing rifles and climbing fifty-foot ropes and swimming the ocean.

In a matter of seconds my entire life plan had been altered. I wept. What would I do with myself? I'd already, in my heart, signed the contract and accepted the warrior lifestyle. I wanted to be a killer, to kill my country's enemies. Now I'd have to take the SATs and visit colleges, I'd have to find a part-time job. I'd never live abroad and chase prostitutes through the world's brothels, or Communists through the world's jungles. I needed the Marine Corps *now*, I needed the Marine Corps to save me from the other life I'd fail at—the life of the college boy hoping to find a girlfriend and later a job.

My father knocked on my door and entered my room before he'd stopped knocking. I tried to look angry rather than sad.

He sat on my weight bench and asked, "How many pounds are on the bar?"

"Two fifty."

"How many times can you lift it?"

"Twelve or fifteen."

"I didn't know you were so strong."

"Lots of guys are stronger than me."

"No, they aren't. As soon as you can sign that contract on your own, go ahead. Until then, I'm responsible for you. I'm not stronger than you, but I know some things about the military that they don't show you in the brochures."

Shortly after this conversation my father left my mother, and a few months later, while he continued to run his business out of the house but slept wherever he wanted, we fought. I'd used his business phone to call a girl I was pursuing. I talked in his office for the privacy it offered, away from my little sister's curious ears and my mother's sad eyes. While using his phone over the two weeks of the failed romance, I'd somehow disabled his answering machine and he'd lost several important phone messages and subsequently a few contracts. When he realized what had occurred, he confronted me, and I first attempted to lie, telling him I had thought someone was breaking into the house and so had used the phone to call 911, but he didn't believe me, and as he spoke to me, he pounded his index finger against my chest. Crying, and telling my father he had no right to touch me that way, I walked backward through the house until I backed my way into the garage, out of the sight of my mother and sister, and I threw the first punch, a solid punch that connected with his jaw and stunned him, and then he punched back, and he connected with me, and for what might have been a minute we exchanged blows, to the face and body, until I fell slowly to the ground, of my own volition, and he continued to hit me, though I curled my body up and covered my face with my arms so his blows connected only with my muscular arms, and these blows were painless.

He stopped hitting me and sat on a workbench stool. He breathed in gasps and might have been crying and I continued to weep and settled my cheek against the broken face of my watch.

He said, "You are stronger than me, but I'm meaner. You don't understand what I've lived through. I'll never touch you again. I'm sorry if I've hurt you, but I believe you can handle anything, especially some soft punches from your old father."

He walked out of the garage and into the house and I heard him tell my mother not to worry about what he had done with his son. The front door opened and closed, and his car door opened and closed, and he started his car and it idled in the driveway for ten or fifteen minutes, while I remained on the floor of the garage, in the same spot where I'd once folded my newspapers, and eventually he drove away.

At the age of seventeen and a half, I signed the enlistment contract myself, though the credit went to a new recruiter, because the recruiter who'd failed with my parents had been transferred to a different station. My new recruiter was Staff Sergeant Erikson, a nice guy who smoked and drank and cursed like a jarhead should and probably hadn't run a 10K in ten years, but still I liked him. He told crude jokes and he too had prostitute stories, and he listed from memory the price of a whore in the Philippines, Guam, Okinawa, Bangkok, Sydney, Hong Kong, and Athens, and on good days, he remembered their names.

Once, when I visited the recruiting station with a pretty girl I was trying to impress—a foolish attempt because what young woman in her right mind in 1988 would've been impressed with a boy joining the Marine Corps?—Erikson pulled me aside and said, "Swofford, I'd drink a gallon of her pee just to see where it came from."

The girl might not have been impressed with Erikson or the Marine Corps, but she became my girlfriend for a short time, and the night before I shipped to boot camp I didn't sleep because we were so busy sweating and fucking in my bed.

The next day my father drove me to the Oakland in-processing station, where northern California men and women joining all of the military services receive a physical prior to basic training. After passing my physical and being sworn in, I'd fly to San Diego to start boot camp. The Marine Corps ran a shuttle from Sacramento to Oakland every afternoon, but my father insisted on taking me himself. On the way toward the Bay Area, we drove through the town of Vacaville, and by the family home at the time of my birth. We also drove past the church where my father and I had both been baptized. We entered Travis Air Force Base, and my father pulled into a parking lot in front of a one-story concrete building. He turned the engine off and we sat for a few minutes in silence. I knew he'd been stationed at Travis after Vietnam, but I didn't know why we'd stopped. It was December, but the sun shone brightly on the closed car, and I felt beads of sweat forming on my forehead and upper lip. I looked at my father as he looked at the sturdy building in front of us.

He patted my knee and said, "I thought you might like to see where you were born. It's not a hospital anymore, it's payroll. But whenever I'm on base, I come up here."

I started to speak, but he blinked hard twice, patted my knee again, and said, "Guess we better get you on the road. There's a drill instructor in San Diego waiting to give you a big wet kiss."

I've never asked my father why he drove us to the place of my birth just hours before I joined the Marine Corps, but I think I know: to remember how he'd once loved our family, to reacquaint himself with his own lost youth and vigor, and also to ask me not to go off and get myself killed.

Sitting on the Berm, the petrol rain falling, I write other letters. I write to Jenn and Katherine, thanking them for their correspondence and support. I write to Kristina, thanking her for her lack of correspondence and her infidelity and for stealing my money and perpetrating other fiendish deeds against me.

I respond to my father's recent letter urging me not to be a hero. He'd written that all of the heroes he knew from Vietnam were dead, and that in the first place they were stupid before dying, doing crazy things such as taking pictures of an enemy assault while standing on the supply warehouse, only to be killed when enemy mortar rounds landed on the roof, blowing all of the shit paper in the region to nothing along with the new hero. All these years later, my father is still unsure why the guy standing on the roof of the supply warehouse taking pictures of VC trying to overrun the airfield became a posthumous hero, but my father remembers wiping his ass with the *Stars & Stripes* for a week while they waited for a fresh shipment of shit paper from the PI. Using brave language, I tell my father that I will only be a hero if the battlefield renders me so, that I will not seek the heroic deed. Whatever occurs, I assure my father, I will not waste my time or my life trying to take pictures of the war, especially not from the vantage point of a stack of shit paper. I also inform my father of my brother's intention to replace me in combat and that I assume this is a product of Jeff's fantasies and wild imagination—a plain lie. I tell my father that I love him and I thank him for my stern upbringing. I begin to write a letter to my mother, but Staff Sergeant Siek calls a muster. I come out from under my poncho like an animal leaving a cave, ready for the hunt.

Three sniper teams are being sent to positions south of the mine-field and east of where Johnny and I were deployed. Because Johnny and I had been out for two days, we'll stay at the Berm. The STA marines not on missions are ordered to clean weapons and equipment and complete various other tasks: confirming the current encryption and retrieving extra batteries and ammunition and chow.

But before we break off, Staff Sergeant Siek advises us to remove any foreign matter from our rucks. By foreign matter he means letters from women or girls other than our wives or girlfriends, and also pornography or other profane materials that wives and girlfriends and mothers might not like to receive after our deaths when our personal effects will be shipped to the States, directly to our home of record. Word has it that two light-armored-vehicle crew members were blown to fuck yesterday by friendly fire—an A-10 Warthog dropped a bomb on them, by mistake, a big fucking devastating bomb, *by mistake*—and that among his personal effects one of the two men carried pictures of dozens of girls and women not his wife, as well as letters from and early drafts of letters to the dozens of girls and women not his wife, along with a healthy dose of pornographic material. And the rules stand that personal effects will not be edited or censored by the marines in the Personal Effects department, so that even if they'd known which pictures were of the dead marine's wife and which were not, and they had wanted to spend the time and energy removing all other pictures and correspondence and miscellany that didn't comply with the rules of marital fidelity and general decency, they wouldn't have been able to do so without breaking the rules of the Personal Effects department and exposing themselves to possible punishment under the Uniform Code of Military Justice, a harsh system of justice, everyone knows.

Crocket begins retrieving from his ruck any and all foreign matter, and we all follow suit. Dettmann and Cortes dig a hole into the Berm and we dump our pictures and letters and other potentially offensive material into the hole and Kuehn pours diesel over the effects and lights a match and we watch it all burn. It's this easy to say good-bye to the Any Marine girls and the pornography, and the hope that they once engendered. We know that if we live through the war, the Any Marine girls and the pornography won't matter, that the product they offered was good only during the buildup. Next war or "conflict" there will be a new batch of Any Marine girls, a fresh helping of home and hope from the heartland, from the cities, from the suburbs, and of course and thank God, pornography never ends.

To better shield myself from the petrol rain, I spend the remainder of the day underneath our Humvee. I read from *The Iliad* and *The Stranger,* choosing a page randomly and reading aloud and then stopping and by memory trying to construct the story before and after the page I've read, as though closing a wound. The psy-ops bastards continue playing the loud rock-and-roll music. I like rock music, but I don't think it belongs in my war. It was fine in the movies, on the boat with Martin Sheen going up the fake Vietnamese Congo or with the grunts patrolling the Ho Chi Minh and as they take a hill and heavy casualties, but I don't need the Who and the Doors in my war, as I prepare to fight for or lose my life. Teenage wasteland, my ass. This is the other side.

Kuehn and Dettmann have challenged one another to see who can collect from the desert floor more propaganda pamphlets than the other, and from under the Humvee, my head at earth level, they look like reptiles searching for the last bits of food after the Bomb. Under the nearby IR netting Welty and Atticus offer a massage to anyone who will give them the same in return. Welty also solicits hugs. He has many takers, and when I finally leave from under the vehicle, I hug Welty and he hugs me and I feel better for a moment. I've never cared much for Welty, a loudmouth, a good marine, and a great shooter, but a very agitating person. But I think his hug idea is sound, and eventually everyone in the platoon has hugged Welty. We are about to die in combat, so why not get one last hug, one last bit of physical contact. And through the hugs Welty has helped make us human again. He's exposed himself to us, exposed his need, and we in turn have exposed ourselves to him, and for that we are no longer simple grunt savages in the desert ready to jump the Berm and begin killing.

Eventually we are all hugging one another, and telling one another that we love each other and pledging faiths of battlefield devotion that need not be spoken but when spoken make us all sound wise and brave and American and young and ready to die.

The final deadline for the total withdrawal of Iraqi troops from occupied Kuwait is nearly expired, and we know that the men we're hugging might within days or hours become corpses—we believe that we will either be a corpse or one day in the future take a trip to a Texas or Iowa or Minnesota or California town to tell someone's mother what a fine marine and man her son was just before he died, alive and brave just before he died, even if this requires stretching the truth or lying.

It's the next afternoon and the entire battalion and all of the First Marine Division combat units—about thirty thousand men and hundreds of tanks and artillery pieces—are mounted in a massive offensive posture, waiting for the word *Go* or *No.*

We're sitting on our rucks in the desert as the nearby oil fires burn black against the sky. Earlier, we spent half an hour taking platoon and team photos. We moved from frame to frame the way a family does at a large reunion, Sergeant Dunn playing the gruff old uncle who calls in the generations and relations in the order he prefers.

Dusk is coming and time is running out. I look at the sky and the petrol rain falling on my uniform. I want the oil in and on me. I open my mouth. I want to taste it, to understand this viscous liquid. What does it mean?

Kuehn says, "Swoff, you better close your mouth. That shit's poison."

I keep my mouth open, and drops of oil hit my tongue like a light rain. The crude tastes like the earth, like foul dirt, the dense core of something I'll never understand. I don't swallow the oil, it sits on my tongue. When I can no longer stand the taste, I wipe my tongue on the sleeve of my blouse.

Fountain has the division freqs dialed on his radio, and we hear over the band that the order to fight has been issued. The word passes around the battalion perimeter like a wave, and when it comes back to us, we might be crushed by the excitement, the pure rage. But we aren't crushed, nor are we excited, even though we know that we're making history, that never before in modern times have so many fighters been massed on a border, waiting for the order to invade after spending nearly seven months training in the same region.

We stand and throw on our rucks and check each other's gear to make sure we're tactical.

Staff Sergeant Siek joins us and says, "The other sniper teams saw some Iraqis come across the minefield and surrender to recon guys. They've got the potential lanes marked through the obstacle belts. Combat engineers are going to blow the way and then we'll cross on trucks and by foot."

On the northern side of the Berm we hook up with the other sniper teams. During their mission they called for fire on an OP and armor positions. Their bombs fell mostly on target and their targets were annihilated and they were happy there wasn't a captain nearby to steal the handset from them. And they tell us about the surrendering Iraqis, twenty or so. The Iraqis looked dirty and defeated, and they clutched propaganda pamphlets in their fists, as though the charred paper were stamped with gold.

The battalion forms in a column behind us. There's little work for us to do other than watch the engineers blow the place to hell and hope they detonate all of the land mines. We hear a call over the freq for a squad of grunts to manually clear a minefield. Now, this is much worse than shitter detail, and no way you can buy your way out of a spot on the mine-prober squad. I consider myself extremely lucky to be in STA Platoon and out of the draw for such poor duty.

The next morning, on foot, we lead the battalion through the cleared approaches. The passages have been cleared with zero friendly casualties.

My battalion is one of four marine task forces from the First Marine Division crossing into Kuwait today. We're Task Force Grizzly, in concert with Taro, Ripper, and Papa Bear. Grizzly and Taro, foot and truck infantry, are in flanking positions, Grizzly to the west, Taro to the east, so that Ripper and Papa Bear, the mechanized units, can motor their way north, first destination, Ahmed Al Jaber Airfield for Ripper and the Burqan oil fields for Papa Bear.

Our forward assault is halted for half an hour while Harriers drop bombs on artillery and troop positions to our front, softening them for our coming assault. Word over the freqs says that many of the Iraqi positions that were supposed to be filled with infantrymen ready to fight are actually abandoned or full only with corpses or squads of men who prefer surrender to combat. We consider this good news.

We also consider the Harriers flying constantly overhead with bombs and the big artillery guns shooting more rounds than we've ever heard good news. In our static position, Johnny tells us to dig shallow shelters into the deck.

Our team has been ordered to the point of the battalion because the staff sergeant and the captain and the colonel have faith in our leadership, but this does not matter. What matters is that the rounds might hit us first. Kuehn complains more than usual, about the heat and all that wasted oil burning up and disappearing in the air. Doc John calls us crazy jarheads and quizzes us on inserting breathing tubes, treating sucking-chest wounds, and administering IVs. Dettmann says something about missing his Harley, Martinez says he wishes he was in Corpus—

—and only feet above our heads the sky splits open as a round passes over. The sound is like a thousand bolts of lightning striking at once.

Kuehn yells, "What the fuck was that?"

Martinez says, "I thought we got their goddamn tanks."

"Stay down!" Johnny yells. "Swoffie, get me visual!"

Rounds pass directly over our heads while I retrieve my spotter's scope from my ruck. As they pass over, it's as though all sound and time and space in their path are sucked into the rounds. A five-ton truck blows one hundred yards behind us. Its water buffalo also blows, into a large bloom of five hundred gallons of water. And another five-ton takes a hit.

I gain visual. The tanks shooting at us are M-60A1s, friendlies.

I yell to Johnny, "It's our own tanks!"

He gets belly-down on the deck and looks through my scope and yells, "It's Ripper!"

The Task Force Ripper tanks are northeast of our position, and even with their naked eyeballs two grand out, they should've known we were friendly. Unlike the minor enemy assaults with artillery and rockets we've experienced over the days prior, we know that our own guys will not stop until the entire convoy and all nearby personnel are annihilated, because that is the way of the Marine Corps. We are fighting ourselves but we can't shoot back.

It's true that we've moved into a flat that an hour before had been a fortified enemy position, but that is no excuse, an hour at war is a lifetime, as a few supply convoy marines have discovered. More rounds pass over.

Johnny dials the Ripper executive officer and asks, *Who the fuck do your tanks think they're shooting at to their southwest, it's fucking friendlies! It's fucking friendlies! It's me, it's my team you're shooting at and our battalion and the goddamn supply convoy, you motherfuckers! You lousy dicks!* And Johnny continues to scream at the man, and I hear in his voice astonishment and rage, because of all the things that Johnny believes in, the superiority of the sniper and the importance of the small unit, first he believes in the Marine Corps and that the Marine Corps takes care of its own, as in doesn't kill its own, and even though he knows different, just like the rest of us he's never experienced the horribly sublime reality of Marine Corps tanks shooting at you and hitting your very own supply convoy, and strangely enough, hearing the loud, screeching friendly fire rounds rip overhead, the rounds pulling all time and space with them, is more mysterious and thrilling and terrifying than taking the fire from the enemy, because the enemy fire made sense but the friendly fire makes no sense—no matter the numbers and statistics that the professors at the military colleges will put up on transparency, friendly fire is fucked fire and it makes no sense and cannot be told in numbers.

Word is that only two men died and six were injured at the hands of the trigger-happy and blind tankers. I don't believe this, because the damage is extreme, three five-tons and a Humvee are burning and marines are swarming around the vehicles. The carnage is only one hundred yards behind me, but it might as well be ten thousand yards away and many years past. I want to run back to the vehicles and make my own body count, but I cannot. I know my job is to forget what I've just seen. Lieutenants and sergeants are yelling up and down the ranks for us to get off our asses and start moving forward, there's still a goddamn war here that we need to win.

For dialing Ripper on the radio and stopping the friendly assault,

Johnny will later receive a Bronze Star. Sometimes I'll think that for yelling, *Tell those motherfuckers, Johnny, tell those motherfuckers they just hit our water buffalo and murdered someone,* I too deserved an award, but I would have plenty on my chest anyway and none of it worth even a few dead shadows floating through the mirage.

Because the surrendering enemy soldiers are clogging our line of approach through the minefields, the attack plan has fallen behind by a few hours. Over the radio we hear of an occasional Iraqi tank squad making the poor decision to fight rather than surrender. Some of the tank battles last less than five minutes, as long as it takes the marine gunner to sight, aim, and send that hell downrange.

Task Force Grizzly remains on foot, a two-mile-long, two-column stretch of ground infantry who feel naked and alone and rather worthless. The Fog of War isn't a fog but a Buzz, a good high fueled by surrendering enemy and their poorly trained and equipped brothers who decided to fight and so died, and the word up and down the columns is that soon we too will fight, that ahead of us two or three klicks we'll encounter firmly entrenched infantry and finally get ours with rifles red-glaring and bayonets fixed for death.

Occasionally an artillery round lands between our columns, but we don't perform immediate action due to the well-established inaccuracy of the enemy fire—you are more likely to walk into one of their rounds than have one of the rounds hit you due to precision fire. We are not only better equipped but we seem also to have the combat luck, an abstract currency you can neither buy nor steal but that you might lose if you're not careful and grateful.

Over concern that the inaccurate artillery rounds might be used to deliver chemical weapons, MOPP level 2 is ordered, the level at which the MOPP suit must be worn loosely, but the gas mask and overboots need not yet be donned. We were supposed to have received desert camouflage MOPP gear before the ground assault started, but this didn't happen. So we look like mulberry bushes marching through the desert. I imagine that before calling in his imprecise rounds an enemy observer might be shocked to see such a bold display of poor camouflage.

We're marching with the overgarment unzipped, and this helps with the heat, but not much, and we sweat and sweat and become exhausted.

In or attached to my ruck, or in my hands, I carry an extra pair of boots and extra fatigues, six MREs, six quarts of water, a disassembled M16, a 9mm pistol, the M40A1 sniper rifle, one hundred rounds of boat-tail ammunition for the sniper rifle, thirty rounds of 9mm ammunition, five hundred M16 rounds, four M67 fragmentation grenades, two smoke grenades, three green star clusters, two replacement sets of gas mask filters, a map and a patrol-order book inside a map case, a compass, and a GPS system. My gas mask is secured to my hip. Sometimes this gear feels like one hundred pounds, sometimes it feels like fifty, depending on how much farther we're told we must march and how often *Gas* is called.

The trucks never do retrieve us, and we will walk twenty miles, and the only enemy we see are those who surrendered, gathered now in concertina-wire circles, and their dead friends in trenches and burnt vehicles, men who might've surrendered, or probably would've surrendered, but in order to coax a withdrawal or surrender you must first prove your might, everyone knows, and you prove your might by destroying weapons and equipment and humans. I've never seen such destruction. The scene is too real not to be real. Every fifty to one hundred feet a burnt-out and bombed-out enemy vehicle lies disabled on the unimproved surface road, bodies dead in the vehicles or blown from them. Dozens, hundreds, of vehicles, with bodies inside or out. Perhaps those two burnt men, one missing both arms, perhaps they were thinking they might make it back to Baghdad and their families for a picnic; and that man crushed under the upended T62 turret, he was running from God knows what to God knows what and of all the godfuckingunlucky space in the desert he stopped and paused right where the turret landed; and he with half a head remaining and maggots tasting through what's left was a staff officer down from Kuwait City to inspect and instruct the troops, to offer morale and support and welfare.

This is war, I think. I'm walking through what my father and his father walked through—the epic results of American bombing, American might. The filth is on my boots. I am one of a few thousand people who will walk this valley today. I am history making. Whether I live or die, the United States will win this war. I know that the United States will win any war it fights, against any country. If colonialism weren't out of style, I'm sure we'd take over the entire Middle East, not only safeguard the oil reserves, but take the oil reserves: *We are here to announce that you no longer own your country, thank you for your cooperation, more details will follow.*

Our rucks are heavy with equipment and ammunition but even heavier with the burdens of history, and each step we take, the burdens increase.

The sky is a dead gray from the oil fires billowing to the north. We hump and hump and look at one another with blank, amazed faces. Is this what we've done? What will I tell my mother?

Troy says to me, "I feel sorry for these poor bastards. They didn't have a chance."

We stop for a water break. A few feet behind me a bombed jeep sits on the road. A corpse is at the wheel, sitting erect, looking serious, seeming almost to squint at the devastation, the corpse's face not unlike our faces—what has happened? Bombs, bombs, big bombs and small bombs, all of them filled with explosives meant to kill you! On either side of the jeep, more corpses, two near me, one not, all belly to the desert, as if they were running from the bomb—as if running would've helped. The back sides of the corpses are charred and decaying, the bottom halves buried in the sand, the sand windsmeared like cake icing against the bodies, and I wonder if the bottom halves of the men are still living, buried by the mirage, unaware that death lurks above. Maybe the men are screaming into the earth, living their half lives, hoping to be heard. What would they tell me? *Run.*

I assume the men were screaming before the A-10 or A-6 dropped its bombs. But maybe they were on their way to Kuwait City for supplies, and it was evening and the men neither saw nor heard the plane that dropped on them. Perhaps one of the men was telling a dirty joke or repeating a rumor he'd heard about the major's wife. But they must have been screaming. I hear them now.

We continue walking. Cortes is having trouble. He's complaining, asking how much farther until we get there, is it over yet, where are the trucks? He still doesn't understand that this is war, not boot camp. As a recruit you can cry about your blisters and occasionally convince a sergeant that even though you are a worthless malingerer and you need a truck to carry you the rest of the way this time, you'll make the next hump. I want to say to Cortes, "This might be the last hump you're ever on, you might die soon. Don't you want to hump hard and long and make all of us proud of you for finally carrying yourself?" But I know that inverse logic could just as easily be applied, and probably is being applied, by Cortes: "This might be my last hump ever, I might die soon, so why not ask for a truck? I'd rather take a ride to my death than be forced to walk my way there." I will not be surprised if Cortes sits down during the next water break and refuses to continue.

My body is sore. My feet are burning, though I will not blister because, as though my feet were made for the Marine Corps grunts, I never do; in the past I have walked forty miles straight without a blister. But my shoulders feel as though fires have been lit on them. My crotch is sweaty and rancid and bleeding. I can feel sand working into the wound. My knees are sore and my back and even my toes hurt, but I will not stop until I'm told to. The sniper rifle, fourteen pounds, is heavy in my fists. I think of the M16 broken down in my ruck, 7.78 pounds, and I again run through a gear manifest in my head, making sure that everything in my ruck is absolutely necessary. Along the road jarheads have discarded pairs of boots and socks and cammies, porn magazines they didn't throw away before, when ordered to, a white-gas stove, a shaving-gear bag. Jettison it if it will not save you.

We stop for chow. I eat the powdered cocoa and dehydrated pears from my MRE and give the main meal, spaghetti, to Dettmann. I put my crackers in my cargo pocket, saving them for later when I will need salt. We are in a slight draw, and I walk up the rise in order to shit in private.

On the other side of the rise, bodies and vehicles are everywhere. The wind blows. I assume this is what remains of an Iraqi convoy that had stopped for the night. Twelve vehicles—eight troop carriers and four supply trucks—are in a circle. Men are gathered dead around what must have been their morning or evening fire. This is disturbing, not knowing what meal they were eating. I am looking at an exhibit in a war museum. But there are no curators, no docents, no benefactors with their names chiseled into marble. The benefactors wish to remain anonymous.

Two large bomb depressions on either side of the circle of vehicles look like the marks a fist would make in a block of clay. A few men are dead in the cabs of the trucks, and the hatch of one troop carrier is open, bodies on bodies inside it. The men around the fire are bent forward at the waist, sitting dead on large steel ammunition boxes. The corpses are badly burned and decaying, and when the wind shifts up the rise, I smell and taste their death, like a moist rotten sponge shoved into my mouth. I vomit into my mouth. I swish the vomit around before expelling it, as though it will cover the stink and taste of the dead men. I walk toward the fire circle. There is one vacant ammunition box, the dead man felled to the side. I pull my crackers from my pocket. I spit into the fire hole and join the circle of the dead. I open my crackers. So close to it, on top of it, I barely notice the hollow smell of death. The fire looks to be many days old, sand- and windswept. Six tin coffee cups sit among the remains of the fire. The men's boots are cooked to their feet. The man to my right has no head. To my left, the man's head is between his legs, and his arms hang at his sides like the burnt flags of defeated countries. The insects of the dead are swarming. Though I can make out no insignia, I imagine that the man across from me commanded the unit, and that when the bombs landed, he was in the middle of issuing a patrol order, *Tomorrow we will kick some American ass.*

It would be silly to speak, but I'd like to. I want to ask the dead men their names and identification numbers and tell them this will soon end. They must have questions for me. But the distance between the living and the dead is too immense to breach. I could bend at the waist, close my eyes, and try to join these men in their tight dead circle, but I am not yet one of them. I must not close my eyes.

The sand surrounding me is smoky and charred. I feel as though I've entered the mirage. The dead Iraqis are poor company, but the presence of so much death reminds me that I'm alive, whatever awaits me to the north. I realize I may never again be so alive. I can see everything and nothing—this moment with the dead men has made my past worth living and my future, always uncertain, now has value.

Over the rise I hear the call to get on the road. I hear my name, two syllables. Troy is calling, and now Johnny, and Troy again. I throw my crackers into the gray fire pit. I try, but I cannot speak. I taste my cocoa-and-pears vomit.

I join my platoon on the other side.

We hump until past dark and form a combat bivouac within about two hundred yards of ten burning oil wells. The flames shoot a hundred feet into the air, fiery arms groping after a disinterested God. We can also hear the fires, and they sound like the echoes from extinct beasts bellowing to reenter the living world. We can feel the heat. We begin to dig individual prone shelters—shallow, gravelike pits, effective protection against small arms and artillery.

Kuehn is especially aggravated by the fires and the constant petrol rain. He asks Johnny if we can use ponchos to build a lean-to of some sort, or if he can sleep under a five-ton. Johnny refuses both requests, and Kuehn begins to scream, he tries to speak, but he's making no sense, flipping out, speaking a lost language of fear.

Kuehn is a large man, and Johnny is small, even gentle, but

Johnny grasps Kuehn's shoulders and shakes him, yelling, "Wake up, Kuehn, come back to me. Come back to us. This is war, baby, this is your war."

Kuehn laughs. "Goddamn, you know I'm here to fight. I just want to get the hell out of this oil." He collapses into the desert. I throw my poncho over him, and I dig his shallow shelter and coax him in.

The oil fires burn and moan all night. The petrol rain falls, and *Gas* is called two or three times, and finally I fall asleep with my gas mask on, a good way to die, but I don't.

The next morning I awake with my gas mask stuck to my face. I peel the mask away, and despite the fires, the morning air is fresh and cool against my skin. Because the moisture inside the mask may have tainted my filters, I replace them.

Johnny and I are attached to Fox Company in order to take part in 3/7's assault on Ahmed Al Jaber Airfield. The remainder of our battalion is supposed to rendezvous with trucks or troop carriers and join the attack in progress. Johnny and I drive with Fox Company in five-tons. The grunts aren't supposed to like us, and they don't. The goodwill that the Golf Company sergeant showed us is many days in the past. We jump on the truck and the grunts eye our rifles with suspicion and disdain, unconvinced that our weapons and our training are superior to theirs. I consider their weapons to be rather filthy, and the men themselves are filthy, and of course I'm filthy too, but my weapon is clean, and I cannot see myself.

I've missed riding five-tons, something I haven't done since joining STA Platoon because we use Humvees. The big, hulky trucks offer an expansive view of the desert, and the same destruction I saw yesterday from ground level is spread out for me in a 360-degree panorama. Death is everywhere at once. The shells of troop carriers and tanks burn, flames rising from the vehicles in a profane tribute to the dead men. Bodies litter the desert as though the men were in a great crowd, chanting with fists raised as they waited for their deaths. Everyone on the five-ton shares the same view, but none of us has anything to say to the others. It's as though we want to keep the carnage to ourselves.

As we drive in the tactical convoy toward the airfield, we occasionally pass a POW internment area, nothing more than a few-hundred-foot circle of concertina wire, and in the center a mass of surrendered men, constrained with plastic thumb cuffs. Marines walk the perimeter with M16s. We drive close enough to the wire so that I see the faces of the POWs, and the men look at us and smile. Occasionally an embarrassing scene of thanks unfolds as a detainee is processed, the detainee kneeling in front of his once enemy and now jailor, weeping and hugging the marine's legs. I suspect the performances are equal parts genuine and dramatic, men genuinely happy at the prospect of not dying and smart enough to please their fierce and potentially deadly jailors with an act of supplication.

It's easier to surrender than to accept surrender. The men who surrender do so with blind faith in the good hearts and justice of the men and the system they surrender to. They are faithful and faith is somewhat easy. Those who accept the surrendering men must follow the rules of justice. This requires not faith, but labor and discipline.

I feel more compassion for the dead Iraqi soldiers I witnessed yesterday than I do for these men, alive and waving the propaganda pamphlets with vigor and a smile as they await processing. These live men were my enemy just before surrendering, while the dead men are quite simply dead. Moments before surrendering, these incarcerated men might have tried to kill me, so until very recently they were capable of receiving my bullets. The dead men have been incapable of killing me for days or weeks or at least hours and so I would not have shot them. When I'd considered my enemy in the past, I'd been able to imagine them as men similar to me, similarly caught in a trap of their own making, but now that I see these men breathing and within arm's reach, witness them smiling and supplicating and wanting to be my friend, *my friend,* even as I am on my way to kill their fellow soldiers, I no longer care for the men or their safety or the cessation of combat. The enemy are caught in an unfortunate catch-22, in that I care for them as men and fellow unfortunates as long as they are not within riflesight or they're busy being dead, but as soon as I see them living, I wish to turn upon them my years of training and suffering, and I want to perform some of the despicable acts I've learned over the prior few years, such as trigger-killing them from one thousand yards distant, or gouging their hearts with my sharp bayonet.

We dismount the trucks two klicks from the airfield. The lieutenant we've been assigned to doesn't know how to use snipers, so Johnny advises him. This problem is common—grunt officers know a sniper might be a good thing to have on the battlefield, but what can they do with the sniper and that fancy rifle? The lieutenant's dilemma is understandable, because he must first decide how to deploy his own grunts. Johnny and I want to be as far away from the grunts as possible. Grunts get antsy and kill the wrong people, just like tankers. Johnny points out a nearby rise to the lieutenant and tells him we'll be there and gives him our freq and our call name.

The lieutenant asks, "What will you do, Corporal?"

Johnny says, "Sir, we will call in air and arty if you need it, and we'll tell you what we see, if anything. We will eliminate targets of opportunity. Sir, we will save you if you need saving."

We hitch a ride nearer the rise with two combat engineers. They're in a Humvee with enough C4 in the back to blow a hole the size of Mecca in anything. The engineers are proud of the work they did at the minefield, as they should be, and they are prepared to detonate a path all the way to Baghdad. The driver has written, on the back of his Kevlar helmet, COMBAT ENGINEERS BLOW YOUR MIND.

Johnny and I dig a shallow hide and settle in for the afternoon. The air control tower is our main target of interest. I read it at eight hundred yards and Johnny agrees. Distance estimation cannot be taught. You can show a marine a target and tell him that it's five hundred yards from him, but unless that five hundred yards is felt, he'll believe you but he'll never know for sure how you came up with that figure; he'll believe you but he won't know. He'll say, I have no idea how you figured that out, it looks like five thousand yards to me, or fifty. He can stare all day at that target and never understand. And another marine, you can tell him that it's five hundred yards away and he'll say, I knew that. This is the marine you want next to you, the marine who understands distance.

We prepare both weapons in the hide, Johnny behind the .50 and me behind the M40A1. That .50 is so damn heavy, and Johnny humped it twenty miles yesterday, that I want him to shoot it as pay-off for his labor. We're above the grunts, northeast of the airfield, and we wait for the battle to unfold. The wind has shifted so that the entire area is blanketed with the thick, dark smoke from the burning wells. Occasional brown pockets of lucidity are available, and they offer a scene of devastation, the landing strip pocked with bomb depressions and disabled vehicles and corpses. The grunts from Fox Company dig their temporary shelters to the south of us. The sporadic radio traffic tells me that to our northwest the other marine task forces are engaged in tank battles and occasional fire-fights with foot infantry.

A recon platoon is situated south of the airfield and 3/7 is entrenched to the east. The Iraqis at the airfield sporadically fire artillery, with their usual lack of precision. *Gas* is called twice and we put our masks on, but by now it has become a chore rather than a lifesaving necessity. I know that within minutes the all-clear will be announced, and I wonder if it isn't the same prick calling *Gas* every time, just for the fun of it.

Enemy soldiers are moving inside the air control tower. An argument is occurring between two commanders. They point at each other's faces and gesture toward the enemy troops, us, and I'm sure one man wants to fight and die and the other man wants to not fight and not die. The men scuffle, and their troops pull them apart.

I request permission to take shots. The men in the tower are perfect targets. The windows are blown out of the tower, and the men are standing, and I know that I can make a headshot. Johnny has already called the dope for the shot. He thinks I can take two people out in succession, the commander who wants to fight and one of his lieutenants. He thinks that the remaining men in the tower will surrender plus however many men are under that command, perhaps the entire defensive posture at the airfield.

The Fox CO tells me over their freq, *Negative, Sierra Tango One—break. Negative on permission to shoot—break. If their buddies next to them—break—start taking rounds in the head—break—they won't surrender, copy.*

I reply, *Roger, roger.* I want to say, *Fuck you, sir, copy.*

I know the opposite of the captain's assertion is true, that when you're sitting in a tower and your neighbor's head becomes a gushing wound, his new wound will be the proper motivation for retrieving the white towel and the propaganda pamphlets from your ruck.

I can't help but assume that certain commanders, at the company level, don't want to use us because they know that two snipers with two of the finest rifles in the world and a few hundred rounds between them will in a short time inflict severe and debilitating havoc on the enemy, causing the entire airfield to surrender. The captains want some war, and they must know that the possibilities are dwindling. The captains want war just as badly as we do. And also, the same as us, the captains want no war, but here it is, and when you're a captain with a company to command and two snipers want to take a dozen easy shots and try to call it a day, of course you tell them no, because you are a captain and you have a company of infantry and what you need is some war ink spilled on your Service Record Book.

The combat engineers blow two breaches in the eastern fence line, and as the dark oil-fire smoke gets darker, and the sky blackens like midnight even though it's only seventeen hundred, the infantry assault companies enter the airfield and we watch. We watch the grunts moving like mules, we watch the smoke, and we hear the resulting confusion, over the freq. The infantry take more rocket and artillery rounds, and it sounds as though a few grunts have shot one another, that one fire team rounded a corner of a building and shot up their buddies, because they couldn't see to know that the movement they heard came from their own platoon. *Gas* is called again, and again we put our masks on, but we don't believe.

At the fence line nearest us, a platoon of Iraqis appears, waving white towels and smiling. There's no one there to accept them, and the men push themselves against the fence, as rioters might at a soccer match, but the soccer match is behind the men and what they are looking for is nowhere to be found. The men sit and stretch out in the sand, as though the war is over.

No one has called Johnny and me for many hours. The airfield assault continues and the fence-line platoon of surrendering Iraqis remains, some of the men smoking casually and eating canned rations. Because I'm angry and frustrated over being forgotten and ignored, I tell Johnny I want to shoot one of the Iraqis, and I spend half an hour hopping from head to head with my crosshairs, yelling, *Bang, bang, you're a dead fucking Iraqi.*

We hear medevac requests over the freq, and mortars are called in to support the grunts, and in a few more hours the assault is over and I've remained a spectator.

The rest of our battalion and platoon arrive at the secure airfield at 2200. The oil fires have decreased visibility and rendered our night-vision devices worthless, and the commanders have made the smart realization that marines who can't see can't fight, or they end up fighting the wrong people, each other, and there has been enough of that already. We sleep amidst an occasional volley of friendly and enemy artillery and again more calls of *Gas.* The only real excitement occurs when the first call of gas comes and Cortes's team is in their Humvee, playing poker. Cortes can't find his gas mask, and he jumps from the vehicle and runs in circles, screaming that he's going to die, and we tell him to stop running and to stop screaming and especially to stop breathing so that he can share a mask with someone until they find his. Finally, Dickerson tackles him and forces his gas mask over Cortes's face, if for nothing else to quiet him. Welty finds Cortes's mask, on the floor of the vehicle, right in front of Cortes's poker seat. Perhaps Cortes has been dreaming for days, putting his mask on and taking it off in somnambulistic splendor, only to be rudely awakened and shocked by this last call of *Gas gas gas!* Cortes has slept through so many training cycles and firewatch duties, there's no reason he wasn't sleeping the war away.

The gas calls continue throughout the night, and because we have nothing better to do, we continue to don and clear.

Though we've been running over the enemy or allowing them to surrender by the hundreds, our final destination is Kuwait City and the commanders insist that the fight for the city will be long and vicious, a protracted house-clearing mission costing many thousands of casualties and much heartache and countless widows and sad mothers of America.

The morning after we bivouac at the airfield, Johnny and I are deployed via Humvee to a hide. Our position is in a corridor about twenty klicks north of the airfield (and the rest of the battalion) and ten klicks west of the Burqan oil fields. Another STA team is ten klicks south of us. Our mission is to call for fire on armor or troops in our area and to snipe officers if they present themselves for such treatment. We spend the day dialing theater-wide freqs and listening to jarheads and army doggies getting a little bit of fight at various other locations. Most of these engagements are either armor to armor, air to armor, or artillery and air dropped on the occasional holdout of enemy infantry. Johnny and I talk about what has kept those enemy soldiers fighting, and we decide that it's probably the same thing keeping us in the fight—pride, bravery, stupidity, fear. As we talk throughout the day and listen to the war unfold on the radio and watch the movement of U.S. troops across massive swaths of desert that until just hours before had been controlled by the Iraqi army, we think the war is ending. We sit and watch and listen, and in the silent stretches between our talking I feel not like a brave and proud and stupid man, but a lucky man, who showed up at the war a boy, with enough training to keep him just ahead of the battle and enough sense to keep him somewhat detached, because the war has been mine to fight but not mine to win or lose, and I know that none of the rewards of victory will come my way, because there are no rewards, not on the field of battle, not for the man who fights the battle—the rewards accrue in places like Washington, D.C., and Riyadh and Houston and Manhattan, south of 125th Street, and Kuwait City.

The fighting man receives tokens—medals, ribbons, badges, promotions, combat pay, abrogation of taxes, a billet to Airborne School—worthless bits of nothing, as valuable as smoke.

Johnny and I listen to the war drone on until all of our batteries die.

The next morning we are supposed to be extracted by Humvee, but the vehicle never shows, and at 0700 we begin patrolling on foot toward what should be the new battalion CP coordinates. We are concerned over the absence of our extraction team, and then, as though to confirm that a slaughter of our battalion has occurred, a squad of enemy tanks moves across the horizon. We kneel in the sand as the tanks head slowly north, and there is nothing for us to do but watch.

I imagine a possible horror—as we took turns sleeping and watching the empty desert, our unit was slaughtered by a renegade enemy force, and Johnny and I will arrive to a mass of fatalities, the only two marines living from a battalion of a thousand men. Who will carry the standard now? Johnny looks afraid, as he did just a few nights prior, as we crawled the rise, ready to engage the enemy who'd shot at us with rockets.

He says, "Swoffie, I don't like this. I've never not had a pickup. Dunn wouldn't allow it. He'd run out here and carry us back on his skinny fucking shoulders."

"Maybe they gave Cortes the map and compass."

"Even Cortes would find us. It's nearly a straight shot. Lock and load. Let's go find out what the fuck."

Johnny assembles his M203 and me my M16 and we fasten our sniper rifles to our bodies with slings.

We patrol tactically the entire route to the assumed battalion coordinates. We speak only in hand signals—Halt, Eyes Right, Decrease Speed, Increase Speed, Shift Right, Shift Left, I Do Not Understand. We are once again undergunned and out of support, two flabby, worthless tits left to jiggle in the wind, most alone in this widest and darkest of lands. I imagine the scene back at battalion, all of my mates dead and dying. I imagine the dubious fame that will come to Johnny and me, the last bearers of the standard: 2/7 is dead. Tell it to the commandant. After such atrocities units are disbanded and marines are banned from mentioning the ghost battalions.

It takes us about three hours to move within two hundred meters of the draw where the battalion should be bivouacked. By 1000 they're supposed to be en route to the next fight or at least packed and ready to roll. But we don't encounter them during the patrol, we don't come upon anyone. We dump our packs and sniper rifles at the bottom of the rise and low-crawl up it. All I can see ahead of me is sand and sky, still some smoke from the oil fires, but more blue than I've seen in weeks. The sand is warm against my body. Johnny pauses and loads a grenade into his breech. I've been on burst the entire patrol, and my finger is still on the trigger, sweating against the trigger.

Nearer the top of the rise we hear music and screaming, and Johnny thinks it must be a trick, a ploy, and we continue slowly, prepared for the worst, prepared for an assault or to witness the results of a great atrocity. We crawl to the top of the rise, and on the other side we see Headquarters & Support Company 2/7 behaving as if they're on liberty. Men are lying naked on sleeping pads, soaking up the sun that bursts between the gray smoke clouds. Weapons and rucks and uniforms are strewn about the camp. Two men throw a football back and forth. A poker game is full of players, and a crowd of bettors surrounds the makeshift card table, the losers arguing as each hand ends. Two gas masks, impaled upon metal fence posts, face us—oh, dreadful but magical skulls!

Johnny and I sit and watch the company live what two days ago, two hours ago, two minutes ago, would've been our wild and dangerous fantasy. We're unable to move, our legs stuck beneath us as under a great weight. We must continue our last bit of war—we know what the commotion means, why First Sergeant Martinez is handing out cigars and dancing shirtless and playing a kazoo when he isn't smoking his cigar, and we know why he's allowing Jimi Hendrix to pipe through the comm towers. But Johnny and I stay on the rise, we sit for an hour or ten minutes or half an hour or all day, watching men we know and love celebrate the end of our little war.

Eventually, I put my rifle on safe, and Johnny removes the grenade from his weapon—he shuts the breech and the sound is like an iron door closing on history. We descend the rise, and the first sergeant is the first to greet us, smiling broadly, and in his face I see his family and the happiness of a family man, this from a marine I've never seen happy except while insulting or degrading a subordinate, and he says to us, "Oh, fuck, you guys got stuck out there, didn't you? I had Siek drive the colonel up north for a look-see. Sorry, guys, you crazy snipers, you crazy bastards, but the war is over, the motherfucker is over." And he slaps us both upon the back and shoves cigars in our faces.

We make our way to the STA area, where everyone apologizes for leaving us out there, but they really did run short of vehicles because of the mad rush of staff officers up to Kuwait City to view the victory. And they are so happy on peace that Johnny and I don't care, we call them bastards and sons of bitches for making us run a tactical patrol for eight klicks without communication while the goddamn war was over, but we really don't care.

The music plays throughout the day, Hendrix, the Stones, the Who, music from a different war. Ours is barely over but we begin to tell stories already. Remember that time. Remember when. Can you believe?

I wonder if we're being fooled. I want to read the news in a newspaper, or hear it on the radio. So much information is bad information.

But by nightfall, after I've heard Siek tell us about the happy civilians he saw on the outskirts of Kuwait City, I begin to believe. Siek has acquired a stack of wooden pallets from an ammunition dump.

We douse the pallets with diesel and light a fire, and we gather in a circle around the flames. We have nothing special to cook and only water to drink, but we have our stories, and these go on for some time. The stories will never end.

Because we don't have liquor, my platoon mates celebrate by chewing tobacco, perhaps the only marine vice I haven't acquired. Atticus swears to me I'll get a buzz, and I realize that I want a buzz, or anything to fill the onset of a nameless emptiness. I try a mouthful of the dark, musty leaves. I chew and suck on the leaves, forming them into a tight ball. My lips and gums go numb. I spit into the fire a few times, just as my mates, and I do feel a good buzz. I swallow some of my spit. I close my eyes, the world spins, and I fall slowly backward off my ammunition box, onto my back. I roll over onto my hands and knees. No one notices me. Their war stories march through my brain like a parade of epileptics. My stomach turns. I vomit. It feels as though I'm regurgitating the last seven months of my life. This is how I welcome the peace.

We spend a few weeks in Kuwait, clearing bunkers, and this is where I will become intimate with the detritus and almost kill myself.

STA 2/7 is ordered to clear three large enemy positions, one artillery and two entrenched infantry. Our mission is to empty the bunkers and trenches of weapons and equipment and especially to look for chemical weapons and any intelligence that might be considered relevant to the debriefing. We know that the only things relevant to the debriefing are the corpses.

The count of the dead: many of them, many fewer of us. This is a good count, these are good numbers. Let's go home.

The cleanup mission is a freelance operation. We gear up in our three Humvees and head out each morning from the battalion bivouac, and the captain only wants to hear from us if something goes wrong, if we engage a sleepy enemy platoon, a group of men who missed the great assault, or if a munitions cache explodes or someone steps on a mine.

We gleefully run through the enemy positions, noting the hundreds of different ways a man might die when five-hundred-pound bombs are dropped on his weakly fortified position or when his tank or troop carrier is blown nearly inside out. Some of the corpses in the bunkers are hunched over, hands covering their ears, as though they'd been patiently waiting. Maggots and whatever other insects enjoy a corpse are busy with the decaying remains. Near some positions shallow graves have been dug. I hope that at the end of the day the casualties were gathered and buried with honor or at least respect. In some positions corpses are stacked on one another, and bottom to top one can tell the stage of decay, a reeking calendar of death. In one bunker I see three different stages of decay on three different corpses, which leads me to believe that the men died at different times, and that the last man alive in the bunker spent a few or many days waiting to die near his two death-bloated friends. I can't understand why he didn't bury the men or at least move them from his bunker, but maybe they were a comfort, a cold comfort— helping him to know his end so intimately, sleeping next to it and smelling it and waiting. Many of the men in the bunkers seem to have died not from shrapnel but concussion, and dried, discolored blood gathers around their eyes and ears and nose and mouth, no obvious trauma to their bodies. A few weeks into the air campaign the United States began employing the daisy-cutter bomb, a weapon originally used in Vietnam to clear helicopter landing zones. Three feet above the ground the daisy cutter detonates its 12,600-pound charge of aluminum-powder blasting slurry. If you were within two acres of the explosion and above ground or even in a barricaded bunker, you were sure to die. The infantry positions look like daisy-cutter test areas. The mouths of the dead men remain open in agony, a death scream halted. Can you hear?

I enjoy sitting in the bunkers and sifting through the dead men's effects. The Iraqis had been in these positions for months, and they made the bunkers comfortable if not formidable, with colorful blankets on the decks and nailed to the plywood roofs, pictures of family propped in shelves dug from the sand. I thumb through their letters, in Arabic, so I can't read them, but I don't need to read the script to know what it says: Please come home alive. We love you. The cause is just.

Near our bivouac, Crocket has found a corpse he particularly disagrees with. He says the look on the dead man's face, his mocking gesture, is insulting, and that the man deserved to die and now that he's dead the man's corpse deserves to be fucked with. And Crocket goes to the corpse again and again, day after day, and with his E-tool he punctures the skull and with his fixed bayonet he hacks into the torso. And he takes pictures. Johnny Rotten orders Crocket to stay away from the corpse, but he doesn't, Crocket is being driven mad by that corpse. I understand what drives Crocket to desecrate the dead soldier—fear, anger, a sense of entitlement, cowardice, stupidity, ignorance. The months of training and deployment, the loneliness, the boredom, the fatigue, the rounds fired at fake, static targets, the nights of firewatch, and finally the letdown, the easy victory that just scraped the surface of a war—all of these are frustrating and nearly unendurable facets of our war, our conflict. Did we fight? Was that combat? When compared to what we've heard from fathers and uncles and brothers about Vietnam, our entire ground war lasted as long as a long-range jungle patrol, and we've lost as many men, theater-wide, as you might need to fill two companies of grunts. Crocket—hacking at the dead Iraqi soldier and taking pictures of the waste—is fighting against our lack of satisfaction.

One morning before Crocket starts his work on the corpse—the body by now a hacked-up, rotting pile of flesh—I bury it. I use my E-tool to cover the dead man with sand. I start at his feet and build a mound that rises six or so inches above his body, and I finish at his mutilated face, the thing no longer a face, his body no longer a corpse but a monument to infinite kinds of loss.

Crocket discovers that I've buried his man, and he calls me a coward and a bitch and an Iraqi-lover. I tell him I've done everyone a favor by burying the corpse, even him, and that someday he'll be grateful I've stopped him.

He says, "Look around, the dead motherfuckers are everywhere. I'll find another one." And maybe he does.

Crocket isn't the only marine desecrating corpses, though. At company formation First Sergeant Martinez says, "Because we are U.S. marines, and honorable, we do not shoot dead men, we do not carve their skulls open with our E-tools, we do not throw grenades into a pit of corpses, and after we don't do these things, we don't take pictures of the resultant damage. If we do take pictures, and the pictures are discovered, we will be punished under the Uniform Code of Military Justice. And if we steal weapons or articles of identification or other battlefield trophies from the corpses, we will also be punished under the UCMJ. Carry on."

One morning we receive a call over the radio that our battalion is in queue for the victory lap through Kuwait City, and that if we want to join the convoy, we should meet the five-tons at such and such coordinates at 1100.

Our convoy rambles through the outskirts of the city, through the poor neighborhoods, where olive-skinned and overweight mothers clutch babies to their large breasts and with one hand wave Kuwaiti and American flags. Their homes are made of stone and held together, it seems, through the creative manipulation of plywood and nails. The only Kuwaitis we see are these women and young children. They chant, "USA, USA," and we wave, and occasionally a jarhead jumps from his truck and hugs a woman or a child while one of his buddies snaps a picture. These must also have been the neighborhoods of the expatriate workers, the workers from the PI and Malaysia and India and Egypt working for cheap with limited human rights, the people whose population, before the invasion, had nearly matched that of the nationals. These Kuwaiti women with their children aren't the ones we fought for: we fought for the oil-landed families living in the palaces deep with gold, shaded by tall and courtly palm trees. These flag-waving women are just like us, these women are our mothers, and those children dirty at the mouth with skinned and bloody knees, they are us and our sisters and our neighborhood friends.

Our convoy is not allowed to drive farther than this ghetto. We're turned around by MPs, stationed at checkpoints preventing us from entering the actual city, from driving through the neighborhoods where in the homes, the palaces, I imagine women and men are busy making lists of the assets and property stolen or vandalized during the Iraqi occupation, while they lived in five-star hotels in Cairo and London and Riyadh.

We turn around and pass the same women and children from earlier, and I assume they've been placed there by the Kuwaiti and U.S. governments, handed the flags, and told to stand in their gravel yards at certain hours while the U.S. troops pass, *and smile and wave your flags and act happy for your freedom.* Maybe I'm wrong, maybe during the occupation they stowed the U.S. flags in their kitchen cupboards, waiting for this glorious day.

One of the hero medals we'll rate will be the Kuwaiti Liberation Medal, a handsome gold medal with what looks to be palm fronds jutting from it. While most medals arrive wrapped in cardboard and plastic, the KLM will be presented in its own collectible box with hinges and a clasp. The rumors will say that the Kuwaiti government offered to pay each American service member who'd served in the region ten thousand American dollars, but the U.S. government refused, claiming the troops weren't for sale. Other rumors will surround the medal: if you pay your way to Kuwait and present your medal upon landing at the airport, untold pleasures await you, pleasures of the flesh delivered by Kuwaiti women—grapes from the vine, wine spit into your mouth from her mouth, her sisters and friends, entering all of the holes like the ancients talked about, the whole sexy deal. Also, the medal is said to be made from pure gold, with a market value of $1,000. None or all of this will be true but I will never know and never care.

After the victory lap we return to the artillery position. I've become comfortable darting in and out of the enemy bunkers, the absent presence of the enemy surrounding me—their colorful blankets and weapons and the Swedish and Russian rations they left behind, the Russian and British munitions, and the pictures of their families and their letters—I've even become comfortable with their corpses bloodied and decayed.

I enter a command position at the southern edge of the perimeter, and as I duck into the bunker, staring at the gun plan affixed to a piece of plywood—the plan drawn on green construction paper with a red felt pen so that it resembles the dark fantasy of a five-year-old boy—I feel a faint tug at my ankle, and my first thought is that someone in his final moments of death, here all these days and finally dying, has reached for me, but I realize that it is a booby trap installed by retreating soldiers. If I continue my forward motion I will trip the trap and die horribly. I realize all of this not in the length of that sentence, but in the length of my life, my life strung out thin along the wire. I stop, back away, and I stare at the goddamn trap and my stupidity and carelessness that hang from the trip wire like a bag of cheap bones. The fragmentation grenade I would've detonated is at head level, tucked into a sand pocket the size of a ripe pear. I can see in the damp sand the finger marks of the man who dug the pocket and carefully rigged the grenade. Of course, I'm familiar with grenades—intimate, even, as I have a few of my own hanging from my body—but this is the first grenade I've heard before it explodes, as though it beats like a heart. I loosely fasten a length of nylon rip cord around the trip wire. I remove the gun plan from the plywood and shove it into my cargo pocket. I back up forty feet from the embrasure, kneel in the sand, as in supplication, and yank the cord as though I'm extracting a life from out of the hole, and the bunker blows, and I own my life again.

I don't enter another bunker, and I tell the rest of the platoon they're insane if they continue the mission, that we've all been insane for ten straight days, and lucky. They seem to think it's natural that I nearly killed myself on a booby trap, but that I detected it and am now safe. No one even asks me, "Are you all right?"

The treasures in the bunkers—correspondence, a bayonet, a beret, a helmet, homemade Iraqi dog tags with the information scrawled by hand with an awl—the worthless treasures call. The platoon continues collecting relics for the same reasons Crocket puts the damage to the corpses—in order to own a part of the Desert, to further scar this landscape already littered with despair and death, and to claim and define themselves, define their histories, to confirm that they are marines, combatants, jarheads, to infuse the last seven months of their young lives with value, and to steal history from the dead Iraqi soldiers who now have nothing to remember.

For this complete absence of memory the dead men are envied their deaths, that perpetual state where they are required only to go on being dead. No other consequences exist for the corpse. The corpse suffers violence and contempt, the corpse is shot and knifed and cursed and burned, but the corpse will not suffer loneliness and despair and rage.

The captain from S-3 suggests STA get together with him and the few enlisted marines from his shop and that we all fire the weapons that STA has gathered from the enemy positions. This means the AK-47s and RPGs. We accept the captain's offer because without his support we won't be allowed to fire the weapons in the psychotic and frenzied fashion the situation requires.

Our cache holds four to five hundred AKs and three dozen RPGs. Our targets, the disabled Iraqi weapons and vehicles, are plentiful. The captain even attempts to get one of the Iraqi tanks running so we can fire it. He spends an hour poking in and around the T-62, but he has neither the knowledge nor the tools to enable the weapon.

The Iraqi soldiers took poor care of their rifles. We've pried the weapons from the hands of dead men who hadn't performed rifle maintenance for days or weeks, but the pitiful state of the weapons—the rust, the filthy barrels, and sand-filled trigger mechanisms—encourages us to curse the men and their poor discipline. Such sloppy soldiering further decreases their stature as our former enemies.

Kuehn says, "These bastards would've gotten about two magazines off before their weapons failed. Jesus, this wasn't an army, it was a pack of assholes with some rifles."

"I haven't seen one set of cleaning gear," Martinez says. "I bet they weren't issued cleaning gear. They probably had to supply their own. This is crazy. Frontline troops with dirty weapons."

I say, "It's as though they wanted their weapons to fail."

"Their weapons didn't fail," Johnny says. "They failed their weapons."

We throw the AKs into a pile, a metal confusion of barrels and stocks and bolts. The RPGs we handle more delicately, placing them in an orderly line. The captain doesn't want us to waste our time attempting to clear failed weapons or changing magazines, and he suggests that when a weapon malfunctions or runs out of ammunition, we throw it in a discard pile. The fire will be a free-for-all; as long as you're safe and remain behind the firing line, you may shoot at anything on the other side of the firing line.

I've studied the AK for years, know its capabilities by heart, and had often assumed that the weapon would kill me in battle. But the battle is over. Now the dirty AKs look like children's toys, and I feel as though I've been fooled again, by myself and propaganda. Also, I feel like a bit of a traitor, holding the enemy's weapon, now firing the enemy's weapon, the *snap snap snap* of the firing pin piercing the shell, the projectiles screaming downrange. I don't care what I hit, in front of me there is desert, and tanks and bunkers and troop carriers and still in some of the carriers, corpses, but I fire, as next to me my platoon mates fire, from the hip, with no precision, as though we are famous and immortal and it doesn't matter that we'll likely hit nothing firing from such an absurd and unstable position, but we burn through the magazines, and when the dead click sounds, meaning the magazine has ended, or a mangle of metal occurs—bolt action stuck in the chamber, like a key stuck in a lock—because the weapon has failed, we throw the rifles aside, watching them leave our hands and land in a tumble, as though throwing aside a disturbing memory that will someday resurface. The RPGs explode with a pop. No one hits a target with an RPG, rather the rounds bounce and flail, exploding finally for nothing. We fire and fire the AKs, a factory of firepower, the fierce scream of metal downrange and discharged cartridges and sand flying everywhere, now all of us shooting in the air, shooting straight up and dancing in circles, dancing on one foot, with the mad, desperate hope that the rounds will never descend, screaming, screaming at ourselves and each other and the dead Iraqis surrounding us, screaming at ourselves and the dead world surrounding us, screaming at ourselves, at the corpses surrounding us and the dead world.

I throw my rifle onto the discard pile and run toward the Humvee, and I dive under the vehicle as the fire line continues to send a wall of metal into the air, and I weep, and I hear my screaming friends, those men I love, and I know we'll soon carry that mad scream home with us, but that no one will listen because they'll want to hear the crowd-roar of victory.

To be a marine, a true marine, you must kill. With all of your train-ing, all of your expertise, if you don't kill, you're not a combatant, even if you've been fired at, and so you are not yet a marine: receiv-ing fire is easy—you've either made a mistake or the enemy is better than you, and now you are either lucky or dead but not a combatant. You will receive a Combat Action Ribbon, and if unlucky enough to have been hit but not fatally, a Purple Heart, or if you're hit fatally, your mother will receive your Purple Heart, but whether you are dead or not, you haven't, with your own hands, killed a hostile enemy soldier. This means everything.

Sometimes you wish you'd killed an Iraqi soldier. Or many Iraqi soldiers, in a series of fierce firefights while on patrol, with dozens of well-placed shots from your M40A1, through countless calls for fire. During the darkest nights you'd even offer your life to go back in time, back to the Desert for the chance to kill. You consider yourself less of a marine and even less of a man for not having killed while at combat. There is a wreck in your head, part of the aftermath, and you must dismantle the wreck.

But after many years you discover that you cannot dismantle the wreck, so you move it around and bury it.

It took years for you to understand that the most complex and dangerous conflicts, the most harrowing operations, and the most deadly wars, occur in the head.

You are certain you'd be no better or worse a man if you'd killed one or all of the men you sometimes fantasize about killing. Probably, you are incorrect, and you would be insane or dead by your own hand if you'd killed one or all of those men. You would've been a great killer. You would've been a terrible killer.

If you'd killed those men, you would've told your mother, "No, I never killed anyone," and even though you have indeed killed no one and have told your mother this, still she has said, numerous times, while weeping, "I lost my baby boy when you went to war. You were once so sweet and gentle and now you are an angry and unhappy man."

After clearing the bunkers, we lived in a tent city near Riyadh, where we were allowed to take cold showers each morning and required to shave our faces and polish our boots. The war ended much faster than it had begun, and while the Pentagon spent six months building the force of five hundred thousand fighting men and women, it would disperse the majority of that same force in less than six weeks, because the host country was now safe, and the need for the protective force had ended, and now we were no longer protectors but intruders.

We spent most of our time in the rear-rear worrying about when we'd be sent home and trying to make sure we didn't get screwed, as we were sure that the first guys in should be the first guys out.

We finally got our plane. We first stopped in Athens, but they didn't let us off, and this was pure torture, looking from inside the stuffy plane at the green hills of Athens, looking at what might have been ancient ruins or contemporary housing, we couldn't tell, but it didn't matter, only that we wanted to be there. Certainly some of us would've stayed in Athens, never to be heard from again, a fact the command must have considered.

Next we stopped in Dublin, and this time they allowed us to debark, probably because armed men patrolled the tarmac. The

flage blouse of indeterminate origin. Tears fell from the man's eyes and rolled down his deeply wrinkled and hurt face, the surface of his face not unlike the topography of the Desert. The man was somewhat drunk, but obviously less drunk than he was used to being. He steadied himself by gripping Crocket's shoulder, and he opened his dry mouth but no words issued forth. The bus quieted. He closed his mouth and licked his cracked lips and yelled to the bus, "Thank you, thank you, jarheads, for making them see we are not bad animals."

Crocket helped the man reenter the crowd. I hoped that even though the spectacle of the excited citizens was worth nothing to me, it might help the Vietnam vet heal his wounds.

Throughout the long drive to base I grasped the dog tags around my neck—not mine, but those that I'd ripped from the necks of three dead Iraqi soldiers. Those dog tags remain in my ruck, in my basement, with my uniforms and medals and badges and ribbons and maps.

Stealing the tags was a crime. I sometimes wonder if the families of the dead men were notified of the deaths, or if the men are listed as missing in action on a stone wall in Baghdad. Probably the corpses were identified with dental records, and probably an Iraqi captain spent a few weeks after the war informing families of their loss, but maybe I am responsible for three Iraqi families living the horror of not knowing what happened to their sons and fathers. Now when I think of these men, I remember their dead faces, and I imagine them wearing their dead faces on a picnic with their families. I am sorry if the families don't know the men are dead, while I know for sure they are dead though not their names. Yes, I'm sorry the men are dead, for many reasons I am sorry, and chief among my reasons is that the men who go to war and live are spared for the single purpose of spreading bad news when they return, the bad news about the way war is fought and why, and by whom for whom, and the more men who survive the war, the higher the number of men who might speak.

Unfortunately, many of the men who live through the war don't understand why they were spared. They think they are still alive in order to return home and make money and fuck their wife and get drunk and wave the flag.

These men spread what they call good news, the good news about war and warriors. Some of the men who spread good news have never fought—so what could they have to say about the purity of war and warriors? These men are liars and cheats and they gamble with your freedom and your life and the lives of your sons and daughters and the reputation of your country.

I have gone to war and now I can issue my complaint. I can sit on my porch and complain all day. And you must listen. Some of you will say to me: You signed the contract, you crying bitch, and you fought in a war because of your signature, no one held a gun to your head. This is true, but because I signed the contract and fulfilled my obligation to fight one of America's wars, I am entitled to speak, to say, *I belonged to a fucked situation.*

I am entitled to despair over the likelihood of further atrocities. Indolence and cowardice do not drive me—despair drives me. I remade my war one word at a time, a foolish, desperate act. When I despair, I am alone, and I am often alone. In crowded rooms and walking the streets of our cities, I am alone and full of despair, and while sitting and writing, I am alone and full of despair—the same despair that impelled me to write this book, a quiet scream from within a buried coffin. Dead, dead, my scream.

What did I hope to gain? More bombs are coming. Dig your holes with the hands God gave you.

Some wars are unavoidable and need well be fought, but this doesn't erase warfare's waste. Sorry, we must say to the mothers whose sons will die horribly. This will never end. Sorry.

Now I often think of the first time I received artillery fire, and the subsequent obliteration of the enemy observation post. I'll never know how many men manned the OP, but in memory I fix the number at two, and though at the time I was angry that the pompous captain took the handset from me and stole my kills, I have lately been thankful that he insisted on calling the fire mission, and sometimes when I am feeling hopeful or even religious, I think that by taking my two kills the pompous captain handed me life, some extra moments of living for myself or that I can offer others, though I have no idea how to use or disburse these extra moments, or if I've wasted them already.

AUTHOR'S NOTE AND ACKNOWLEDGMENTS

This book describes a number of people reacting to the difficulties of life, war, and service in the U.S. Marines. I'm grateful to these individuals for sharing their lives with me. I've changed certain names and biographical details.

Deepest thanks: first, to my editor, Colin Harrison, who worked with me page by page in exactly the way I'd been told Manhattan book editors no longer do and so proved wrong those who insisted that the editor is extinct; also at Scribner—Nan Graham, Sarah Knight, Laura Wise, Steve Boldt, and Veronica Jordan; my agent, Sloan Harris at ICM; also, Katharine Cluverius at ICM; my teachers at the Iowa Writers' Workshop.

I am indebted to Harold Schneider, Jack Hicks, Katherine Vaz, John Callahan; William Wann, Clifton Hall, Douglas Ahim-Bisibwe, D. Foy O'Brien, Sachiko Tamura; Les and Susan Freeman, and especially my parents and sisters. And Sarah Elisabeth Freeman.

I thank the Corporation of Yaddo and Caldera for time and space.

AUTHOR'S NOTE AND ACKNOWLEDGMENTS

I wish to express my gratitude to James Michener and the Copernicus Society for their generous support of my work.

For Gulf War theater—wide chronology, order of battle, U.S. and Iraqi weapons nomenclature, and an understanding of the support and dissent of the U.S. citizenry and media, I consulted the following works: *Order of Battle: Allied Ground Forces of Operation Desert Storm*, Thomas D. Dinackus (Hellgate Press, 2000); *Against All Enemies: Gulf War Syndrome: The War Between America's Ailing Veterans and Their Government,* Seymour M. Hersh (Random House, 1998); *Gulf War: The Complete History*, Thomas Houlahan (Schrenker Military Publishing, 1999); *The March to War*, edited by James Ridgeway (Four Walls Eight Windows, 1991); *The Gulf War Reader*, edited by Micah Sifry and Christopher Cerf (Times Books, 1991). The definition of the word *sand* (pages 175 and 187) is from *Webster's Third International Dictionary.* The epigraph is taken from *The Cantos of Ezra Pound* (New Directions, 1998).

Anthony Swofford served in a U.S. Marine Corps Surveillance and Target Acquisition/Scout-Sniper Platoon during the Gulf War. After the war, he was educated at American River College; the University of California, Davis; and the University of Iowa Writers' Workshop. He has taught at the University of Iowa and Lewis and Clark College. His fiction and nonfiction have appeared in *The New York Times*, *Harper's*, *Men's Journal*, *The Iowa Review*, *NOON*, and other publications. A Michener-Copernicus Fellowship recipient, he lives in Portland, Oregon. He is at work on a novel.